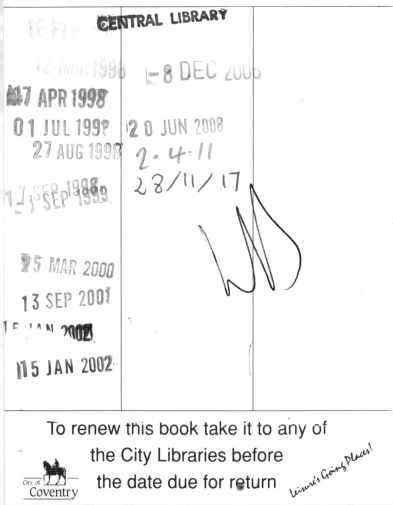

W. G.

W. G.

A LIFE OF W. G. GRACE

Robert Low

RICHARD COHEN BOOKS
LONDON

British Library Cataloguing in Publication Data:
A catalogue record for this book is available
from the British Library

Copyright © 1997 by Robert Low

ISBN 1 86066095 9

First published in Great Britain in 1997 by
Richard Cohen Books
7 Manchester Square
London WIM 5RE

1 3 5 7 9 8 6 4 2

Designed by Humphrey Stone

Typeset in Imprint by
Palimpsest Book Production Limited,
Polmont, Stirlingshire

Printed in Great Britain by
Mackays of Chatham plc, Chatham, Kent

CONTENTS

ACKNOWLEDGEMENTS

I owe three people a huge debt for their part in the writing of this book. To my wife, Angela Levin, I owe the idea in the first place, despite her admitted dislike of cricket. She also put up nobly with my absences while I was researching the book and with the many evenings and weekends when I shut myself in my study to write it. Richard Cohen has been the ideal publisher, always supportive and encouraging even when his own problems setting up and running an independent publishing house were far greater than mine. Tom Chesshyre carried out a great deal of valuable research for me; without him I could never have met my deadline, nor included so much detail about W.G.'s life.

I must also thank my agent Jonathan Lloyd, managing director of Curtis Brown; Stephen Green, curator of the Lord's Library and Museum, and his assistant, Michael Wolton, for allowing me to use their facilities and for their courteous help and advice; Roger Mann for many of the photographs used in this book and for allowing me to see letters in his magnificent collection of cricket memorabilia at Torquay; Bert Avery, curator of Gloucestershire County Cricket Club's museum; Clive Ward, formerly chief librarian, the University of Bristol Medical Library; Pat Chetwyn of Richard Cohen Books; my copy-editor Barbara Ellis; Wendy Wimbush, for compiling the index; and Alan Watkins. I also used the British Library; the British Newspaper Library; the London Library; and Bristol Public Library's Newspaper Archive.

I dedicate this book to my parents: to my mother, Agnes Low, who washed my cricket whites more times than I care to remember and has always been a stalwart supporter of my professional and sporting activities; and my late father, Walter Low, who instilled in me a lifelong passion for cricket and, like W.G.'s father, put up a net on the lawn so that he, my brother and I could practise to our hearts' content all summer long. It gave me quite a jolt to realise that as W.G. lay dying in September 1915 at home in Mottingham, near Eltham, where London peters out and Kent begins, my father, then aged four, was living just up the road in Belvedere. I wondered if the little boy was awoken by the noise of the bombs dropped by a Zeppelin on Woolwich barracks which so upset cricket's old warrior; and surely my grandfather, a keen club cricketer, must have taken the odd afternoon off to watch the ageing W.G. playing for his London County side at the Crystal Palace? The thought of grandfather enjoying a few of the twilight hours of the greatest cricketer this country has ever produced gave me a deep satisfaction.

Drawings of W.G. by Harry Furniss

I · INTRODUCTION

MUCH was written about W.G. Grace, who was born on 18 July 1848, during his full and active lifetime and much has been written since. We have an image of him: a huge, bulky bearded man, glowering at the camera from beneath a striped cap which looks faintly ridiculous on such a massive head. Or perhaps posing at the crease, in one of those stilted Victorian photographs. Or preparing to bowl, still with his cap on, his arm much lower than anything you would see today. The image is that of a man who was very far from being an athlete, yet everyone who knows anything about cricket knows this: W.G. Grace was the greatest cricketer England has ever seen.

What else could they tell you? After all, cricket followers can recite statistics and relate them to individuals at the drop of a floppy white hat. Len Hutton? He scored 364 against Australia in 1938, a world record which stood for nearly thirty years. Jack Hobbs? Most centuries – 197, to be precise. Ian Botham? In 1981, his two whirlwind centuries against Australia turned the tide and won back the Ashes. Jim Laker? He took a record nineteen wickets in a Test match in 1956. I wrote those down without consulting a single reference book, and I could do the same for many more players, both English and overseas.

Before I embarked on this biography of W.G. Grace, I could not have told you anything much about him except that he was a large, corpulent man with a beard, a doctor of medicine, an all-rounder who dominated the game of cricket in his day. Above all, he was a character, a bit of a rogue, a batsman who hated to leave the crease, a player who hated to lose, a man who bent the rules to suit himself. The one story everyone knows about him is of his dismissive retort to an umpire who had just attempted to give him out: 'They've come to see me bat, not to see you umpire.'

As I set about the task of retelling his life, I frequently asked myself what the point of it was. Did the world need a new biography? Plenty had been written, some during his life, a massive, rambling Memorial Biography compiled by the game's great and good soon after his death in 1915, several at regular intervals since, notably by Bernard Darwin, better known as the father figure of modern golf writing, in 1934, by A.A. Thompson (my own favourite) in 1957, and Eric Midwinter, academic, social historian and cricket buff, whose blend of interests produced an interesting portrait in 1981.

My frequent doubts would be offset by the number of people who, on finding out my project, (a) declared that it sounded a very interesting idea, and (b) revealed that they knew absolutely nothing about W.G. beyond the sort of sketchy brushstrokes I have mentioned above. It encouraged me to plough on, in the growing belief not only that Grace's life was a fascinating one but that it deserved to be told again, and perhaps reinterpreted, for a new generation. And the more I looked into his life, the less like the usual caricature it appeared to be.

Beyond a Boundary by C.L.R. James, the great West Indian writer on cricket, history and politics, should be required reading for anyone interested in the game and how it developed in the Caribbean. A Marxist, but utterly devoid of the dogmatism normally associated with people to whom that adjective is applied, James devoted two fascinating chapters of *Beyond a Boundary* to W.G. and his key place in the Victorian era. Most of what he wrote is brilliantly perceptive and reads as freshly as if written yesterday. His central thesis was that Grace was 'a typical representative of the pre-Victorian Age' who nevertheless came to be one of a trio who symbolised Victorian culture, the others being Thomas Arnold, the great headmaster of Rugby, and Thomas Hughes, author of *Tom Brown's Schooldays*. Yet you would search through the history books of the period in vain for any mention of Grace, an omission which James deplored.

Viewing him in purely cricketing terms, he also saw Grace as the founder of modern batting, and the man who almost single-handed and 'by modern scientific method . . . lifted cricket from a more or less casual pastime into the national institution which it rapidly became'. What are the missing words in that sentence? 'This pre-Victorian' – James was infatuated with the notion of Grace springing from a pre-industrial Arcadia and somehow rising above the Victorian hurly-burly to impose his will upon his sport.

While I am convinced by most of James's elegant proposition, I cannot see Grace as a pre-Victorian, and not only because Victoria had already been Queen for eleven years before he was born. Neville Cardus was surely right to have characterised him as the archetypal Eminent Victorian, perhaps the one public figure who was instantly recognisable to the common man. For my part, the more I have immersed myself in Grace's life, the more modern he seems to be. The overriding impression he leaves is that he would have been as successful in the late twentieth century as he was in the equivalent period of the nineteenth.

There were always two sides to Grace. He may have been an amateur, in name at least and certainly by nature, but in reality he was the ultimate professional in every respect, almost from the beginning. He was reared to be a cricketer, by a family whose obsession the game was – two of his brothers were among the finest players of the age alongside him, his father helped to shape the game in the West Country and even his mother was devoted to the game and the fortunes of her offspring.

Throughout his long career he earned more money from the game than any of the so-called professionals with whom he played. Indeed, so bitter did they become at this that five of them finally threatened to go on strike over the issue before the Oval Test match of 1896, and two declined to play when their demands were refused. Although much is made of his simultaneous medical career, he was only too glad to abandon it in his early fifties, just when he might have been thought to be about to settle down to the life of a full-time doctor, in order to devote himself entirely to cricket, as secretary-captain of the new London County Club.

Equally, there were two faces of W.G., the cricketer. There is the familiar, bulky figure to which I have already referred and which still dominates our image of him – but there is an altogether different face which, I believe, has become neglected and obscured by the later one. This one is the Grace of his late teens and twenties: a tall, slim, graceful, athletic figure, whose long black beard contained not a fleck of grey and who rewrote the record books in the decade or so between the mid-1860s and mid-1870s. This Grace resembled a fierce young prophet, or a Zionist pioneer. He slightly resembled the young Theodor Herzl, who imposed his own will on a different field of play.

He is as different from the older Grace as the young Botham of 1981 was from the man whose international career was virtually over only a decade later. Incidentally, how Grace would have loved to have played with Botham! And what high jinks that pair might have got up to after play was over for the day. But whereas Botham was effectively finished as a cricketer by his mid-thirties, W.G. went on and on, his career bursting into life again in his late forties like one of those ancient plants that suddenly and unexpectedly produce a glorious flower when it was thought to be incapable of doing so again.

Cricketers who play on well into their forties at the highest level are not unknown in the modern age. One thinks of Cyril Washbrook, gloriously recalled to the England colours at the age of forty-two and responding with 98, of Bill Alley saving his best until the late autumn of his career when he scored more than 3,000 runs in one season (1961), also aged forty-two. In our own era, Graham Gooch is also going strong at forty-three and in 1996 passed W.G.'s mark of 124 first-class centuries. But what distinguishes Grace from anyone else is that he provides a bridge from the old world to the new. In 1863, at the age of fifteen, he played for a Bristol Twenty-Two against William Clarke's professional circus, long before there was such a thing as a county championship. In 1899, at the age of nearly fifty-one, he was opening the batting for England against Australia with C.B. Fry and matching the arch-Corinthian stroke for stroke, if not in fleetness of foot between the wickets. He played with and against the ageing John Lillywhite in the 1860s and the young Jack Hobbs at the turn of the century.

In between, he rewrote – or perhaps I should say wrote, for there was nothing much before him – the record books. The statistics are awesome. He scored 54,211 first-class runs in a career that lasted an incredible forty-three years, from 1865 to 1908 (the exact number of runs is disputed by cricket statisticians, some of whom appear to have dedicated the best part of their lives to trying to trace every run he scored). Only four batsmen have made more – Jack Hobbs (61,237), Frank Woolley, Percy Hendren and Phil Mead. Of later players, Walter Hammond had a total of 50,551, Herbert Sutcliffe 50,138, Geoffrey Boycott 48,426 and Graham Gooch had accumulated 44,472 by the end of 1996. But statistics tell only part of the story. In the first half of his career, Grace played on pitches which were often atrocious by modern standards, when scores were far lower than they became from the 1880s onwards. In those circumstances, his achievements were remarkable. For instance, in 1871 he scored 2,739 first-class runs, the first man to clear 2,000 in a season.

Compared with Grace in that season, only one other batsman topped 1,000 (Harry Jupp, with 1,068). In 1873, W.G. made 1,805, when nobody else could manage 1,000 (the dogged Jupp failed by 4). In his great year of 1876, W.G. made 2,622, including 839 in eight days, a spell which included two triple-centuries. Nobody had ever managed even one before and only one other batsman scored more than 1,000 that summer. The previous month W.G. had scored 400 not out against *twenty-two* fielders at Grimsby. Yet nineteen years later, in 1895, he was still good enough to become the first batsman to score 1,000 first-class runs in May and to rattle up 2,346 runs in the season. How many might he have scored on the shirt-front wickets of modern times, or if he had toured abroad more than three times (twice to Australia, once to Canada and the USA)?

He also made more than 45,000 runs in club and other minor fixtures. Did he score more than 100,000 runs in all forms of cricket? Some believe he falls short of the magic figure by a tantalising few but, just as I like to think of Mallory and Irving disappearing into the clouds just short of the summit of Everest but getting to the top before perishing on the way down, so I like to think of W.G. having reached his 100,000, despite what the dry race of statisticians says.

He was a highly effective bowler, taking 2,808 first-class wickets, first as a brisk round-arm seamer, then slowing down with age to become a purveyor of gentle leg-breaks which lured successive generations of batsmen to a destruction they all thought impossible against such soft stuff – and he diddled out a further 4,500 or so in minor cricket. But statistics, while imposing, tell less than half the story. For W.G. *was* cricket for the Victorian public, the most recognisable face in the country along with Gladstone (Monsignor Ronald Knox playfully suggested they were one and the same person).

His participation in a match was guaranteed to add thousands to the gate. If the news spread round London that he was batting at Lord's or The Oval, offices would empty and the cabs stream up the roads to St John's Wood or Kennington. If he was playing at Trent Bridge, Old Trafford or Sheffield, the workers would leave factory or furnace to walk miles for a sight of him batting. And how rarely would he let them down. Of plain country stock himself, he had an instinctive empathy with the common man. The spontaneous displays of affection, the crowds spilling over the ropes to chase him to the pavilion at the end of a great innings, or merely the day's play, were evidence of his huge popularity. Twice national testimonials were organised on his behalf, once by the MCC, once by the *Daily Telegraph*, and on both occasions the public was unstinting in its generosity to a man who had already done well out of the game financially, although he was never one to turn down money.

This sense of comradeship with ordinary people was most marked in his work as a doctor in Bristol. There are many stories of his kindness to poor people, of his little gifts to those in trouble and his efforts to get them help or work. But he was no saint: he had a violent temper, which it was easy to provoke. In 1889 he battered a youth with a cricket stump after the lad had the temerity to ignore W.G.'s orders not to practise on the new county ground at Bristol, and was fortunate to escape legal proceedings. In the event, an apology was enough to settle the matter. He had to apologise in similar fashion to settle a huge row with the Australian touring side of 1878 whom he had outraged by kidnapping Billy Midwinter, the Australian player also registered with Gloucestershire, from Lord's and taking him off to The Oval for a county match on 20 June. That was W.G. all over – quick to rouse, and usually quick to make up, or regret his actions. The most obvious example is his resignation from the Gloucestershire captaincy in 1899 with a withering letter of contempt and hatred for the committee who, he believed, had forced him to take such a step unnecessarily. But he regretted it ever afterwards, and was delighted when fences were mended a few years later.

Indeed, he was often pathetically reluctant to give offence or to dredge up old quarrels. His books of memoirs are utterly devoid of contentious material, and it is difficult to believe they could have any connection with the man who had been involved in so many confrontations on and off the field in England and Australia. It was almost as if he preferred to believe they had never happened. In old age, he was even unwilling to get involved in nominating his greatest XI, a harmless exercise if ever there was one, for fear of giving offence to someone. Behind that brooding, off-putting facade there may have lurked a rather uncertain personality.

He could also be tolerance itself, especially if children were involved. When he arrived at the county ground, Bristol, one morning in 1896 for a match starting at 11.30 a.m., there was already a crowd of about thirty boys waiting outside. He opened the door himself and the boys asked if they could pay him. He let them in and told them to go back and pay when the gates opened. As he walked off, he asked his companion and team-mate, Robert Price, 'Think they'll come back and pay?' Price replied, 'I don't think they will.'

'No, I shouldn't,' replied W.G., laughing.

When a visitor to Bristol paid for his family to get into the ground at Clifton under the mistaken impression it was Clifton Zoo, the gatekeeper refused to give him his money back. Spotting W.G.'s unmistakable face, the man went up to him and told him of his error. W.G. took him back to the gate, made the keeper refund him and pointed out the correct way to get to the zoo.

As he grew older he became more and more autocratic. His family virtually founded Gloucestershire County Cricket Club and were instrumental in making it an instant success and leading it to a glorious first decade of existence never since equalled. He captained the team for twenty-nine years but would not change his selection policy or his way of doing things when the county hit bad times in the late 1880s and early 1890s. The subsequent parting of the ways was inevitable, for he was never a man to compromise.

Not only did he quit Gloucestershire County Cricket Club, he left the county of his birth, and the practice of medicine, for ever and moved to London. The abruptness of his departure is intriguing. Did he ever really enjoy being a doctor? Did he perhaps go into medicine out of a sense of family duty? His father and three older brothers were doctors and it seems to have been considered inevitable that W.G. would follow suit. Whether he was ever consulted about it is another matter.

His medical studies took him the best part of a decade to complete, which is hardly surprising given that at the same time he was in his prime as a cricketer and made two overseas tours. But even so it does not speak of great aptitude for the work. He practised medicine in Bristol for nearly two decades, mainly in the winter, for he continued to play cricket during the summers with undiminished enthusiasm, and was greatly loved by his patients. But at the age of fifty-one he gave it up at short notice and never went back to it.

This was premature by any standards. His father and brothers, for example, practised medicine almost until their dying days. In various memoirs, W.G. never wrote a word about his medical work and does not seem to have missed it at all, particularly once his financial future was secure, thanks to his second testimonial. Perhaps he went along with the study of medicine in the 1870s out of respect for the memory of his father, Dr Henry Grace, who died in 1871, and felt free to abandon a doctor's labours after the death of his eldest brother, Henry junior, in 1895.

He was not a complicated man. Like most of the Grace brothers, he adored practical jokes and schoolboy japes, even in his fifties. His idea of a lark was to suggest to his fellow-players staying at the Grand Hotel, Bournemouth, to race up the stairs to the top of the hotel and back, the last man to stand drinks all round – and this at one o'clock in the morning. He took part, naturally, and did not have to pay for the round. Then they did it all over again, to the consternation of the other guests, who by now thought the hotel must be on fire. As several of his contemporaries noted, he was really just an overgrown schoolboy. Indeed, he was never happier than in the company of children. One of his granddaughters remembered sitting on his knee and tying ribbons in his beard, to his huge amusement.

He left Bristol for ever in 1899 but there were many in the city nearly half a century later in the 1930s who could still remember Dr Grace on his rounds putting down his bag and joining in a snowball fight with the local boys, or an impromptu game of cricket. He would round up a few youths to bowl at him in his garden or before an innings on the county ground, always tipping them generously. For while he was notorious for demanding and getting what he thought he was worth as a cricketer he was equally free in dispensing his money to anyone, young or old, who did him a favour. When a youth found his purse in the street and took it to his surgery, W.G. gave him the purse and all the money in it, which was enough to buy the lad a new suit.

He seems to have spent his life in perpetual motion. When he wasn't playing cricket or attending to his patients, he was out following the beagles or, in later life, playing golf or bowls. He adored beagling, a recreation he pursued all his life (he had to give up riding to hounds when he got too heavy for a horse). His stamina was remarkable and so was his strength, as one Gloucestershire farmer discovered when he tried to block W.G. from pursuing the beagles into his fields. W.G. simply picked up the man, tucked him under his arm and strode across his land, depositing him on the other side with a threat to smack his bottom if he misbehaved himself further. When another farmer rejoiced at the sight of W.G. falling headlong into a ditch as he raced after the dogs, W.G. got up, grabbed him and sat him down in the water too. 'He picked me up as if I'd been a new-born baby,' the farmer is said to have remarked wonderingly when told the identity of his huge assailant.

Such stories are all part of the Grace legend, and there are a thousand such anecdotes about his cricketing life which have gone into the game's folklore. Many of them involve Tom Emmett, the doughty Yorkshire left-arm seam bowler who was involved in many a long battle with W.G. 'He ought to have a littler bat,' was his comment during one epic innings. Another left-armer who came in for a lot of punishment from W.G. was Nottinghamshire's James Shaw, who made the immortal remark: 'I puts 'em where I likes, and he puts 'em where *he* likes.'

The commonest perception of W.G., which persists to this day, is that he was a cheat, that he bent the rules to suit himself, and would simply ignore an umpire's decision if he did not agree with it. 'He would stretch the laws of cricket uncommonly taut in his own favour,' wrote Lord Hawke, 'but nobody bore him a grudge.' Whether W.G. behaved very differently from anybody else playing then or now is a moot point. I was writing some of this book to the accompaniment of the radio commentary on the climax of the first Test between Zimbabwe and England in December 1996, when Zimbabwe deliberately bowled wide to prevent the England batsmen from scoring the last few vital runs. I have no doubt that had W.G. been captaining the fielding side in such a situation he would have ordered his bowlers to behave in a similar fashion.

He played to win, although he could accept defeat gracefully. He undoubtedly tried to intimidate umpires into giving marginal decisions in his favour but, again as I write, the England team in Zimbabwe has just been warned by the match referee for that very offence. When Gloucestershire played Essex at Leyton in 1898, W.G. infuriated the Essex fielders as the game built up towards a tight finish by refusing to accept the umpire's initial verdict of 'out' for what he thought was a bump-ball return catch. On that occasion, the umpire backed down, but just as frequently umpires did not, sending W.G. on his way despite his grumbles. Once he enquired, as he left the wicket, which leg the umpire thought the ball had struck for an lbw decision. 'Never mind which leg,' replied the umpire. 'I've given you out and out you've got to go.'

To another umpire who had also given him out leg before, W.G. complained, 'I played that ball.'

'Yes,' retorted the umpire, 'but it was after it had hit your leg.'

In these days the sports pages are full of batsmen who never touched the ball but were given out caught behind, or off bat and pad at forward-short-leg, and often we are none the wiser after watching the television replay half-a-dozen times.

So, while W.G. may frequently have stretched the laws as far as he could, the idea that he invariably disregarded the umpire's verdict if he did not agree with it is an exaggeration. He once prevented a Gloucestershire batsman from leaving the pavilion to go out to the wicket at Bristol because he believed the last man out, Gilbert Jessop, had not been fairly caught on the boundary. The game was held up for half an hour while the argument raged but the umpires had their way in the end.

W.G. was essentially a cricketer who liked to win and occasionally crossed the barrier between fair and foul play in tight situations, like many others before and since. He was involved in a number of notorious incidents in first-class cricket, such as when he ran out the Australian batsman Sammy Jones in the legendary match at The Oval in 1882 when Jones wandered up the pitch to do a spot of 'gardening'. Most people – including the batsman – thought the ball was dead but the umpire bowed to W.G.'s appeal.

Tony Greig did something very similar to Alvin Kallicharran in 1974, and the umpire agreed with *him* too. Such was the outcry that the appeal was withdrawn and the West Indian reinstated, but when people think of Greig today they don't think of him primarily as a cheat but as occasionally over-enthusiastic for the best motives. (Incidentally, had Kerry Packer existed in W.G.'s day, he would have been strongly tempted to throw in his lot with Packer, as Greig did, for W.G. was always keen on money. He would have made a great limited-overs player too.)

Like players today, he behaved worse than normally if he

thought the standard of umpiring was low, as it probably was on his two tours of Australia where he repeatedly took umbrage at the umpires' decisions, and thereby earned the hostility of press and public, though interestingly not of the Australian players. They knew a tough competitor when they saw one, and probably didn't think much of their own officials either.

Nothing W.G. got up to in Australia was anything like as bad as the row between the England captain Mike Gatting and the local umpire Shakoor Rana in Pakistan in 1987 which helped to sour cricketing relations between the two countries for years.

Many of the stories about W.G. and umpires stem from club matches where nothing was at stake and where the crowd undoubtedly wanted to see the legendary figure in action. He went out to open the innings in a charity match, attended by a large and expectant crowd, only to see the second ball remove the off bail. W.G. bent down, picked it up and replaced it, saying to the wicketkeeper in his inimitable Gloucestershire accent, 'Strong wind today, Jarge.' No one queried his action and he went on to hit 142 – which is what everyone had hoped to see.

His contemporaries had no doubt about his stature. Those two cricketing peers who dominated the councils of the Victorian game, Lords Hawke and Harris, produced very similar verdicts on him. 'As a cricketer,' wrote Hawke,

I do not hesitate to say that not only was he the greatest that ever lived, but also the greatest that ever can be, because no future batsman will ever have to play on the bad wickets on which he made his mark and proved himself so immeasurably superior to all his contemporaries.

According to Harris,

he was . . . always a most genial, even-tempered, considerate companion and of all the many cricketers I have ever known the kindest as well as the best. He was ever ready with an encouraging word for the novice, and a compassionate one for the man who had made a mistake . . . It is difficult to believe that a combination so remarkable of health, activity, power, eye, hand, devotion and opportunity will ever present itself again.

There is much more anecdotal evidence about his kindness to young players and modesty about his own achievements.

If he had a weakness, it was as a captain. While he was a dab hand at enticing a batsman out with a crafty bit of field placing, he had a tendency to let things drift along when imagination and daring were called for. He was no innovator, but an instinctive conservative, and he brooked no opposition to his way of doing things. His record was patchy. He led Gloucestershire with great success in the first years of the county's official existence but that was due more to his own overwhelming dominance with bat and ball, ably backed up by his brothers E.M. and G.F. The county's fortunes declined and W.G. failed to bring on enough new players to restore it to its previous eminence.

But of his own playing ability there will never be any doubt. In our century, Gary Sobers was a purer all-rounder and Don Bradman a greater run-getter, although there are some interesting parallels between Bradman and Grace. Both were country boys who displayed a fierce dedication from a very young age, while their adult play was characterised by enormous patience and discipline. Neither was a stylist; instead, they were brutally effective, deriving an almost sadistic pleasure from reducing a bowling attack to rubble. Bradman's career batting figures (first-class average: 95.14, Test average 99.94) were far superior to Grace's but he played on much better pitches. Perhaps the greatest similarity between them was that they represented more than cricket to the common man in his own country. Bradman was the personification of an Australia emerging from the dominance of its colonial master, Grace the hero to the working class of industrial Victorian England.

W.G.'s abiding legacy, however, is that no single cricketer has since dominated the game so totally as he did for more than thirty years. English cricket these days could do with someone possessing one tenth of his talent, discipline and will to win.

2 · THE GRACE FAMILY

THE year is 1858, the scene the garden of a large house in the village of Downend, near Bristol. The big lawn is shaded by several spreading chestnut trees. It is an early summer's day, clear and bright, a light breeze chases a few clouds quickly across the blue sky. In the garden, a stocky teenage boy in shirt-sleeves is driving three cricket stumps into the grass at the end of the lawn nearest the house. A strip of grass has been mown shorter than the rest to make a pitch. A single stump has already been set up some twenty yards away.

Another young man, sporting a dark moustache, is rolling up his shirt-sleeves. Two older men, well into middle age, talk with each other as they take off their jackets and lay them on the grass. A little boy of seven capers around the lawn and begs to be allowed to play with the grown-ups. A peal of laughter comes from the edge of the lawn under a large chestnut tree where stand a middle-aged lady and her daughters – two young women and two much younger girls in their early teens, in blouses and demure ankle-length skirts. Occasionally they bend to stroke two dogs lying at their feet, a golden retriever and a pointer. Another pointer crouches near by, wagging its tail and watching the activity on the lawn intently as if waiting for an invitation to join in.

There is one other person on the lawn: a boy about ten years old, kneeling as he straps a pad on to his leg. That done, he picks up a bat from the grass beside him, stands up and walks to a position just in front of the stumps. He is a slim, slight figure compared to the adults, with jet-black hair and intense dark eyes that stand out against his pale face. He has an air of seriousness, watchfulness and concentration.

The middle-aged men and the smallest boy stroll to positions around the lawn. The young man with the moustache walks up the wicket, exchanges a word with the dark-haired boy and proceeds to crouch behind the stumps. The teenager picks up a cricket ball, waits for the dark-haired boy to take guard, then runs a few paces to the single stump and delivers the ball with a round-arm slinging action. The boy picks his bat up cleanly, plants his padded left leg down the wicket and strikes the ball on the off side towards the young women chatting under the chestnut. As it speeds towards them, bouncing off the uneven surface of the lawn, the black dog at their feet snaps out of his crouch and leaps at the ball as it breasts him, knocks it down with his chest and pounces on it. At this, the girls laugh and clap and the men cheer. 'Well stopped, Ponto sir!' shouts one, as the dog picks the ball up in his mouth and trots towards the bowler, his tail wagging furiously. Turning towards the batsman, one of the older men says quietly, 'And well hit, Gilbert.' The older woman, who has been watching the episode closely, nods approvingly.

Lost in a world of his own, the dark-haired boy does not appear to have noticed the dog's antics, nor heard the word of praise from his father. William Gilbert Grace rehearses the off-drive again, then resumes his guard, waiting for the next delivery.

As we near the end of the twentieth century there is much discussion and soul-searching in many British sports about how to spot, train and develop children with sporting talent. In tennis and cricket particularly, games invented in Britain and which used to spawn a steady stream of great players, there seems a dreadful dearth of potential world-beaters. If by chance a good cricketer is unearthed, there is reluctance to blood him in the demanding arena of Test cricket. Yet in other countries bright youngsters are pitched into international matches while still in their teens. In Australia the country's most promising young players are invited to attend the National Cricket Academy of excellence in Adelaide and submitted to a demanding year-long training programme to prepare them for greater things, with notable success. After England had lost several successive Ashes series in the 1980s and 1990s by embarrassing margins, the cry went up: Why can't we do the same?

Perhaps these things don't have to be done by governments or governing bodies. A century and a half ago, William Gilbert Grace was born into a home-grown sporting academy, whose record would stand comparison with any official institution charged with turning out good sportsmen. His father and favourite uncle were keen cricketers, his four brothers all fine players. Of the five Grace boys, three became among the best cricketers in England, and Gilbert the greatest the game had ever seen. Even their mother was, untypically for the Victorian age, an enthusiast who was highly knowledgeable about the game and followed her sons' progress keenly.

Their father, Henry Mills Grace, was born on 21 February 1808, in the Somerset village of Long Ashton. His own father, also called Henry, was said to have been an Irish footman at Long Ashton Court who married the daughter of the chief steward. It is attractive to think of the Grace boys having Irish blood. Certainly, they displayed all the classic Irish traits of athleticism, physical courage, wit and good-natured cheek. Henry Mills Grace's was a typical rural childhood of the age: he grew up well versed in the traditional country pursuits, particularly riding, but he also acquired an early interest in cricket and, as a boy, played the game as much as he could. His distinguished son later described with sympathy the problems young Henry had in practising the game as much as he clearly would have liked. 'If he had had the opportunities afforded to his children he would have attained a good position as an all-round player,' wrote W.G. in 1891. 'Clubs were few in number in his boyhood and grounds were fewer still.'

Sport was not yet the integral part of the school curriculum that it was to become in the mid-Victorian era so Henry's cricketing development was restricted. Like many a father before and since, he was determined his own sons should not suffer the same lack of facilities, which helps to explain the intense devotion he was later to lavish on their sporting education, with such remarkable results. A sturdy 5 ft 10 in tall, weighing 13 stone, Henry Grace was not a man to be put off by anything.

Settling on a career in medicine, he was articled to a surgeon in Bristol, after the custom of the times, but did not allow his studies to interfere with his cricket. Two or three times a week he and some friends would rise early in the morning to head for Durdham Down, a large expanse of open common ground to the north-west of the city, where Gloucestershire were to play their first county match against Surrey many years later in 1870 with Henry Grace's sons among the participants. On Durdham Down, Henry and company would practise their cricket between five and eight o'clock, Henry batting right-handed but bowling and throwing in left-handed.

He undertook further studies at the combined medical school of Guy's and St Thomas's Hospitals in London and on qualifying embarked on the life of a country doctor which he was to be for the rest of his life. Henry was twenty-three when he married Martha Pocock in 1831. Born on 18 July 1812, she was barely nineteen on her wedding day but was a perfect match for the energetic, hard-working young doctor.

She was a spirited girl from a decidedly eccentric background. Her father, George Pocock, was proprietor of a private boarding school at St Michael's Hill, Bristol, and as fervent about religion as Henry Grace was about cricket. So keen was he to spread the word that he toured the West Country in a horse-drawn trap, erecting a tent which he called his 'itinerant temple' in places where there was no church but a likely supply of worshippers.

He was also obsessed with box-kites. Family legend had it that he and his daughters once drove from Bristol to London in a carriage drawn by a kite, overtaking the Duke of York's more conventionally-powered coach on the way. That may have been the same journey as one he reportedly made in 1828 to the Ascot races where his kite-carriage was said to have greatly impressed George IV. Pocock was also said to have designed a kite-borne chair, which sounds like an early prototype of a hang-glider, in which young Martha was once strapped and transported across the Avon Gorge.

Martha grew to be a most remarkable woman, and more than

a century after her death remains possibly the most influential in the history of cricket. Even today cricket is overwhelmingly a male-dominated sport, and women who are both passionate and knowledgeable about the game are regarded as something of an oddity by many men. However, the informed cricket woman is to be seen, instantly recognisable, at Lord's or any county ground, as much a part of the scenery as the players, umpires or scorers. Martha Grace was the archetype, and has yet to be improved upon. The great cricketer Richard Daft said of her, 'She knew ten times more about cricket than any lady I ever met.'

She was an imposing figure, 'of magnificent physique and indomitable will', and W.G. strongly resembled her physically. Quite where her love of cricket sprang from is uncertain; perhaps from her brother Alfred ('Uncle Pocock') who was also a key figure in the Grace boys' cricket education. At any rate Martha took as much a part in the coaching of her sons as her husband and closely followed her talented sons' progress. She watched them play whenever she could and was forthright in her criticisms. In her old age she regularly attended Gloucestershire's matches and was noted for her pithy comments on the play and the players. Indeed it appears to have been part of a Gloucestershire's batsman's duties, once dismissed, to pay his respects to Mrs Grace as she sat in the stand and to listen attentively as he was told just where he had gone wrong. For some reason she disliked left-handed batsmen and fielders who returned the ball underarm (which would presumably have doubly disqualified David Gower from her pantheon).

Throughout her life she demanded to be kept informed of her sons' performances: when they were playing away from home, they would post to her the day's scoresheets or send her a telegram informing her of their achievements that day, which would arrive the same evening. She cut out all newspaper reports of their doings and pasted them in large scrapbooks. She was their greatest supporter, and author of the most famous letter in English cricket. This was to George Parr, captain of the All England XI in which she recommended her third son, Edward Mills Grace, for selection in the England team, and added that she had a younger son who would eventually be even better because his back-play was sounder and he always played with a straight bat.

There is a touching vignette of the old lady watching the Lansdown Club in 1884 playing the American tourists, Gentlemen of Philadelphia, and being offered a chair by a player who did not recognise her. As they talked of the game, she said, 'I taught my sons to play. I used to bowl to them.'

Henry Grace and his bride settled in the Gloucestershire village of Downend, four miles outside the bustling city of Bristol, and never moved from it thereafter. Grace was a highly conscientious doctor and a good surgeon, whose practice extended for a twelve-mile radius around Downend. He covered it on horseback and was often not back home until midnight. He was surgeon to the Royal Gloucestershire Reserves and did much work for the underprivileged as medical officer to the Poor Law. A jovial and popular man, he ranged easily over the classes. He was a friend of the Duke of Beaufort and a frequent visitor to Badminton to hunt during the winter.

His obituary in the *Lancet* noted: 'Few better horsemen ever rode to cover.' He was also a man of strong views and principles. W.G. wrote of him: 'He took great care that the foxes were preserved and was so strict that he used to say that a man who would kill a fox would commit almost any crime.' He seems to have been decidedly progressive in many ways. He never smoked, and drank but little, 'a glass of wine with his dinner and a little whisky and water at night', reported W.G., also a lifelong non-smoker – apart perhaps from the occasional cigar – but liked a glass of whisky at lunchtime during a cricket match and enjoyed champagne too.

The Graces' first home was Downend House, on whose lawn the doctor lost no time in laying down a cricket pitch in front of the house where he could practise. However, having his own pitch was never going to be enough for the cricket-mad doctor. Interest in the game was growing to such an extent in Downend and the surrounding villages, as elsewhere in the country, that Dr Grace and his friends decided to set up their own club. They found some common land at Rodway Hill at Mangotsfield, about a mile to the

19

east of Downend, and cleared, levelled and fenced in some forty square yards of it to create their own ground.

Thus was born the Mangotsfield Cricket Club, with Dr Grace and Arthur Pocock its two leading lights. Pocock, a good racquets player, was a novice at cricket but took to it with a will and was soon an accomplished all-rounder. He was a great one for practice, a habit he was to pass on to his nephews. The club prospered, aided by two of Mrs Grace's nephews, William Rees and George Gilbert, who came to stay at Downend House during the summer holidays for several years and showed themselves a cut above the average local player. At around the same time, the West Gloucestershire club had been founded at Coalpit Heath, a couple of miles north of Downend, by another local enthusiast, Henry Hewitt. The two clubs became fierce rivals, with West Gloucestershire at first holding the advantage. Mangotsfield, however, gradually overhauled their rivals and in 1847 the clubs agreed to pool their resources. The new club went under the name of West Gloucestershire but was based at Rodway Hill, where it played for twenty more years. West Gloucestershire became the dominant club of the area; the only other team to pose a regular challenge was Lansdown.

Henry and Martha Grace lived at Downend House for nineteen years, during which time Martha gave birth to eight of their nine children, five sons and four daughters. The four boys born there were Henry, the eldest, (31 January 1833), Alfred (17 May 1840), Edward Mills (28 November 1841) and William Gilbert, who arrived on 18 July 1848, his mother's thirty-sixth birthday. The girls were Annie, born in 1834, Fanny Hellings (1838), Alice Rose (1845) and the youngest, Elizabeth Blanche, who like W.G. was known by her second name, and was born in 1847. By 1850, with their last child on the way, the Graces needed a bigger house and moved across the road to The Chestnuts, where George Frederick ('Fred') was born on 13 December 1850 to complete the family.

Downend is no longer a self-contained village but part of the straggling suburbs of Bristol. Downend House still stands there, although its ground floor has been extensively remodelled and in 1996 was home to offices of a lift firm and a catering company. It bears a small plaque which states that 'Dr W.G. Grace, Famous Gloucester Cricketer, was born here on the 18th July, 1848'. Another plaque proclaims it to be part of the Kingswood Heritage Trail.

The Chestnuts (or The Chesnuts as the Graces eccentrically spelt it) was much more suitable for the large and lively family than the relatively cramped conditions of Downend House. It was, according to a contemporary description, 'a square, plain building . . . ivy creeping all over, with pretty flower garden, and numerous outhouses . . . Walking up the carriage drive, past the lodge and old summer house, you come to the main entrance . . . beyond, the orchard, some 80 yards in length, high wall on the left.' Still farther beyond was a view of barley and oat fields stretching away to the villages of Frenchay and Stapleton in the far distance.

Alas, the house no longer exists. On its site stands a spectacularly hideous British Telecom building, dating from 1968, and adorned with an antenna tower for mobile telephones. Next to it is a 1980s shopping parade, decorated with a portrait of W.G. Behind the buildings, there is a field divided into allotments, which must be the garden of The Chestnuts. It still presents an attractively rural aspect.

The apple trees in one of the orchards – for there were, in fact, two – stood in the way of Dr Grace's ideal: his own cricket pitch. With Arthur Pocock and eldest son Henry, by now a strapping teenager, he set to and felled most of them. Edward Mills (later better known, like W.G., by his initials E.M.) took over the job with relish as he grew older, making the cricket field bigger and better – he was always a keen organiser, as he showed when he ran Gloucestershire C.C.'s affairs for nearly forty years. A piece of canvas, hung on three poles like a beach windbreak, was put up behind the batsman's end to do the job of wicketkeeper and the stage was set. Here the Grace family practised with a dedication bordering on the obsessional, in the early morning or late in the evening, co-opting anybody and everybody to help: maids, the bootboy, but only very occasionally one of the Grace sisters, despite a legend that grew up when W.G. was young that the girls fielded with enthusiasm while the boys batted. One young

Downend man called Alf Monks was regularly invited to bowl. As an incentive, the Grace boys put two-shilling coins or half-crowns on the stumps and told Alf he could keep any that he knocked off. Although he rarely succeeded, he was usually compensated with five shillings for his efforts, so he rarely lost out.

What a fortunate childhood! 'It was as natural for me and everyone at home to walk out to the ground as it is for every boy in England to go into his nursery,' W.G. mused later. 'And what boy with a choice at his command would prefer the latter?'

The most remarkable participants in the family practice sessions were the Graces' dogs, Don and Ponto, the two pointers, and Noble, the retriever, and by all accounts the best cricketer of the three. Family legend had it that the dogs were connoisseurs of the game. They were said to position themselves behind the bowler and if the ball was pitched on the off side they would make off in that direction even before the batsman had hit it. If he pulled it from outside off stump to leg they would decline to run after it. One suspects the notorious leg-pulling of the whole Grace clan behind this story.

W.G. – 'Young Gilbert' – had the best of all worlds as a boy. His older brothers were still around for practice and his father and Uncle Pocock still in the prime of life and eager to coach him. Gilbert was fielding for them all from the moment he could run around, and he soon picked up a bat too. Uncle Pocock took a special interest in coaching him and was to be a big influence on the boy. W.G. was always at great pains to emphasise that his uncle insisted he played with a straight bat from the first. Perhaps this was out of guilt that he and Dr Grace had allowed E.M. to develop bad habits through not having the correct-sized bat. Uncle Pocock worked on W.G.'s stance and his footwork and for years insisted that he do no more than defend his wicket. 'There must be no playing or hitting wildly,' was the instruction and Gilbert applied himself with total dedication. He claimed he was not a 'natural' player to whom the art of batting came easily; but his uncle had obviously spotted something in the boy. He insisted he learn to bat the right way: left shoulder forward, head over the ball, and watch the ball all the way. Gilbert applied himself

hounds several times a week, and was famous throughout the district for his flair and daring. He was once claimed to have jumped a thirty-foot-wide stream on an Irish thoroughbred, and it was said of him that for thirty years he never had to buy a hunter of his own, but was given the most difficult horses to ride by his friends. He was an immensely popular figure, often referred to in local literature as 'the hunting doctor'. The wonder is that he was able to find time for all his interests. He was the only smoker of the five brothers, yet he lived the longest: he died in 1916, aged seventy-six.

If W.G. had never existed, old Dr Grace could still have boasted of siring one of the finest cricketers in England. At his adult height of 5ft 7 ¾ in, E.M. was the shortest of the brothers and the liveliest. His love of cricket manifested itself from an early age. Local lore had it that he was spotted staggering towards the West Gloucestershire ground clutching a full-sized bat before his first birthday, which sounds like another tall story dreamt up for seekers after Grace myths.

Whatever the truth, he certainly practised when young with a bat that was too big for him – the cause of his unorthodox batting style. He did not play straight but hit most deliveries to leg with a cross bat, and continued to do so as an adult. At school he owned his own set of stumps, presumably a gift from a father delighted that his third son should be as passionate about cricket as himself. If events were going against him E.M. would simply hurl himself over the stumps and refuse to allow the game to proceed. While he never went that far in later life, he was always a fierce competitor who hated to lose.

He developed into a great all-rounder – a brilliant batsman, a shrewd and effective bowler and, by general consent, the best fielder in England, always at point, his speed, athleticism and eye making a lethal combination. There were numerous stories of him appearing to pick the ball almost off the face of the bat. One such victim was Surrey's Bobby Abel, who cut a ball from W.G. with a full swing of the bat and started running up the wicket. No one else moved, and W.G. roared 'Where's the ball?' E.M. calmly fished it out of his pocket and Abel was given out caught, although nobody had seen E.M. catch him. Similarly, in a match at Clifton College, E.M. stopped a rocket of a shot, turned and pointed towards the boundary. Cover-point ran off in that direction while the batsman started off up the wicket. At that, E.M. strolled up to the stumps, ball in hand, knocked off a bail and ran him out.

His MCC biography described him as 'one of the most successful batsmen that ever appeared, and the rapidity with which he can score is something marvellous, being a tremedous hitter . . . Is overflowing with cricket at every pore, full of lusty life, cheerily gay, with energy inexhaustible.'

The story of his first appearance in the celebrated Canterbury week in 1862 gives a flavour of the man. Still only twenty, he was acquiring a considerable reputation and the Kent secretary, his side being a man short, asked Dr and Mrs Grace, who were in town for the cricket, if E.M. would make up the eleven. Dr Grace consented on condition the young man was asked to play in two matches. Summoned to Canterbury by telegraph, E.M. arrived on the second day of the first game but made a duck. In the second innings, he made up for it with 56 not out.

When he was invited to play for MCC against Gentlemen of Kent in the next match a row broke out, some of the Kent players objecting to the fact that E.M. was not an MCC member, to Dr Grace's ire. The Kent secretary, who was away from the ground when the complaint was aired, returned and confirmed the arrangement. So E.M. guested for MCC and made the Kentish men pay for their punctiliousness. Opening the innings, he carried his bat for a superb 192 not out and demolished Kent with the ball in their second innings, taking all ten wickets. Earl Sefton, President of MCC, presented him with a bat and the Hon. Spencer Ponsonby sent him a ball mounted on an inscribed stand commemorating his feat. There is no record of what the Gentlemen of Kent thought of it all, but the episode typified E.M's fiery nature: if any man tried to do him down, he responded explosively. It is not hard to imagine what an influence such a larger-than-life character must have had on the young W.G., seven years his junior.

E.M. toured Australia with George Parr's team in 1863/64

although he did not do himself justice there, mainly because of an injured hand. He played once for England, in the historic first Test match in England, against Australia at The Oval in 1880. He was by then thirty-nine years old and would undoubtedly have played far more often for his country had Test cricket existed while he was in his prime.

He qualified as a doctor in 1861 – one of the examiners wrote, 'Dr Grace is requested not to write with a stump' – and first practised at Marshfield before moving two years later to the village of Thornbury, twelve miles from Downend, where he was to remain for the rest of his life. Like his brothers, he was deeply involved in the life of the community: he too was surgeon to the local workhouse, parish medical officer and public vaccinator. He was also Registrar of Births and Deaths, and Coroner for East Gloucestershire from 1875, and known to the cricketing press and public as 'The Coroner'.

He was quick to take offence at a slight, real or imagined. Playing for Gloucestershire against Somerset in the 1890s, he batted with a badly damaged thumb which was further injured by deliveries from the Somerset bowler Sammy Woods. As play was held up while he was being treated, a spectator shouted, 'Why don't you hold an inquest on him?' E.M. muttered, 'I can't stand this' and headed off in the heckler's direction to exact retribution. Seeing him approaching, the man ran off, with E.M. pursuing him all the way to the gate. Then he returned to the wicket and completed an innings of 70.

On another occasion, he was batting with W.G. and both were scoring very slowly, unusually for them as both liked to get on with it whenever possible. The crowd began to barrack them, and their criticism intensified as the players returned to the pavilion at an interval. Furious, E.M. reached into the crowd and grabbed one of his barrackers. A spirited tussle ensued, and as the man's friends dragged him away, one of them told E.M. in a deep Gloucestershire accent, 'Look yer, Crowner, thee canst sit on carpse with twelve men to help tha, but thee cassent sit on a live man.'

The story was told of E.M. playing in an away match for Gloucestershire and receiving a telegram requesting him to return at once to Bristol to hold an inquest. As the county had only eleven players, W.G. advised him to reply, 'Impossible to come today – please put corpse on ice.'

He bowled both round-arm seamers and tricky under-arm lobs and his impatience extended to batsmen who treated the latter with too much reverence. To one such, in a club match, who was simply blocking and not scoring, he eventually shouted, 'I'm not bowling for you to play pat-ball. Hit 'em, man!' The man did so and ran up an impressive score after which E.M., bearing no grudge, congratulated him with the words, 'If you hadn't taken my advice, you would have been in still, poking about.'

Like all the Graces, he was a keen huntsman. A boy playing a scratch game of cricket with some friends at Dursley remembered E.M. arriving on the scene with the Berkeley Hunt. Forgetting the chase, he leapt off his horse and joined in the game, promising a shilling to anyone who could bowl or catch him. Nobody did, but they still got their money.

E.M. was heavily involved in non-medical matters too, as chairman of the parish council and school board, the last Mayor of Thornbury (the post was abolished under local government reorganisation), chairman of the local Conservative Party and the Tariff Reform League. As Gloucestershire secretary, he had a near-photographic memory for members' names and faces, which came in handy as he wandered round the club's many grounds on match days collecting subscriptions. He was married four times, and fathered eighteen children, thirteen by his first wife and five by his second. He died in 1911, aged sixty-nine, and a huge crowd followed the coffin the twelve miles from Thornbury to the family plot at Downend where he was buried.

Finally, there was Fred. He was the archetypal youngest child, loved by everybody in the family and beyond. However, being the youngest was something of a handicap because by the time he was getting keen and eager to practise on the lawn his two older brothers had married and moved out to different villages, while E.M. was often away playing cricket. For much of the time Fred had to make do with the bootboy's bowling and his mother's coaching. An attempt to rope in a nursemaid called

Tibbie Jones ended after the poor girl was forced to bowl and field for a day, after which she retired hurt for good. Still, Fred prospered, once he had been persuaded not to bat left-handed, as he wished. Presumably the chief opponent of this was Mrs Grace, and while her prejudice would be disapproved of these days Fred's subsequent record justified her insistence. 'He showed promise of excellence at quite as early an age as I did,' wrote W.G. 'He was strong for his age and played with a determination worthy of a much older boy.' (This trait is common among children with much older siblings whom they are desperate to emulate.) He played in his first local match when he was only nine and took thirteen wickets, ten of them clean bowled. By his mid-teens he was known throughout the county and like his brothers grew to be a fine all-rounder, a hard-hitting batsman, a fast round-arm bowler and a brilliant fielder; he too played for England, and studied medicine. But at the age of twenty-nine, he died from pneumonia brought on by a chill, a terrible blow to the family and to the cricket world for he was a handsome, dashing and popular figure.

As Gilbert grew older, his love of the countryside developed and was never to desert him. Fred, being only two-and-a-half years younger, shared his enthusiasms; they were constantly together. They learned how to use a gun, at first shooting at small birds and going on to hares, but the hunt for the latter on one occasion led them into disgrace. To distract the local harriers (the hare hunt), Gilbert, Fred and Uncle Pocock laid a circular trail of aniseed around the district to put off the hounds and leave the field for themselves. Unfortunately for them, when the dogs came round for the third time, suspicion as to the reason started to grow. The two Grace boys legged it, leaving Uncle Pocock to face the music.

Life in Downend and the area between the village and Bristol was not to be a rural idyll for much longer. The Industrial Revolution which had transformed the great cities of the North and Midlands had not bypassed Bristol entirely. In the first half of the nineteenth century its population more than doubled, from 72,000 in 1801 to 166,000 in 1851. The city's most explosive growth was reserved for the second half, the population more than doubling again to reach 356,000 in 1901. In the latter period, its older

31

industries were redeveloped and a host of new ones arose beside them. The symbol of the new Bristol was Isambard Kingdom Brunel, originally a Londoner who came to Bristol in poor health and in search of cleaner air, and swiftly recovered to mastermind the laying down of the Great Western Railway between Bristol and London, which started operations in 1841. In 1844 the line between Bristol and Birmingham was inaugurated, opening up access to the Midlands and the North for the south-western city, and the same year a line to South Wales was approved. (Incidentally, these new lines were to be a major factor in the spread of professional cricket, bearing the players from one end of the country to another in hitherto unimaginable speed and comfort.) The railways' gargantuan appetite for iron and coal was partly fed by the mines of the Forest of Dean, where iron production rose from 9,800 tons in 1828 to 170,611 in 1871. From the forest's coal mines came 100,000 tons in 1800; by 1856, that had risen to 460,000 tons and by the end of the century to more than a million. In 1851, 3,600 people were employed in engineering in the whole of Gloucestershire. Fifty years later there were 7,850 in Bristol alone. Entire new industries were born: non-ferrous metal-bashing, boot- and shoe-making, leather-working and tanning supplied by hides from the rich agricultural land around the city. Figures for the port of Bristol confirm the city's dynamic growth: between 1850 and 1900 the annual registered net tonnage of ships using it rose from 129,254 tons to 847,632. More significantly, the cargo they unloaded had increased from about 175,000 tons in 1850 to more than 500,000 by the 1870s and topped 1.3 million in 1900.

Most of the city's industrial and population growth was eastwards, eventually devouring villages like Mangotsfield. The population of Bristol's eastern area rose from 23,000 in 1801 to 61,000 in 1851. From then until 1901, virtually the exact period that W.G. lived in Downend as a child and a man, the population soared to 177,000. The area accounted for nearly 80 per cent of the city's nineteenth-century population increase. W.G. grew up, not in a static, unchanging pastoral world, but on the edge of a dynamic, fast-growing industrial landscape, with all the benefits and evils which that world brought with it. Most importantly, as far as he was concerned, there developed a new urban working-class who increasingly looked for sports and pastimes to play or to watch which would give them a break from their grimy, unhealthy and gruelling workplaces. In the latter half of the nineteenth century one game above all caught their imagination – cricket.

3 · BOY WONDER
1854–1869

WHAT was the state of cricket in England when Gilbert Grace was a boy in Downend? In the 1850s it was at a crossroads, in between its birth in the previous century as a village game and its development as a national sport in the second half of the nineteenth century, with the county championship at its apex. Several county clubs had been set up (the first was Sussex in 1841) and an informal championship began in 1864. This left large areas of the country where the only cricket was played between village teams such as Dr Grace had set up in Gloucestershire, but there was a growing number of good professionals whom the public were keen to see. In the absence of a proper county championship, how were they to do so? The answer came in the form of touring troupes of the top professionals, of which the first and most notable was the All England Eleven set up by William Clarke in 1846.

It is fitting that W.G.'s first experience of cricket outside the charmed world of The Chestnuts was in 1854, when he was six years old. He was taken to Bristol to see a match between Clarke's All England team and twenty-two men of West Gloucestershire. The game was organised by his father, who also captained the local team. So the first match seen by the boy who was to be the century's greatest cricketer involved the man who was the century's most innovative cricketer until that point.

William Clarke was as significant a figure in his day as Kerry

34

Packer was in ours and with much the same aim: to capitalise on the growing public interest in the game and establish regular employment and a decent market rate for professional cricketers, whose job prospects had hitherto been precarious. The means Clarke devised to do this was to recruit the best cricketers in the country for All England and tour the country playing any local teams who cared to arrange a venue.

A Nottingham man, Clarke was first a bricklayer and then an innkeeper. He first played cricket for the Notts Eleven at the age of eighteen and became well known in the North and Midlands as a slow bowler who delivered leg-breaks from waist height. He had a shrewd eye for business, for a good horse and a good deal: he married the widow of the proprietor of the Trent Bridge Inn and laid the foundations of the Trent Bridge ground by buying and developing the adjoining land. He was a late developer on the national cricket scene: his first appearance at Lord's, for the North v the South, was in 1836 when he was thirty-seven. Ten years later, he was invited by the Marylebone Cricket Club to come to London as a practice bowler at Lord's. That year he made a belated debut for the Players v Gentlemen (in which he was to play several more times) and in the 1847 fixture he shared all twenty wickets with John Lillywhite, both matches being played at Lords.

By then, Clarke, ever on the look-out for a good business opportunity, had set up his All England Eleven. As he had predicted, it was a huge success. Invitations came in from all over the country and Clarke's circus took the cricketing message to places until then starved of top-class cricket, going to remote spots as far afield as Cornwall, Lincolnshire and Ireland, travelling long hours in the most uncomfortable circumstances, by stagecoach if there was no railway line.

The welcome they received everywhere more than made up for the hardship involved. The financial rewards did not, however, and in 1852 several of his professionals departed to set up a rival team, the United All England Eleven, in protest at Clarke's refusal to pay them a decent wage. Local clubs were required to put up a fee of about £70, yet Clarke, who had a reputation for tight-fistedness, paid his players only £5 each (or a grudging

£6 for long journeys) from which he deducted their travelling expenses.

He retained the loyalty of most of his players, however, and for the visit to Bristol he could still muster a formidable Eleven, including some of the greatest names in English cricket: George Parr, 'the Lion of the North', another Nottinghamshire man, gritty and determined, a natural leader who took over the All England team from Clarke and led two of the first three overseas tours by English teams; Julius Caesar, whose magnificent name belied both his origins (he came from Goldalming, in rural Surrey), his small stature and his intensely nervous nature, but who was a fine batsman, a great exponent of the drive and the pull; the durable and evergreen Sussex wicketkeeper Thomas Box; William Caffyn, also of Surrey, a talented all-rounder known at The Oval as 'Terrible Billy'; John Bickley, the Nottinghamshire medium-pace bowler who the previous year had taken 8–23 against England at Lord's; Edgar 'Ned' Willsher, the Kent left-arm opening bowler who eight years later was to write his name in cricket history by being no-balled by John Lillywhite for overarm bowling, which led to its legalisation; and there was Clarke himself, at fifty-six nearing the end of his long career, and his son, Alfred, a capable enough batsman. So superior in ability were Clarke's men to the local amateurs that they were quite happy to play teams of eighteen or twenty-two, and generally beat them. A visit from Clarke's Eleven was a great social occasion, eagerly anticipated for months beforehand by a public with an appetite for good cricket that had never previously been served. Special entertainments were devised for the evenings to keep the spectators amused.

The players wore spotted or striped shirts, ties or scarves, white trousers held up with thick belts and round bowler-style hats. They bowled four-ball overs in the round-arm style which had gradually developed in the first half of the century despite fierce opposition from defenders of the old underarm fashion and was legalised in 1835 (it was not until 1864 that the MCC finally sanctioned fully overarm bowling). Scores were usually low by modern standards, for batting was often a slow and laborious process largely because pitches and playing fields were usually primitive and sometimes downright dangerous. Richard Daft, one of Clarke's players, remembered the great Fuller Pilch mowing one wicket with a borrowed scythe and another player running into a covey of partridges when fielding the ball at Truro.

The ground found by Dr Grace for his great match was in this tradition. It lay behind the Full Moon Hotel at Stokes Croft (quite near the centre of Bristol nowadays) and until the previous autumn had been a ploughed field. Dr Grace's gardener and some other men had prepared it; the pitch was said to be 'first rate' but the rest of the ground 'rough and uneven'. Uncle Pocock and Alfred Grace played along with Dr Grace; little Gilbert watched with his mother who 'sat in her pony-carriage all day'. W.G. remembered little more about the occasion than that some of the England team played in top hats, but doubtless the talk in the Grace household was of little else for months before and after the match. Despite being outnumbered two to one, Clarke's Eleven won by 149 runs.

The fixture was repeated the following year. Clarke was unable to play because of eye trouble – he had lost an eye playing fives at the age of 30 – but Dr Grace had three of his sons playing with him: Henry junior, Alfred, aged fifteen, and thirteen-year-old E.M., who understandably made little impression at the crease against such distinguished opposition (he scored 1 and 3). Long afterwards, E.M. remembered: 'I was very small indeed then, and when an appeal for lbw was made against me from a ball which hit me high up in the stomach, I felt that I wasn't tall enough to be able to doubt the umpire's word.' However, he fielded so well at long-stop in difficult conditions that after the match Clarke presented him with a bat and his mother with a book *Cricket: Notes by W. Bollard, with a letter containing practical hints by William Clarke,* in which he wrote: 'Presented to Mrs Grace by William Clarke, Secretary All-England XI'. One can imagine seven-year-old Gilbert's pride that his mother and brother should be singled out by such a great man. It has survived; in 1996 it fetched £4,600 at auction.

West Gloucestershire, all twenty-two of them, made only 48 in their first innings (top score: Henry Grace, junior, 13) and 76 in

the second (top score: Henry Grace, senior, 14), losing by 167
runs. Alfred Grace collected a 'pair'. Julius Caesar, who relished
inferior slow bowling, made top score (33 and 78) in both of All-
England's second innings to emphasise the disparity between the
two sides. Bickley took sixteen wickets in West Gloucestershire's
first innings; indeed, only three of the home side got into double
figures in the entire match. To look at the scorecard is to realise
what a primitive game cricket was in those days – one can visualise
the clumsy swiping that would have characterised the Bristolians'
play and the huge gap that existed between their play and that
of the wily professionals. Little did they know that the dark-eyed
little boy watching from the sidelines would in little more than a
decade transform the face of the game, and almost single-handed
overthrow the supremacy of the professional cricketer.

The All England team returned to Bristol the following year to
play a Bristol and District XXII, this time on the Clifton ground,
and won again but only by twelve runs this time. By the end of the
century, the field behind the Full Moon was built over.

There is a Gracean postscript: the All England team went into
decline in the 1860s and its demise was hastened by the rise
of another wandering team, the United South of England. The
large gates it attracted were attributed mainly to its greatest star:
W.G. Grace.

Gilbert continued to develop his talents on the pitch at The
Chestnuts under his uncle's careful tutelage, and at his boarding
school. All three of his older brothers had started their cricket
careers with West Gloucestershire and in 1857, at the precocious
age of nine, it was Gilbert's turn. The Bristol cricketing community had become used to the idea of precocious Graces.

By then, Gilbert had acquired a reasonable defensive technique
and was learning how to play the ball away with a bit more power,
still largely on the back foot. 'Playing with a straight bat had
become easy to me; and my uncle told me I was on the right
track, and patiently I continued with it.' He made his debut for
his father's club on 19 July, the day after his ninth birthday, against
Bedminster. Batting last, he made 3 not out. He played twice more
that summer, both times against West Gloucestershire's keenest

rivals Clifton, adding only one more run to his career total. By the following summer, he was learning how to play forward as well as back, but was yet to play attacking shots off the front foot, and he found the going against grown men just as tough, making 4 runs in five innings in 1858, and 12 runs in nine innings in 1859.

So far, there was little sign that Gilbert was anything special but that all changed in 1860, his twelfth year. He scored 9 in West Gloucestershire's first game against Clifton but really came into his own in the return, a two-day affair played on 19 and 20 July. The Clifton bowling was softened up by E.M. and Alfred Pocock, who put on 126 for the first wicket, the nineteen-year-old E.M. going on to score a chanceless 150. Gilbert went in at number eight and by the close of play on the first day had scored a solid and patient 35 not out. The next day the twelve-year-old completed his half century and was finally out for 51. His father also distinguished himself by taking all ten Clifton wickets, nine clean bowled and the tenth caught by Alfred Grace. The following weekend W.G. made 16 against a combined team from Gloucester and Cheltenham, who were beaten by an innings and 27 runs.

He had also been working hard on his bowling and was occasionally called on by West Gloucestershire to turn his arm over, though, as he was first to admit, only when all else had failed. His batting of 1860 was something of a false dawn: the next season he made only 46 runs in ten innings, never once managing to reach double figures. He had shot up and was now tall for his age but his greater reach proved of little help that season. Perhaps his strength had not caught up with his height; more likely the opposition had got wise to his talent and did not wish to be shown up by a thirteen-year-old. The year, he recalled, 'was not an encouraging one to me or my teachers'.

The next year, 1862, was a little better: Gilbert managed to score 24 not out against twenty-two men of Corsham and 18 against Gentlemen of Devon, totalling 53 in five innings. That year he left Rudgway School and went back home; his subsequent education consisting of private lessons with his brother-in-law, the Rev. John Walter Dann, a graduate of Trinity College, Dublin, who had married his sister Blanche and became the much loved and respected vicar of Downend for half a century, and a devoted supporter of local cricket.

Then came a severe setback. Gilbert contracted a bad case of pneumonia and was bedridden for several weeks. In those pre-antibiotic days, pneumonia posed a real threat to life and for a while it was touch and go for the boy. He made a slow recovery but when it came it produced a rapid change. As if in reaction to the physical battering he had taken, he suddenly shot up several more inches in height, taking him to over 6 ft tall. By his fifteenth birthday in 1863, he was the tallest of the Grace brothers by several inches, and the strongest: he settled one fraternal argument by picking up his eldest brother Henry, by then a sturdy thirty-year-old weighing 12 stone, and dropping him somewhere else. He eventually grew to 6ft 2 ½ inches tall, towering over most of his contemporaries, another important factor in his superiority over them.

Fully restored to health and grown to adult size, he made a real impact on the club game in the West Country that summer, scoring 350 in nineteen innings, at an average of 26.12. His top score came in his first innings of the summer in July when he hit 86 against Clifton. A few days later he scored an unbeaten 42 against Lansdown and in August made an unbeaten 52 for an embryonic Gloucestershire side got up by his father to play Somerset at Sydenham Fields, Bath. He had made great strides with the ball too and was now considered one of his club's leading performers. Against Somerset he took 4–17 and 2–26.

The most notable event of the year for W.G. was that he was considered good enough to be matched against some of the best professional bowlers in the country. He was selected to play for Twenty-Two of Bristol and District against the All-England touring side at the Clifton ground at the end of August, the same fixture which he had watched enthralled as a boy of six nine years previously. It was every schoolboy's dream and Gilbert was well aware of the enormous honour bestowed on him. He practised even more keenly in the weeks beforehand. 'I knew right well that the contests in which I had played the last year or two were not to be compared with the contest on this occasion,' he wrote later.

The game rated a small mention in the weekly *Clifton Chronicle*, which on the same page reported the discovery by some children of the body of a newly-born baby on Brandon Hill, a packed residents' meeting to discuss a proposed new road from Bristol up to Clifton, then as now a genteel suburb, and the ticket prices for the new Bristol and South Wales Union Railway (the charges from Bristol to Stapleton Road, where Dr W.G. Grace would open his first practice nearly twenty years later, were 6d, 4d and 1½d for first, second and third class respectively).

William Clarke had died in 1856 but the All-England operation continued under the direction of George Parr. The team which came to Bristol consisted of some familiar faces – Julius Caesar, Ned Willsher and Alfred Clarke – plus some of the most outstanding professionals of the age. They included George Tarrant, the Cambridgeshire round-arm fast bowler, his county colleague Tom Hayward, a slim but graceful batsman, H.H. Stephenson, the Surrey all-rounder whose selection to lead the first tour party to Australia in 1861/2 greatly upset the northern professionals, the great Nottinghamshire fast bowler and the terror of Lord's, John Jackson, R.C. Tinley, the lob bowler also of Nottinghamshire, and W.H. Moore, an amateur who had recently scored a century against the North. The Bristol team included the four oldest Grace boys: Henry, Alfred, Edward and Gilbert.

Opening the innings, E.M. smashed a swift 37 in his usual swashbuckling style before being given out lbw to Jackson. W.G. was down to bat at number ten, half-way down the order. Lunch was taken just before he was due to bat and Tarrant, nicknamed 'Tear'em' or 'Tearaway' because of his menacing appearance as he raced in to bowl at high speed, offered to give the youngster some practice. This act of kindness was all the more surprising as Tarrant was notorious in the game for his moodiness and short temper. (Interestingly, he became a close friend of E.M. when they toured Australia and New Zealand with George Parr's team the following winter. Perhaps the fact that both operated on a short fuse helped to cement the relationship.)

When W.G. walked to the wicket Tarrant and Jackson were bowling, an awesome prospect for a fifteen-year-old but one which W.G. took in his stride, though he confessed to suffering from nerves before going out to bat. After a couple of overs Tinley was brought on to bowl his under-arm lobs. They held no terrors for W.G., who was well used to batting against E.M.'s lobs at home. He played the first over cautiously, then showed his mettle in the next over, pulling Tinley into the scoring tent. The crowd's enthusiastic reception is easy to imagine. Unfortunately for the teenager, the success went to his head. In the next over he gave Tinley the charge, missed and was bowled, not the first or last time a headstrong young batsman has been undone by a wily pro. Still, W.G. walked off with a highly respectable 32 to his credit and professed himself thrilled with his performance. He had made the fourth best score, and fared better than his other brothers: Henry made a duck and Alfred 3 in a total of 212.

All England performed poorly against the enthusiastic Bristolians and were forced to follow on after making only 86 in their first innings, E.M. taking five wickets. The England stars fared little better in their second knock. When Edwin Stephenson, of Yorkshire, no mean batsman, came in, E.M. handed W.G. the ball, told him to toss it up and took himself off to the outfield. Sure enough, Stephenson swallowed the bait in W.G.'s first over, E.M. pulling off a magnificent catch to give the young man a distinguished first scalp at top level. All England were all out for 106, E.M. taking another five wickets. The Bristol XXII had won by an innings and 20 runs in under two days, although three had been set aside for the match. The result indicated the improvement in the Bristol players' standards over their past decade, thanks in no small part to Dr Grace's efforts. By now, E.M. was recognised as one of the finest players in the country.

W.G. finished off his season for West Gloucestershire in the autumnal conditions of October with 35 and 2 against Cheltenham College. But, for all his burgeoning self-confidence, he and his family cannot have realised just how rapidly he was progressing. That he was to demonstrate in style the following summer.

He was still only fifteen years when in June 1864 he was invited to play for the All-England XI against Lansdown. That the invitation was extended at all indicates that he must have mightily impressed the canny old All-England pros during his brief knock against them the previous summer. Perhaps it was a tribute to the Grace family's influence, though E.M. was absent, still making his way home from Australia after the completion of Parr's tour. His oldest brother Henry played for Lansdown. W.G. batted at number six and found himself at the wicket with the great John Lillywhite, who made a nonchalant century. W.G. batted with care, scoring 15 in half an hour until he had the misfortune to be run out by Lillywhite, the teenager presumably not daring to countermand the great man's call. 'I did not mind that,' he manfully recalled. 'I had played for the All England Eleven.' The professionals duly won by an innings and 22 runs.

It was E.M.'s continuing absence that led to W.G.'s first game in London ten days later. For years various members of the clan had been invited by the South Wales Club to join its annual tour to London, the Graces being popular figures on the cricket fields of the principality. Henry suggested that W.G. take E.M.'s place and the young man was off to the capital for the first time in his life. His journey was nearly in vain. The first game was at The Oval against Surrey. When the brothers arrived, the Welsh captain, Mr J. Lloyd, took Henry aside and asked him if his brother would mind stepping down for the second match, against Gentlemen of Sussex at Hove, as he wanted to include a more experienced player. He reckoned without the Graces' unflinching sense of family solidarity. Henry was firm: Gilbert would play in both matches or neither. Indeed Henry went further: if Gilbert wasn't picked, he himself would not play and no Graces would ever appear for South Wales again. Lloyd backed down. W.G. scored 5 and 38 but the real fireworks came on 14, 15 and 16 July at the historic Hove ground, one of cricket's most splendid arenas, and left Lloyd looking very stupid indeed.

In the event South Wales played with only ten men so the whole unpleasantness had been unnecessary but it meant W.G. was under some pressure to do well. He responded in extraordinary fashion, confessing that the events at the Oval had placed even greater pressure on his shoulders. E.M.'s ship was known to be nearing England and W.G. hung on to the hope that his inspirational older brother might turn up at Hove and help out. He need not have worried.

South Wales won the toss and W.G. went in first wicket down, joining Lloyd in the middle. There he proceeded to give the captain a close-up demonstration of just how mistaken he had been. He scored 170 out of a total of 356 for nine, hitting 19 fours and dominating the day's proceedings before wearily chopping an attempted cut on to his stumps.

W.G. claimed it was chanceless but one of the Sussex bowlers thought he should have been caught at point going for a fourth consecutive boundary. Lloyd contributed 82 but was eclipsed by his young partner. W.G. had arrived on the big stage with a bang. That afternoon he heard that E.M. had in fact arrived back in England that day.

In South Wales's second innings W.G. dominated again, scoring 56 not out in a total of 118–5, though the Welshmen failed by 16 runs to win the match. The Gentlemen of Sussex presented W.G with a bat to mark his epic performance. He treasured it all his life; it marked the real beginning of his magnificent career. He was not quite sixteen years old.

Six days later the prodigy made his first appearance at Lord's, again for South Wales, against MCC and Ground, and again he made a huge impression. He went in first wicket down and made 50, the second highest score. This would have been quite an achievement by any standards, but it was made all the more meritorious by the dreadful conditions the batsman faced, even at the home of cricket. The pitch, uncared for, full of holes and covered with small pebbles, was lethal; that very summer Sussex refused to play there because of it. Surrey had done the same in 1859. The creases were not marked with chalk but were inch-deep trenches which deteriorated rapidly. W.G. himself recounted that an over might contain three 'shooters' but also balls that hit the stones and reared up at the batsman. The only boundary was if a ball hit the pavilion rails; otherwise everything had to be run. One spectator was Charles Alcock, secretary of Surrey cricket club and editor of Lillywhite's *Annual*. He was mightily impressed by the youngster, as he wrote years later:

I can recall his form as if it were yesterday; his straight and true bowling – much faster than it is now, and not quite so high in delivery – the wonderful straightness of his bat, and the wonderful push off the leg stump, the stroke that has made him famous above every other cricketer of the age.

It may have been a relief to go on from the Lord's pitch north to Southgate in Middlesex, where W.G. made 14. Then he returned to Lord's for a two-day game against I Zingari, the last of the London season. It opened on 28 July, W.G.'s sixteenth birthday, and to celebrate he and E.M., opening the innings together for the first time, put on 81 before W.G. was out for 34. He made 47 in the second innings to round a memorable first expedition to the capital. For South Wales that summer he averaged 48, and in all matches he topped a thousand runs (totalling 1,079), including 126 for Clifton v Fownes's XI in August. He had forced his way on to the national cricket stage, and was not to take his leave until the next century. John Lillywhite's *Companion* commented soberly: 'Mr W.G. Grace promises to be a good bat; bowls very fairly.'

W.G. spent the winter of 1864–5 in customary fashion, hunting, shooting and fishing with his brothers. He always walked long distances too and in this way he kept fit for the cricket season. Now that he had suddenly exploded on to the scene, W.G. was in great demand in the summer of 1865. Everybody wanted the extraordinary youth from Gloucestershire in their team. Was he really as good as his performances the previous summer appeared to indicate?

With Henry and E.M., he turned out in June for a Lansdown Club Eighteen against the United All England Eleven, the professional touring troupe set up by disgruntled former members of William Clarke's All-England outfit. E.M. was the dominant figure of the match, hitting a magnificent 121 including a six into the river Avon. The Grace brothers had the distinction of taking all the wickets in each of the opposition's innings, All England being dismissed for the paltry totals of 99 and 87.

When W.G. accompanied E.M. to play against Marlborough

College, one of the school team was R.F. Miles, who later played with them for Gloucestershire. He recalled W.G. as 'a long lanky boy, who bowled very straight with a good natural leg curl.'

W.G.'s first chance to display his progress away from the West Country that summer came with an invitation to play for the Gentlemen of the South against the Players of the South at The Oval, starting on 22 June 1865. Such was the Gentlemen's confidence in the prodigy that he went in first wicket down, an honour which he himself felt was unjustified. Perhaps weighed down by the responsibility, he was soon back in the pavilion, out, stumped for a duck. But this failure was more than outweighed by his success with the ball. Bowling unchanged through both the Players' innings, he took 5–44 in the first innings and followed up with the extraordinary figures of 8–40 in the second to secure victory for the Gentlemen by an innings and 58 runs. The opinions of the professionals at being skittled by a sixteen-year-old were not recorded. The Surrey club presented him with the ball, inscribed and mounted.

Ten days later, on the same ground, W.G. made his first appearance in a match which he was to dominate for the next forty-one years, the fixture that embodied the yawning social gulf that divided the game, Gentlemen v Players. The fortunes of the two teams charted the progress of the sport. For the previous decade, it had been dominated by the professionals; the Players had beaten the Gentlemen in nineteen consecutive games since 1854 (in those days the fixture was played twice a season, at Lord's and The Oval). It is no exaggeration to say that W.G.'s arrival transformed it: his last appearance for the Gentlemen would be in 1906 at The Oval and in that time they lost only four more times. He was to dominate the fixture as no one else before or since, scoring 6,008 runs and taking 276 wickets. He made fifteen centuries, more than any other batsman, and frequently carried his team to success on his own shoulders.

W.G.'s debut at The Oval was the first time Lord Cobham had seen him. He provided this impression of him:

46

He was a tall, loose-limbed lean boy, with some appearance of delicacy and, in marked contrast with his brother E.M., quiet and shy in manner. He looked older than he was, and indications of the great beard which subsequently distinguished him through life were even then apparent.

W.G. turned in a solid all-round performance, again impressing more by his bowling than his batting: and catching the eye with a superb display of fielding at cover-point. He batted eighth and scored 23 and 12 not out, impressing one of the 5,000 spectators with his 'excellent form'. At least he outscored E.M., who opened the batting but made only 8 and 10. In the Players' first innings W.G. had figures of 40–9–65–4, in the second 35–12–60–3, a lot of bowling and a highly economical performance in a high-scoring game. It was his assessment that the batting of the teams was about equal but the professionals' bowling was far superior, even though they were without all their northern stars, who had refused to take part. They still won comfortably enough, by 118 runs.

It was a different story five days later in the return match at Lord's. This was a much more low-scoring affair, because of the dreadful pitch, 'almost unplayable' according to R.D. Walker of the Gentlemen. It was dominated by the ageing George Parr, who scored 60 for the Players in his last appearance in the fixture he had graced since 1846, and the irrepressible E.M. There was a fitting circularity about the appearances of Parr and W.G. When Parr was first picked for the Players he had been only eighteen and the selection of one so young was thought to be exceptional. Now, as he bowed out, a similar prodigy who was even younger had arrived.

The Players won the toss and batted but were all out for only 132. W.G. opened the bowling but took no wickets. It was the first time C.E. Green, later a great figure in Essex cricket, had seen W.G. in action. He described his bowling action at the time:

In those days his arm was as high as his shoulder – that is as high as it was then allowed by cricket law – and while his delivery was a nice one, his action was different to what it was in his later days; it was more slinging and his pace was fast medium. He had not then acquired any of his subsequent craftiness with the ball. He used to bowl straight on the wicket, trusting to the ground to do the rest.

47

W.G. and E.M. opened the batting for the Gentlemen but the partnership was short-lived: W.G. was run out for only 3. E.M.'s innings was typically explosive: he hit a six through a bedroom window of the old tavern and was then given out lbw for 24 'at which decision dissatisfaction was loudly expressed by some of the spectators', according to *The Times*. The Gentlemen made 198, E.M. taking six wickets, and then dismissed the Players for 140, leaving themselves only 75 to win. The Grace brothers saw to it that the target was reached without trouble, W.G. making 34, E.M. 30. The Gentlemen's eight-wicket victory was their first in nineteen fixtures. The tide had turned.

There was plenty more action for W.G. at the top level that summer. A week later he played for The Gentlemen of England v The Gentlemen of Middlesex at Islington, Middlesex's county ground, where E.M. continued his rich vein of form with 111 in the second innings. W.G. contributed 48 and 34. His highest score of the summer was 85, for South Wales against I Zingari and he was disappointed not to have made a century. He even found himself playing for Suffolk when he popped into Lord's one day and was pressed into service by the county, who were two men short for the match against MCC, underlining the casual nature of much of cricket in those days. There was no fairytale ending, alas: W.G. failed in both innings with the bat and had to watch in the field while E.M. (who else?) struck a refulgent 82.

Further recognition came with selection for England v Surrey at The Oval in the last major match of the season, although his was clearly not yet a household name: in its preview *The Times* called him Mr N.G. Grace. Several thousand spectators were in attendance to see him opening with E.M. He batted solidly for 35, the brothers putting on more than 80 before being parted. Rain denied W.G. the chance of another knock, causing the match to be abandoned on the second day. The season ended on a note of low comedy, with E.M. inevitably at the centre of a highly controversial incident, which threatened to spoil a benefit match between a Gentlemen of the South of England XVIII and the United South of England, played at The Oval to raise money for the professional bowlers attached to the ground.

E.M. had already scored half-centuries in each of the Gentlemen's innings and was clearly in high spirits. The renowned stonewaller Henry Jupp was at the wicket, determined to save the game in the final innings. All else having failed to remove him, E.M. announced that he knew how to do so. He was variously reported as saying 'I'll give him a high toss' and 'I can do it with a lob.'

Whatever the precise words, the intention was clear: E.M. delivered a high under-arm lob which rose some 15 yards into the air before descending towards the startled batsman. Jupp hit it away for 2 but E.M. was not put off. He ignored the booing of a section of the crowd and his next ball was a similar one. The difference was that Jupp left it alone. Unfortunately for him it landed on his wicket and the umpire gave him out. He walked, albeit reluctantly, but the crowd was was incensed. The game was held up for an hour while the spectators made their displeasure known in the frankest terms. So menacing was the atmosphere that E.M. and a couple of his team-mates grabbed stumps with which to defend themselves in case a riot started. Eventually the crowd quietened down and the game restarted. After it E.M. was presented with two bats to mark his half-centuries, for the seventy-fifth time. What he did with all his bats is unclear – probably the hammering they received meant their lives were short.

The season had been a constant learning curve for W.G: he found professional bowling a very different proposition from the amateur stuff he was used to, and it required all his patience to adjust to their consistent length. 'I took no liberties,' he gravely observed. The difference between first-class and other bowling was evident in his batting averages for 1865. In all matches, he scored 2,169 runs at an average of 40. But in his eight first-class innings, he managed only 189 runs at an average of 27. Still, as the summer came to an end he felt he was making progress.

Over the winter W.G. continued to grow and by the start of the 1866 season, he stood 6 ft 1 in tall and weighed nearly 12 stone. He warmed up for the first-class season with the usual round of local matches, hitting two centuries for Clifton and another for Bedminster. Then he made his first journey away from the south

and west to sample cricket in the North. E.M. had been asked to
captain eighteen Colts of Nottingham and Sheffield against the
might of the All England XI at Sheffield, but when E.M. was
unable to fulfil the engagement his brilliant younger brother was
invited to take over. It was both an honour and a challenge for a
seventeen-year-old, particularly in an alien atmosphere.

W.G. found it a strange experience. He and his team had to
climb a steep hill to get to the Hyde Park ground, which he
found very primitive, though he had no criticism of the pitch.
The industrial landscape of Sheffield was obviously an eye-opener
to the country boy from Gloucestershire. 'I felt as if I had got to
the world's end, and a very black and sooty one it seemed,' he
wrote later. The youthful XVIII was soundly beaten but W.G.
scored 9 and 36 and performed creditably enough as captain.

His next major engagement was for the Gentlemen v the Players
at Lord's, beginning on 26 June. Before a crowd estimated at
between four and five thousand the Players won the toss and
batted. E.M. and W.G. bowled through most of the innings,
including a spell of eighteen overs in which they conceded only
3 runs. They shared all the wickets, six to E.M., four to W.G.

The Players made only 116 but the Gentlemen only 20 more,
W.G. top-scoring on the usual difficult Lord's track with 25, all
singles. Thanks to a magnificent 122 by Tom Hearne in their
second innings, the Players ran out winners by 38 runs (W.G.
taking two more wickets but contributing only 11 runs in the
Gentlemen's second innings).

The return match started next day at The Oval, W.G. contributing greatly to victory for the Gentlemen by taking nine wickets in
the game, though he did little with the bat. It was the Gentlemen's
first win at The Oval since the fixure had been played there, and
the secretary of the Surrey club presented each member of the
team with a bat to mark the milestone. W.G.'s mediocre form
made his performance, when once again invited to play for an
England XI against Surrey at The Oval at the end of July, all
the more unexpected. Batting at number five, he scored 224, his
first double century and the highest individual score at The Oval
until then. He had just turned eighteen. In that massive total there

50

were only two fives and eight fours. All the runs were literally that, reflecting W.G.'s superb state of fitness.

He was in his physical prime, tall but slim and brilliantly athletic, so much so that his captain, the great Middlesex all-rounder, V.E. Walker, benevolently allowed him to take the second afternoon of the game off, while his side was fielding, to compete in a big athletics competition, the National Olympian Association meeting, at the Crystal Palace, several miles away. Perhaps he thought the young man deserved a rest. Shrugging off the effects of his mammoth score, W.G. won the 440 yards hurdles in 1min 10 sec, considered then to be a fast time, before returning to The Oval, although he need not have bothered. In their two innings the eleven men of Surrey were unable to equal even his score, never mind England's, and lost by an innings and 296 runs.

Between 1866 and 1870 W.G. was almost as keen on running as playing cricket, and with E.M., he was an enthusiastic competitor at athletic meetings throughout the summer, usually in Bristol and neighbouring towns like Cheltenham, but sometimes travelling to London for major events. Races were often sponsored by public houses and held on the road, with handicaps, substantial prizes for the winners and a great deal of betting from the spectators. The main venue in Bristol for organised meetings was the Zoological Gardens at Clifton, where the organisation was frequently chaotic.

W.G. was an excellent sprinter and hurdler, who would run in sprints ranging from the 100 yards (in which his best time was a highly creditable 10.45 seconds) to the 400 yards (52.15). He would sometimes enter field events such as the long jump, the high jump, the hop skip and jump (as the triple jump was then called), and throwing the cricket ball, in which he was a mighty performer with a best of 117 yards.

In 1869 when he recorded seventeen firsts and nine seconds he was at his peak, but the next season, in which he competed in fewer meetings, turned out to be his last. He also played the growing game of rugby football a few times, and must have been a formidable performer, but one crushing tackle from an opponent of similar proportions convinced him that he could endanger his cricket career if he carried on, a surprisingly modern approach.

His epic knock at The Oval was no flash in the pan, and may even have been bettered in terms of quality by his display at the end of August for the Gentlemen of the South against the Players of the South, at The Oval, rapidly becoming his favourite ground. The Gentlemen were acknowledged to be fielding an under-strength side but that only served to inspire the young Gloucestershire colossus. First he rattled through the Players with the ball, taking 7–92, including the obdurate Jupp for the third time in major matches that summer. Then he surpassed that – and himself – with the bat, scoring a brilliant 173 not out, of 240 while he was at the wicket, with two sixes, two fives, 14 threes and 16 twos. Cricket reports in the newspapers of the day were apt to be curt affairs, detailing little more than the scores and conveying little or nothing of the atmosphere of the day's play. But *The Times* correspondent was roused to rare superlatives:

A finer innings could not be witnessed; good bowling (with several changes) being tried against him; but his runs were gained in admirable cricket form, not even the shadow of a chance for a catch being given. During the play he was frequently applauded; but upon retiring the applause was general.

The bowling, moreover, was of the highest class, including James Lillywhite and Ned Willsher. But perhaps the most interesting fact about his innings was that it showed how thoughtful and thorough – one might even say professional – W.G. was about his cricket. During that summer, he had given a lot of thought to field placing in the first-class game. The prevailing othodoxy was that batsmen should play straight bowling defensively. Consequently, there was no need to have anyone fielding in the deep because big hitting was almost non-existent.

The Grace brothers broke from this with a vengeance. E.M. was the first to cock a snook at the theory: to him, every ball was fair game, to be hit out of the ground if possible in his own unique flailing style. Observing his success, frequently from the non-striker's end, W.G. determined to copy his example, and put it into practice against the Players of the South.

Every time I had a ball the least bit overpitched, I hit it hard over the bowler's head, and did not trouble about where it was going. My height enabled me to get over those that were slightly short and I played them hard: long-hops off the wicket I pulled to square leg or long-on, without the slightest hesitation.

The Surrey club rewarded his display with a fine silver-plated bat. It was after this that he was first called 'the Champion'.

Precocious though W.G. was, another Grace was already hard on his heels. Fred, still only fifteen, was thought promising enough to be invited to join his older brother for Gentlemen of the South against I Zingari at Canterbury on 10 August, the second match of the Canterbury Week. But he was pressed into service to play for them against the North in the opening match of the week when the Kent slow bowler 'Farmer' Bennett was stuck in a train *en route* to the game.

Fred batted at number eleven and made 1 and 5 not out. Against I Zingari W.G. scored 30 and 50 while Fred – 'quite a youth' remarked *The Times* – chipped in with 17 in the second innings.

W.G.'s run aggregate in all matches for 1866 was remarkably similar to the previous season: 2,168, making him already the most prolific batsman in the country, with more than 600 in hand over the next man, C.F. Buller. His average significantly improved, to 54. And in his fifteen first-class innings his progress was apparent: a total of 640 runs at an average of 42.

Around this time, there were rumours that Dr Henry Grace had made enquiries about the possibility of his son going up to Gonville and Caius College, Cambridge. Perhaps there was no substance in it for when a cricketing cleric, Canon E.S. Carter, tried to persuade him to go up to Oxford in 1866 W.G. told him regretfully that he did not think his father would allow him to spare the time from his impending medical studies. Judging by his protracted studies at Bristol Medical School and elsewhere, W.G. might have had trouble in satisfying the Oxford or Cambridge examiners, but he would certainly have rewritten all the university cricket records. He always enjoyed playing the universities, putting their young attacks to the sword for the MCC year after year, and nothing gave him greater pride in later life than attending the University match at Lord's in 1895 to watch his eldest son, W.G. junior, gain his first Cambridge Blue.

But if he hoped to dominate the batting scene in the 1867 season, he was to be disappointed. It started badly and never really got going. First he suffered a sprained ankle and a split finger early in the season. Hardly had he regained fitness than he was struck down by scarlet fever in the middle of July and was off for six weeks. Even when he returned he was still feeling the effects of the illness and the rest of the season was a virtual write-off. Despite all his problems, it was W.G.'s best-ever season with the ball: he took thirty-nine first-class wickets at an average of only 7.51, bowling much more briskly than he was to do in later life.

His performance with the bat in his first big match of the season, for England v Middlesex, was promising enough. It was Middlesex's first game against an England XI, played for the benefit of the professionals on the Lord's staff. Four thousand spectators turned out to support it, and W.G. treated them to a sparkling 75 in a dashing partnership with the Old Etonian Alfred Lubbock, who hit 129. W.G. then proceeded to take 6–53 as Middlesex were demolished by an innings.

The dreadful state of the Lord's pitch was demonstrated by his next two appearances there. South of the Thames played North of the Thames, a game put on to replace the North v South fixture, which had to be cancelled because of the schism betweeen the northern and southern players. The general standard of batting had improved but three innings had been completed by the end of the first day, the South being skittled for only 32 in their first knock, the North for 61. Set 73 to win in their second innings, the North were all out for 46 on the second day, W.G. taking 6–28 and E.M. snaffling four brilliant catches in his habitual position of point.

It was much the same story when the Gentlemen met the Players at Lord's on 8 July. Again thirty wickets fell on the first day, eleven of them to W.G. (three in the first, eight in the second). There was no doubt about the culprit: *The Times* dismissed the wicket as 'a kind of tessellated, lumpy sward, where patches of rusty yellow strive with faded green'. Faced with 55 to win, W.G. and Alfred

Lubbock saw the Gentlemen to an eight-wicket victory, W.G. hitting the winning runs with a cut for 3 to the grandstand.

But when the teams squared up again at The Oval a week later, W.G. was missing, struck down with scarlet fever. It was six weeks before he was fit enough to return to the fray, for England versus a joint Surrey/Sussex team at The Oval on 26 August, in a benefit match for Tom Lockyer, the Surrey wicket-keeper. W.G. took eight wickets in the match and was loudly cheered by a large crowd, delighted to see their young hero recovered when he walked out to join E.M. at the wicket, though he was caught at slip for only 12.

Despite his truncated season Lillywhite's *Annual* was unstinting in its praise for W.G.: 'A magnificent batsman, his defence and hitting powers being second to none and his scoring for the last three years marvellous. Plays for Gentlemen v Players and is a host in himself. A splendid fielder and thrower from leg.'

The summer of 1868 was a long, hot one, producing fast, dry pitches and a series of remarkable scores. At Clifton College, one E.F.S. Tylecote, for instance, amassed 404 not out, albeit in an inter-school match, which would not have gone unnoticed by local boy Gilbert Grace. The high scoring led to fears that bowlers were not good enough to restrain the batsmen (the low scores of the previous summer being conveniently forgotten). The same worry is voiced nowadays whenever batsmen look like getting the upper hand, giving rise to the thought that cricketers and those who follow them do not change much.

W.G. wasn't complaining: he was now at the peak of his ability and to prove it rattled up three first-class centuries. While other bowlers toiled, he mopped up forty-four first-class wickets at an average of only 16.38. He also became the first batsman for more than half a century to score two centuries in the same first-class match. An exotic addition to a memorable season came in the shape of a touring team of Australian Aboriginals who, although not of the highest class, won hearts wherever they went and also entertained the crowds with exhibitions of boomerang throwing.

It was around this time that the teenaged Lord Harris remembered being taken to Lord's with a few other members of the Eton

XI 'for the express purpose of seeing W.G. bat and thereby having our own ideas improved'. It was a damp morning and the sight they were treated to was not of their hero (who was in fact only three years older than Harris) batting but of a young man in an overcoat arguing with the groundsman that the pitch was not fit to play on.

The MCC v England fixture was revived in June at Lord's for the first time for twelve years as a benefit for the Marylebone Cricketers' Fund, the Lord's professionals, and W.G. showed his superiority over his batting contemporaries with 29 out of 96 in England's first innings and a superb 66 out of 179 in the second. Later that month he recorded his first century for the Gentlemen v the Players, 134 at Lord's out of a total of 193. He himself regarded it as one of the best innings he ever played – even a half-century on the dreadful Lord's square was a creditable achievement. The pitch that day was described thus: '. . . in nine cricket grounds out of ten within twenty miles of London, whether village green or county club ground, a local club could find a better wicket, in spite of drought and in spite of their poverty, than Marylebone Club supplied to the Players of England.' Although the wicket was its usual skittish self, it was also hard and fast, which suited W.G.'s attacking style admirably. He went in at first wicket down after E.M. was run out for only one and, said *The Times*, 'played one of the finest, and most assuredly the most prolific, innings at Lord's during the present season'. Hardly anything passed his bat and to rub salt into the professionals' wounds, Grace took 10–81 in the match to set up an eight-wicket win for the Gentlemen, which they followed up with a comprehensive innings and 87 runs victory at The Oval, their fourth in succession.

His historic pair of centuries – 130 and 102 not out – came at one of his happiest hunting grounds, the St Lawrence ground at Canterbury, for South of the Thames against North of the Thames, which again replaced the old North v South game. The only other time it had been performed was back in 1817 by the great all-rounder William Lambert, playing for Sussex v Epsom at Lord's, hardly a comparable fixture. Grace modestly described his achievement as much easier than his 134 at Lord's as there were boundaries at Canterbury and he did not have to run so much. Oddly enough, his side still lost.

Perhaps the most significant match he played in that summer was a two-day affair at Lord's on 25 and 26 June, the first game played there by a club bearing the Gloucestershire name (it was not properly constituted until three years later). Appropriately for the family which was to dominate the county's formative years, three of the Grace brothers played: E.M., W.G. and young Fred, still only seventeen but a batsman of the greatest promise. Their opponents were Middlesex Club and Ground, and the Graces bowled every ball against them, Gloucestershire emerging victorious by 134 runs. Although it would be another two years before they engaged another county, Gloucestershire were on their way.

In the summer of 1869, W.G. reached two landmarks: his twenty-first birthday and membership of the MCC. So eager was the club to enrol the young tyro that he was proposed by the Treasurer, T. Burgoyne, and seconded by the Secretary, R.A. (Bob) Fitzgerald (also spelt FitzGerald), who had been a vigorous reformer since taking up the post in 1863 and who was to be a stout friend and ally of W.G. Indeed, his championing of W.G. can be seen as evidence of his radical ways, for while there was no doubt that he was the finest batsman in the land, his somewhat obscure origins (to the metropolitan eye at least) would not normally have qualified him for MCC membership.

W.G. did not disappoint his patrons, making a century on his debut, 117 against Oxford University on Magdalen College's ground at Cowley Marsh, and three more before the end of the season, against Surrey, Nottinghamshire and Kent. It was the start of a long and distinguished association in which W.G. was to score 7,780 runs, including nineteen centuries. In all matches in 1869, he scored nine centuries and was universally regarded as the finest batsman then playing the game. In its summary of the season, Lillywhite's *Annual* went further: Grace was 'generally admitted to be the most wonderful cricketer that ever handled a bat'. Young Fred was not far behind that summer, with five centuries to his name, including one score of 206.

Such was W.G.'s dominance of the bowlers that his occasional

failures were greeted with astonishment. The North v South
fixture was resumed that year, though some diehard Northerners
– Parr, Carpenter and Hayward – refused to participate. The
teams played each other three times, once in the Canterbury
Festival, and W.G. was unexpectedly bowled third ball by J.C.
'Jemmy' Shaw, the Nottinghamshire left-arm pace bowler. The
Daily Telegraph commented: 'Imagine Patti [the famous opera
singer] singing outrageously out of tune; imagine Mr Gladstone
violating all the rules of grammar – and you have a faint idea of
the surprise created by this incident.' The writer added that he
fancied Mr Grace to take his revenge in the second innings, and
the great man concurred. 'I fancy I'll do a little better this time,'
he said as he walked out to bat again and indeed he did, with a
whirlwind 96 out of 134 in partnership with Jupp.

The remark is evidence that the shy teenager of a few years
earlier had matured into a self-confident young man. It was
much the same story when MCC met Nottinghamshire. In the
first innings W.G. was run out for 48 (still top score in an innings
of 112) and was thoroughly outshone by the great Notts batsman
Richard Daft, who scored an unbeaten 103. An essential element
of W.G.'s make-up was his unrelenting competitiveness, whatever
the standard of the match. He bet Daft that he would do better
than him in his second innings and he was as good as his word.
He thrashed a rapid 121, untypically offering several chances.

The news of Grace's exploits had naturally spread all over the
country but there were few opportunities for cricket lovers in
many areas to see him in action. His appearances at that time
were reserved for a relatively few venues: club grounds around
Bristol, where he was well known, Lord's and The Oval in London,
and a few county grounds in the south such as Canterbury and
Hove. Gloucestershire were not yet part of the informal county
championship, apart from that. The cricket season consisted of
a motley collection of first-class fixtures: the MCC played the
counties, the Gentlemen played the Players twice and sometimes
more, the North played the South, Gentlemen of the South played
Gentlemen of the North, and so on.

At that stage of his career Grace rarely ventured out of the south or west. Thus the North v South fixture at Sheffield attracted great interest and a large crowd, for many of whom Grace was the chief attraction. (His *Memorial Biography* mistakenly described it as 'his first appearance locally', forgetting that he had captained the XVIII Youths of Nottingham and Sheffield there in 1866.) He did not let them down: opening the innings he rattled up 122 against a very strong attack. Charles Alcock later described it as 'perhaps his most meritorious achievement' of the season.

I remember well, how, in the short space of two hours, against the bowling of Freeman, Emmett, Iddison and Wootton, he scored 122 runs on a wicket in every way suitable to the Northern bowling, and with George Freeman – then at his best – in such deadly form that no other Southern batsman could so much as look at him.

The measure of W.G.'s superiority was that his ten team-mates contributed only 51. Then he took 6–57 when the North batted.

Almost as great a performance came in the Gentlemen of the South v the Players of the South at that favourite hunting ground, The Oval, in mid-July. On a perfect pitch and in perfect weather the Players clocked up 475, batting through until after lunch on the second day of what was only a three-day match and W.G. had no more luck than anyone else with the ball. But the Players' huge score proved to be no more than an aperitif for the main dish. W.G. opened with B.B. Cooper, who was to pop up in opposition to him in Australia a few years later. Less than four hours later they had put on 283 to break the first-class record for the first wicket, a record which stood until 1892. W.G.'s share was 180, Cooper's 101. The *Daily Telegraph*'s observations provide a striking description of Grace in action at the crease:

He has made even larger scores than the 180, but we doubt whether a better innings has ever been played by a cricketer past or present. The characteristic of Mr Grace's play was that he knew exactly where every ball he hit would go. Just the strength required was expended and no more. When the fieldsmen were placed injudiciously too deep, he would quietly send a ball half-way towards them with a gentle tap and content himself with a modest single. If they came in a little nearer, the shoulders opened out and the powerful arms swung round as he lashed at the first loose ball and sent it away through the crowded ring of visitors until one heard a big thump as it struck against the farthest fence. Watching most other men – even good players – your main object is to see how they will defend themselves against the bowling; watching Mr Gilbert Grace, you can hardly help feeling as though the batsman himself were the assailant.

The Gentlemen eventually totalled 553 all out and the match inevitably petered out in a draw.

It was not success all the way for Grace that year. He took a Gloucestershire XI by train to play the boys of Marlborough College and on the way wagered that he would score a century and hit the ball into Sun Lane, a massive blow which had only ever been achieved once before. This was one bet that W.G. lost: he was bowled for only 6 by a boy named Kempe, who thus achieved what the cream of English cricket would have dearly loved to have done. The boy, a fast bowler, also dismissed the next batsman cheaply, who on returning to the pavilion remarked that he would have coped easily but for the bad light. To his great credit, Grace replied: 'It was just the opposite with me. I could see it perfectly but I couldn't play it.'

To cap it, he attended evening service in the chapel, where 'Sweet Saviour, Bless Us Ere We Go' was sung. To the amusement of all, it contained the highly appropriate line:

> The scanty triumphs Grace hath won
> The heathen in his blindness bows down to wood and stone.

4 · THE NONPAREIL
1870–1872

IN the years 1870–6 W.G. developed from the age of twenty-one to twenty-eight. He was at the very peak of his powers during that time. His achievements as a batsman were prodigious – and while he was to remain at the summit of English cricket almost until the end of the century he never quite repeated the almost effortless accumulation of runs that flowed from his bat in this high summer of his career. He dominated the scene as no batsman had ever done before. The suspicion that this tall, dark and superbly athletic young man from the West Country was the greatest practitioner of his craft yet seen had been growing for several years. Now it became reality. He was the champion, the nonpareil, feted in prose and poetry, adored by the public, admired and feared by his playing contemporaries.

His rise to the top coincided with the rapid growth and expansion of cricket itself. Previously the structure of the sport had resembled a series of small self-enclosed worlds that had very little to do with each other. Comparatively few players strayed out of their immediate circles, playing the same teams year after year, seeing the same old faces. But by the start of the 1870s this collection of amoebae was starting to coalesce and take on the shape that has persisted relatively unchanged to the present era. In particular, more and more county cricket clubs were being formed, and 1870 was notable for the creation of Gloucestershire as a proper county club. Inevitably, the driving force behind it was Dr Henry Grace.

The idea of a county club had been germinating in his mind for some years. As far back as 1862, he had formed a Gentlemen of Gloucestershire side to play Gentlemen of Devon on 8 and 9 July on Durdham Down, where he had once practised with his friends in the early morning before dragging himself off to his medical classes. E.M. made 57 and the Gloucestershire men won by an innings and 77 runs.

The following year the Gloucestershire fixture list had grown to three, two against Devon plus the match against Somerset at Bath, in which W.G. had made an unbeaten half century. That year a rival would-be county outfit, the Cheltenham and County of Gloucester club, was set up, presided over by Lord Fitzhardinge, reviving the memory of a short-lived organisation with a similar name (the County of Gloucestershire and Cheltenham Cricket Club), founded in 1842 and closed in 1846.

Like its prototype, the Cheltenham-based club failed to prosper. It never approached the playing standard of its Bristol rival, largely because of the presence in the latter of the Grace brothers, three of whom featured in the Gloucestershire side which went to Lord's and beat MCC and Ground in 1868.

But it was not until 1870 that the Graces' Gloucestershire club played its first inter-county game, against Surrey, in front of a huge and appreciative crowd – and a band – on Durdham Down. W.G. made 26 and 25 but it was with the ball that the Grace brothers were irresistible: W.G. had match figures of 9–92 and G.F. 7–87. The home side won the historic fixture by 51 runs. With the inspirational figure of W.G. carrying all before him, Gloucestershire's first season went like a dream, for they won both their other fixtures by massive margins. In the return at the Oval, they crushed Surrey by an innings and 129 runs, the high spot being the county's first century, inevitably scored by W.G., with 143.

To show the capital that this result was no fluke, Gloucestershire went to Lord's to demolish MCC by an innings and 88 runs thanks largely to W.G.'s magnificent 172 out of his county's total of 276. In front of a small crowd, he and C.S. Gordon opened the batting and put on 73 in fifty-five minutes before a violent thunderstorm forced the players to retreat. The rain fell solidly for three hours, and when play resumed at 5 p.m. it was a sodden pitch and in appalling light. Nevertheless, Grace blazed away and with the total on 208 was 133 not out at stumps, having lost five partners including Fred, unfortunately run out when he slipped on the damp turf. Next day W.G. continued in the same vein, before holing out to point. 'Thus one of the grandest innings ever played by "the champion" was brought to a conclusion, after a duration of four hours and a quarter, in which was some of the finest hitting and brilliant batting under most disadvantageous conditions of ground and light that has ever been seen in any match,' was the *Sportsman*'s breathless summary. The *Sporting Gazette* agreed: 'It was a marvellous performance even from the best batsman whom England has ever seen.'

The performances of the Graces' Gloucestershire team in 1870 seem to have been enough to convince their Cheltenham rivals that it was pointless to continue. In March 1871 the club was wound up and Lord Fitzhardinge became a vice-president of Dr Grace's Gloucestershire, which was officially constituted the same year.

The year 1870 was an important one in several other respects. The laws were changed to allow a bowler to change ends twice in an innings, compared to once allowed previously. The rift between the northern professionals and the south was healed and almost all the top northern pros played in the South v North game at Lord's in early June, which was also notable for being the forty-four-year-old George Parr's last game at headquarters.

There was some dispute as to which was W.G.'s greatest innings in the summer of 1870. The conventional wisdom was that it was his 215 for the Gentlemen v the Players at The Oval, played between 14 and 16 July. Admittedly the Players did not field a strong bowling attack, but Grace was still majestic in his dominance once he had survived a sharp chance to Willsher at slip off the first ball of the third over. Had it been held, noted the *Daily Telegraph*, 'it would have saved the Players an immensity of trouble and toil'. It was the highest innings ever recorded in the fixture until then, although Grace himself managed to better it by two the following year. It even included one eight, a mighty hit for seven past the Racket Court and, to crown it, an overthrow. W.G. was at the wicket for five hours and 'never gave a ghost of a chance'. Said the *Telegraph*: 'Independent of its numerical excellence, it is an innings that, for complete mastery over the bowling and for judicious "placing" the ball, never was surpassed.' Another observer wrote that it was a 'leviathan score' obtained by 'the most marvellous combination of defence, brilliant hitting, and truly wonderful rapidity of scoring ever witnessed'.

Nor was it the last the Players saw of him that season. In the return match, Grace was again the only batsman able to cope with the notorious Lord's pitch, hitting 109 out of 182. He was then the first victim of a hat-trick, remarkable in that the second was Fred Grace, clean bowled by a typical Lord's 'shooter'. The third was nineteen-year-old Charles Francis, just down from his first year at Oxford, a useful all-rounder who had taken seventeen wickets for Rugby v Marlborough at Lord's the previous summer. The bowler, who presumably dined out on his achievement for the remainder of his short life (he died four years later, aged only forty-one), was Tom Hayward the elder.

But those who saw it reckoned that another of Grace's knocks that summer was much greater than any of his nine centuries, five of them in first-class fixtures. This was his second innings for MCC against Yorkshire, the strongest county that season, on another shocking Lord's pitch. MCC were shot out for only 73 in their first innings by George Freeman (6–25) and Tom Emmett (4–39), who were considered to be the most effective opening attack of the time. W.G. made 10.

In the second innings the Yorkshire fast bowlers were again a terrifying prospect, delivering bouncers and shooters in about equal proportions, but Grace stood up to them with heroic stoicism for a dogged 66 before being caught at point by Roger Iddison off Emmett (exactly the same way as he had been dismissed in the first innings). 'Just before I was out, last man, Emmett bowled a ball which hit me very hard on the point of the left elbow, the ball flew into the air, and we ran a run before it came down into short-leg's hands,' Grace remembered, 'but I could not hold the bat properly afterwards, and was glad when the innings was over.'

'Mr Grace was a good deal hit about the body by the fast bowling – thanks, of course, to the bad wickets, but nevertheless he played throughout with unfailing pluck and was apparently as fresh at the close as he was at the commencement of his batting,' said the *Sporting Gazette*. 'A great display of skilled and successful batting played against A1 bowling on a difficult and false playing wicket. It was a masterpiece indeed,' commented the *Daily Telegraph*. 'Although hardly as fast as some of his efforts . . . one of his best and soundest of his many brilliant performances,' added the *Sportsman*.

C.E. Green was the only batsman to stay with him for any length of time, for 51. Nearly half a century later he wrote: 'We were both cruelly battered about; indeed to this day I carry a mark on my chest where I was struck by a very fast rising ball from Freeman.' His assailant also recalled the match many years on:

Tom Emmett and I have often said it was a marvel the doctor was not either maimed or unnerved for the rest of his days or killed outright. I often think of his pluck when I watch a modern batsman scared if a medium-paced ball hits him on the hand; he should have seen our expresses flying about his ribs, shoulders and head in 1870.

Grace absorbed his punishment as defiantly as Brian Close accepted his battering by Wes Hall and Charlie Griffith in 1963. Like Close, W.G. was 'loudly cheered' as he returned to the pavilion with his body bruised and raw but his spirit undefeated. He himself inclined to the belief that it had indeed been his finest innings.

He made another 66 for Gentlemen of the South v Players of the South and a fine 77 for the same side against Gentlemen of the North at Beeston, near Nottingham. This innings was memorable for being entirely outshone by the eighteen-year-old Fred, with a blazing innings of 189 not out, and a massive partnership with I.D. Walker, another of the prolific Walker clan (Middlesex's answer to the Graces) who made 179 not out. One oddity of the southerners' score was that the other eight batsmen totalled only 19 runs in a score of 482.

The Grace brothers treated the people of Lincolnshire to a

batting exhibition with an opening partnership of 166 for a United South XI against a Sleaford XXII in June. To W.G.'s amusement, the Yorkshire lob-bowler, Roger Iddison, who was guesting for Sleaford, placed a man at short leg and kept moving him closer to the bat until he stood only four yards away. Sure enough, when Iddison overpitched, W.G. cracked the ball straight at the unfortunate short leg, hitting him square on the ankle. The force of the stroke was underlined by the fact that the batsmen then ran four. To Grace's astonishment (and admiration), the fielder gave no immediate sign that he was hurt. 'He was a rare plucked one and never winced,' as W.G. put it. But next over, out in the deep field when he thought nobody was looking, he began rubbing his ankle and so bad was the injury that he hardly appeared next day. 'I think it cured Iddison of placing a man so near when bowling lobs,' commented W.G. laconically.

Only two days later W.G. saw that cricket injuries could be much more serious. He travelled back to London to appear for MCC against Nottinghamshire, and once again proved to be the one MCC batsman who could cope with the dreadful Lord's pitch, scoring an unbeaten 117 of a total of 183. The only other batsman to equal his mastery was his great rival, Richard Daft, who made exactly the same score for Notts. But the incident for which the match would always be remembered came early in the Notts second innings. George Summers, a young Nottinghamshire professional and a promising batsman, was at the wicket when the MCC fast bowler, Platts of Derbyshire, came on. His first ball reared up and struck Summers on the cheek. Summers collapsed and W.G. swiftly went to his aid, feeling his pulse and pronouncing: 'He is not dead.'

Summers was carried off, still unconscious, but appeared to have made a good recovery. MCC's wicketkeeper George Burton thought that the ball might have struck something on the pitch, perhaps a stone, 'for it came up with exceptional quickness. Summers was naturally standing sideways and received the ball on the thinnest part of the skull.' The next day was a hot one and although Summers was not well enough to play, he sat in the sun watching the match. Then he took the train back to Nottingham, where he died shortly afterwards. Grace was convinced that the combination of sun and a bumpy train ride aggravated Summers's concussion with fatal consequences. So alarmed was Richard Daft by the state of the Lord's pitch that, when the next man in after Summers was carried off, he walked out to the middle with two towels wrapped round his head, possibly the first recorded example of a helmet. Daft was more than a century ahead of his time.

An example of Grace's superiority over his fellows, especially on a bad wicket, came in a match for a Worcestershire XXII (county qualifications were pretty lax in those days) against a United North of England XI. Grace made 74 out of 114, and his last nine partners failed to contrive a single run between them. Worcs won by thirteen wickets!

Grace just could not stop scoring that summer. In sixty-seven innings in all cricket he totalled 3,255 at an average of 48; thirty-three of them were in first-class matches in which he made 1,808. Oddly enough, his average was six runs per innings higher, at 54. He also took 50 wickets at 15.70 each. One admirer was moved to write a poem in praise of the champion, apparently addressed to a future cricket 'widow':

> The turf is as verdant as spring, love,
> The air is seductively calm;
> Why echoes the jubilant ring, love,
> With rattle of palm upon palm?
> The lovers of 'glorious cricket'
> Stint not their exuberant glee,
> When quietly walks to the wicket
>   Great W.G.
>
> Who is he? Ah! sure, not to know, love,
> Must argue yourself as unknown.
> When fielders are sulky and slow, love,
> When bowlers are beaten and blown,
> When Lord's is alive with applause, love,
> When the telegraph figures are three,
> Then ask anybody the cause, love –
>   Tis W.G.

Who smiles at all Southerton's striving,
And Wootton's most murderous shots?
Who glories in cutting and driving
The bowling of Yorkshire and Notts?
Who stands to the hot ones unshrinking?
Who hits with the powder of three?
And in general goes it like winking?
    But W.G.

We'll wish him a cricketer's luck, love,
In life, a long innings and stout;
By Fate never bowled for a duck, love,
Or by time prematurely run out.
May he muff none of Fortune's best catches
And – eh? that's your sex to a T –
May he win in the sweetest of matches,
    Our W.G.

The season of 1871 saw W.G. again at his superlative best. Statistically it was his greatest summer with the bat: 2,739 first-class runs with ten centuries (two of them double hundreds) and the extraordinary average of 78. In all matches he made 3,696 runs. But it was the manner of scoring that demonstrated how he was now effortlessly head and shoulders above everyone else playing the game. The second man in the first-class table averaged 44 fewer runs per innings – and that was Fred Grace.

W.G. described how he felt at the crease: 'Nearly all nervous feeling at the commencement of an innings had left me; but I guarded against over-confidence and invariably played the first over or two carefully until I got my eye in. Grounds had improved wonderfully everywhere and I aimed at placing every ball, however straight and good the length of it; for that was about the only way to score at all rapidly against the crack bowlers of the day . . .'

The cracks didn't get much of a look-in against W.G., with the exception of Jemmy Shaw, who twice dismissed him for a first-over duck. On both occasions W.G. took his revenge at the first available opportunity: in the second innings.

The first game in which this happened was the South v the North on 31 July-2 August, a benefit for H.H. Stephenson, the former Surrey captain. W.G. was dismissed by the first ball of the South's innings, when Shaw's appeal for lbw was upheld by the umpire, John Lillywhite.

W.G. was not happy with the verdict, claiming he had hit the ball before it struck his pad, and Fred, standing at the non-striker's end, agreed. W.G.'s obvious dissent caused something of a sensation in the sporting press. The *Sporting Gazette* backed Lillywhite and remarked sternly: 'The decisions of the umpire must not be subjected to a test more or less rigorous, according to the celebrity of the player who happens to be subject himself thereto. A batsman is out or not, whether he be Mr W.G. Grace or the tenth man in the All Muggleton team.' The writer went on to wonder that Grace was not dismissed leg before wicket more often because of 'the peculiarity of his pose' while waiting for the bowler to deliver and 'were his eye to fail him' he would be highly vulnerable. But he had to admit: 'Only his eye so very seldom does fail, or his bat either.'

Both were back in working order by the time Grace marched out for his second knock in the late afternoon of the second day, the South holding a first-innings lead of 16. W.G. produced probably the finest display of sustained batting yet seen, to make the highest individual score in a first-class match since William Ward's 278 at Lord's in 1820. So determined was he not to gather a 'pair' that he laboured for six overs before getting off the mark. He made up for his slow start with a tremendous display of hitting and by the end of the day had scored 142 out of 195-2, paying as he put it 'special attention to J.C. Shaw'. At the close of play Grace had to race back to the pavilion to avoid the spectators who rushed to congratulate him.

A large crowd gathered for the final day, looking forward to a good finish, and their champion did not let them down. He had made 11 more runs when he offered a chance to the wicket-keeper but it was the only blemish in the entire innings. He scored a further century before lunch, at which he stood 246 not out and when finally caught behind off his gloves had made 268 at nearly a run a minute out of 377-4. 'Of his play nothing can possibly be written that can savour of exaggeration, as the cricket he displayed was throughout superb, and his batting faultless,' commented the *Sportsman*. It was 'one of the most marvellous exhibitions of batting that have ever been seen against a combination of seven bowlers, comprising most of the very best bowling of the year . . . His hitting was as well timed as ever and his placing irreproachable.'

Stephenson, the beneficiary, gave him a gold ring as a memento of his performance. Stephenson was naturally delighted: the great man's performance had brought in thousands more than he might otherwise have expected to swell the gate receipts and the collection. W.G. always did his best to play in benefit matches and was disappointed if he did not perform at his best in them: he had a massive sense of responsibility to his fellow players' welfare.

Thus there was keen expectation that John Lillywhite's benefit match in August would be the occasion for another W.G. spectacular. It was an extra Gentlemen v Players game at the old Hove Ground and a good crowd turned out in beautiful weather only to see Grace's off stump knocked out first ball by Jemmy Shaw again. Seventeen years later, Grace recalled the occasion clearly as one that taught him a valuable lesson – that a cricketer should always allow plenty of time to acclimatise himself to the state of the weather and ground. He arrived at the ground just before he was due to bat, and faced Shaw bowling from the sea end.

There was a glare on the water, delighting the artistic eye I have no doubt, but to me shifting and dancing like a will o' the wisp . . . I was all abroad to his first ball and knew it had beaten me before it came within two yards of me . . . The dazzling light, the railway journey, and want of five minutes' practice did it.

It was a lesson he took to heart. He apologised profusely to Lillywhite, who replied, 'Better luck next time.' For some reason, Grace related, he did not feel confident he would repeat his feats of The Oval. But Lillywhite did: he gave Grace two sovereigns (two pounds) and said he would take sixpence back for every run Grace scored in the second innings. It was a subtly calculated challenge. (For the decimal generation it should be explained that with 240 pennies to the sovereign, Grace would need to score 80 before

Lillywhite was in profit.) It certainly helped to dispel Grace's uncertainty about his prospects.

Opening the innings next day he lost his partner with the score at 35 and was joined by his brother Fred. They put on 240 together before Fred was out for 98, described by one observer as 'a grand and faultless exhibition of superfine cricket from first to last, his play being remarkable for some of the cleanest hitting of the season'. W.G. was still there at the end of the day on exactly 200 not out, having been dropped by Daft off a skyer when he was on only 21, to the relief of the thirteen thousand spectators crowded into the ground. When Grace got back to the pavilion, Lillywhite said: 'I'll trouble you for five pounds on account.'

W.G. himself provided two contradictory accounts of what happened next. In his book, *Cricket*, published in 1891, he claimed to have replied: 'All right Lillywhite, here it is, but if you do not let me off for the rest of the bet, I shall knock down my wicket first over tomorrow!' Lillywhite then agreed to call it quits, he claimed.

But in the massive *Memorial Biography*, published in 1919, W.G. is quoted verbatim as giving a rather different version, though no source is provided:

At the end of the day's play I had scored two hundred and had completely forgotten my compact with John. On my arrival at the pavilion he quietly came up to me and said: 'I will thank you for £5 on account.' I handed over the fiver with rather a woebegone air I suppose, for with a merry twinkle in his eye, he said: 'I'm quite content to cry quits on the bargain as far as it has gone if you are.' I was, I don't mind confessing, as I was in rare batting fettle and the wicket was like a billiard table. After all, I should have only had to give him 8s 6d more, as I only got 17 runs the next day.

No mention there of knocking his wicket over if the bet wasn't called off, which makes one wonder at the veracity of some of Grace's other stories about himself. There is no dispute however that he scored 217 runs although so great were people's expectations of Grace by now that even a double century was not enough: it had to be a good one. The *Sporting Gazette* commented: 'It was not a great performance. Indeed for fine batting the younger Mr

Grace's display was greatly superior. Only the latter portion of the 217 was quite worthy of Mr W.G. Grace . . .' He also took seven wickets in the match. At its end he was presented with a bat bearing an inscribed gold plate, on behalf of the Surrey club in recognition of his 268 at The Oval. His speech in reply was brevity itself: 'Thank you,' he said, for he was not fond of public speaking. He and Fred also received bats from Sussex.

Yet W.G.'s two double centuries were merely the icing on the cake. Wherever he played that summer and whatever the state of the wicket, the runs flowed and there were other competitors for the title of Grace's Greatest Innings. For another big benefit, that of Ned Willsher, the rarely played fixture of Single v Married was staged at Lords's in mid-July for the first time since 1858. W.G. carried his bat for 189 out of 310 against a strong attack and on a wicket made even more difficult than usual by rain.

Once more he took a long look at the bowling, taking a quarter of an hour to score his first run, but after that he was simply devastating. He himself rated it as one of his best and so did other observers. The *Sporting Gazette* called it

. . . the best display he has made during the present "aquatic" season. Two days sun and wind had sharpened up the wickets and he was himself again, at home to every sort of attack – master of every kind of bowling . . . He is not the prettiest bat living, but he is the most marvellous. When he is at his best he rises superior to the laws which govern ordinary cricketers, and hence, perhaps, much of the wonder which his defiant manipulation of the ball rouses in the mind of the average spectator.

The figures tell much of the story: the next highest scorer was Fred Grace with 33, while the married men contributed 159 and 78 between them. The *Sporting Gazette*'s commentator quoted a remark by John Lillywhite that aptly summarised Grace's power: 'There! Did you see that? I could never score off such a ball. I was content to stop it. Gone for three.'

Others regarded Grace's performance for the South v North at Lord's over Whit weekend as the equal or better. Sir John Lubbock's Bill granting the populace a day's holiday on Whit Monday had just been passed and cricket lovers took full advantage of their new day off to converge on Lord's. 'Such a crowd as which was attracted to Lord's on Whit Monday has, perhaps, never been seen on the old ground since its establishment,' wrote the *Sporting Gazette*. 'It rolled up and formed itself into a ring long before the game commenced.' When the lunch bells rang, the crowd, estimated at eight thousand, made a dash for the one exit gate that was open and such was the crush that no one could get in or out. (How interesting to note that the Lord's authorities' curmudgeonly treatment of its paying customers has such deep roots.) If any of the crowd were still disgruntled at missing their lunch, W.G. restored their spirits with a magnificent 178 not out, much of it in partnership (yet again) with Fred, who scored 83, 'showing good sound steady batting, as well as an amount of patience for which few had credited him', as the *Sportsman*'s correspondent wrote. W.G. was 'irreproachable . . . both his timing and placing were more remarkable than usual, his manner of scoring off leg-balls that would, we venture to say, have disposed of any less accomplished batsman, being marvellous'.

The centuries came all season: 181 for MCC v Surrey at Lord's (when turnstiles were in use for the first time and Grace's highest score on the ground thus far); 146 in the return fixture at The Oval; 118 for Gentlemen of the South v Gentlemen of the North on the Middlesex County Ground at West Brompton; 162 (out of 255) for Gentlemen of England v Cambridge University on his first appearance at Fenner's; 117 for MCC v Kent at Canterbury; and he was run out two short of his century, also for MCC, against Yorkshire at Lord's.

Whenever W.G. ventured out of Bristol or London the anticipation was intense. Everyone wanted to see the champion, and the publicity for a match in which he was playing was entirely centred on him. Huge posters featuring his name were plastered all over walls and hordings. 'His coming is heralded by local journals with as much gravity and "circumstance" as would be used in notifying the coming of Marimon herself,' sniffily commented one metropolitan scribe.

On his first appearance at Trent Bridge, for Gloucestershire, in August, he pulled in a crowd of ten thousand on the first day and made a dogged 79 in the first innings (out of 140). His great adversary Richard Daft remarked to him afterwards that he ought to have gone on to make a century as it would have been the first in a first-class match on the Nottingham ground. 'Why didn't you tell me before and I would have done it,' replied Grace with a laugh and promised to rectify matters in the second innings. In customary fashion he was as good as his word next day, scoring 116 before an even bigger crowd, estimated at twelve thousand. There was little work done in the local factories for those three days, the men decamping in droves to Trent Bridge to see the almost mythical W.G. bat. 'It was chiefly the prospect of beholding the great batsman perform which drew together these enormous crowds and therefore swelled the exchequer of the county club in such a wholesome manner,' said the *Sporting Gazette*. The men surely returned to work well satisfied, for they had witnessed both Grace in his pomp and the powerful Nottinghamshire team win with ease.

There were plenty of sparkling Grace vignettes too: 59 out of 83 in forty minutes against Sussex at Lord's; a powerful 78 in an opening partnership of 134 with E.M. in the first Gloucs–Notts match, played at Clifton College, Bristol; 81 not out in a total of 141 against Kent at Maidstone and 42 not out in the second innings. In this match he bowled through both innings and took ten wickets. There was little danger of his being taken off as it was his own scratch XI, in a hastily-arranged second benefit for Willsher, the first having been disrupted by rain. Thus in Willsher's benefit matches he had scored 312 runs without being out. His enthusiasm for the game was always intense.

When a game at Lord's finished early he went off to Harrow to watch a school match, only to witness a tragedy. The star of the Harrow School first XI was taking his turn as square-leg umpire when he was hit behind the ear by a pull-shot. Grace rushed to his aid but to no avail: the boy was dead.

Grace's bowling through the summer of 1871 should not be entirely overshadowed by his extraordinary feats with the bat. He took seventy-nine first-class wickets at an average of 17 but in the opinion of the *Sporting Gazette*, 'Mr W.G. Grace would not earn his salt as a bowler.' He was good enough, however, to deal with lesser mortals, as he showed when playing for the United South of England v a local XXII at Uppingham in July, a sort of missionary expedition to take the game to a region which saw little top-class cricket. Most of the spectators hoped to see W.G. in form with the bat but were sadly disappointed: he was out for a single in the first innings and run out for a duck in the second. Perhaps eager to compensate the crowd, he took twenty-five wickets (fourteen in the first innings, eleven in the second) and five catches at point.

W.G.'s enormous fame aroused such expectation among spectators that there was enormous pressure both on him to succeed and on the umpires to allow him to. An example of this came during the Canterbury Festival in August when he appeared for South v North. He made 31 in the first innings (having been prevented from opening the innings by a late train), a trifling amount by his standards, leaving him keen to do better in the second. He was in such good form that he swiftly got to 40 and, according to one observer, 'seemed fairly set for three or four hundred runs, at the very least'. So when he was given run out by umpire Royston in dubious circumstances, the crowd, many of whom had attended just to see W.G., was upset and voiced their opposition vociferously. W.G. was as surprised as they were. He hesitated, queried the decision before departing, and felt aggrieved about it for the rest of his life. The *Sporting Gazette* had no hesitation in declaring it a mistake and went so far as to accuse Royston of being overcome by the heat or the wish for a cool drink.

Lillywhite's Companion summed up his season: 'The batting of him who has earned the title of the champion cricketer – and most certainly his equal has never been seen – has been the leading feature of the season. His defence has been more stubborn, his hitting more brilliant and his timing and placing of the ball more judicious and skilful than during the previous summer and it is a common occurrence to see him defy the combined efforts of the best bowlers in England for the whole of an afternoon. He is also unsurpassed in the field, not infrequently a successful bowler, and always an excellent general and tactician.'

The *Sporting Gazette* had a sly dig at Grace's superiority to the rest of his county colleagues (Fred excepted): 'It is true that Mr W.G. Grace has again witched the world with noble run getting, but then that sort of thing has become such a matter of course with Gloucestershire – we beg pardon, with Mr W.G. Grace – that the most devoted admirers of the great batman must really be pardoned if they tire of applauding.'

But W.G.'s greatest season thus far had a sad postscript. His father, Dr Henry Grace, died two days before Christmas at the age of sixty-three. His love of hunting and dedication to his profession were contributory factors. He insisted on riding out with the hounds despite suffering from a heavy cold, and then stayed up all night with a patient. The combination was fatal. Death was attributed to 'inflammation of the lungs': pneumonia. The *Clifton Chronicle* recorded:

Few better sportsmen existed, and by the members of the Beaufort and Berkeley Hunts, and by the lovers of field sports generally in the county and neighbourhood his loss will be generally lamented. Mr Grace, himself a fine cricketer, was the father, and we almost think we may add, instructor of the eminent amateurs bearing his name, who have obtained such renown as champion players in both hemispheres. In private life he was beloved for his professional kindness towards the poor, no less than for the generosity of his disposition, and the cordial and genial way in which he demeaned himself towards all with whom he came in contact.

He was buried in the church at Downend. As well as being a pillar of the local community, much loved by his patients, he had had the satisfaction of founding two cricket clubs (Mangotsfield, which became West Gloucestershire) and being the main inspiration behind a county team which was rapidly being built up into a force in the English game. But above all he had sired the most formidable family and the greatest individual yet to play the sport. His boys certainly inherited both his spirit and his total devotion to the cause in hand.

For W.G., the English season of 1872 was truncated at the beginning by bad weather, including snow and sleet in May, and at the end by his selection, along with eleven others, to tour Canada and the United States, the party departing in August.

His first appearance outside the West Country was for MCC v Hertfordshire at Chorleywood on 10 May, where he began inauspiciously with a duck, but followed up with 75 in the second innings.

The bad weather meant that pitches were difficult to bat on in May and in common with most batsmen Grace found the runs hard to come by at first and he had to admit defeat from the rain. As one columnist put it:

Even Mr W.G. Grace, who cares rather less for the rain than a young sheldrake, and would bat for a week in the heaviest conceivable downpour, if he could get anyone to bowl to him – even the champion himself was early brought to admit that playing under such circumstances was impossible.

He also fell foul again of umpire Royston when appearing for MCC v Surrey at Lords, in the opening first-class match of the season in mid-May, dismissed lbw fourth ball without scoring, although he did not dissent from this decision.

The match was remarkable for the use of a tarpaulin cover to protect the pitch from the drenching rain. It failed in its appointed task but it was a pointer to the future. The wicket was eventually pitched 20 yards from the usual square and was rapidly reduced to a mudpatch. Grace was not alone in his failure: as the *Sportsman* put it, 'the discomfiture of the great batsman was the forerunner of one of the most extraordinary freaks of fortune ever witnessed in a first-class match'. At one stage MCC were 0–7 and were grateful to reach 16 all out. The match, scheduled to last three days, finished within one, Surrey winning by five wickets. The *Sporting Gazette* commented: 'Even the champion himself was early brought to admit that playing under such circumstances was impossible . . . W.G. is never himself upon a slow wicket. Nothing brings him so near to the level of an ordinary batsman as a few hours rain.'

As well as covers, there were other experiments in 1872. A match, in which Grace took part, was played at Lord's with the wickets an inch higher and broader, there being a belief that batsmen were having it too much their own way. Predictably, W.G. did not agree. The experiment proved inconclusive and was not repeated. Four stumps were tried out in a match in Lancashire but that too failed to find favour.

Grace still managed two centuries in May and 87 for the South v North at Prince's but he did not really get into his stride until July when within the space of eight days he hit 306 in three innings for the Gentlemen v Players. In the first match, at Lord's from 1 to 3 July, he made a chanceless 77 in the first innings, 47 of them in the first hour, displaying 'some of the grandest cricket shown by the great batsman during the present season', according to the *Sportsman*. He did even better in the second innings, with 112, which the *Sporting Gazette* described as his finest display of the season and which led to a seven-wicket win for the Gentlemen. Its writer summarised the finale of the match thus: 'The Alfred Jingle phraseology might be fairly adopted: "Bowling beaten – punishment awful – very".'

The return match, held at the Oval immediately afterwards in front of a crowd estimated at between six and seven thousand, followed much the same pattern. The Gentlemen demolished the Players inside two days, this time by nine wickets. Grace made 117, the highlight of which was a hit for six over long-on into the trees near the rackets court. He failed by only two to make a century before lunch. The *Sporting Gazette* thought it would 'rank among his finest exploits' but took him to task for restricting the match to two days. He had 'again played the mischief with the gate money. Had he . . . been content with an average share of the runs the struggle might have been prolonged into the third day, and the coffers of the club thereby benefited.'

Two days later he was back at Lord's to make 170 not out for England versus a combined Yorkshire/Nottinghamshire side, an innings which included slashing cuts and a 6 to the nursery wall after he had completed his century. The innings took him only 225 minutes and was made out of 283. Although not entirely faultless – he gave sharp chances to short-leg and cover-point – it was nevertheless described thus by the *Sportsman*: 'as superfine and irreproachable a display of batting as he has ever shown in his career . . . Those who have witnessed this performance are to be congratulated on their fortune in seeing such an innings . . . The unnerving precision of his defence and hitting proved he retains in every way the marvellous skill shown of late years.'

The *Sporting Life* provided a rather sniffier description of the admiration Grace commanded from ordinary cricket-lovers, which perhaps unwittingly showed the divide between those who ran the game and those who paid to watch it:

With that extraordinary love of mobbing celebrities that seems indigenous to the British public, especially that portion of it which frequents cricket grounds, Mr Grace had to pass to his dressing room through a living lane of excited hand-clapping people, who had, directly the last wicket fell, rushed to the pavilion enclosure like a swarm of bees to applaud and stare at the Gloucestershire gentleman. That the applause was well merited we grant; but was the manner of giving it pleasant to the recipient or delicate on the part of the donors? However, Mr Grace must now be well used to such scenes.

He played another memorable innings when he led Gloucestershire against Yorkshire at Sheffield – his first appearance on the ground – in a benefit for the all-rounder Roger Iddison. It was a huge challenge for Gloucestershire, only recently formed and composed entirely of amateurs, to take on the mighty Yorkshire on their home territory but with W.G. at the helm anything was possible. One columnist wryly described the team as 'the three Graces and their eight assistants'. Eight thousand people crammed in to Bramall Lane to see him and his opening partner, T.G. Matthews, open the batting on a dull morning. An additional hazard was smoke from adjoining factories spreading over the ground to such an extent that the spectators could sometimes barely see the players. (The smoke was so sooty that when the southern team fielded their white flannels rapidly became filthy; the Yorkshiremen were canny enough to wear darker strip.)

The Gloucestershire openers put on 208 on the first day without being parted. W.G. hit two balls out of the ground into Harwood Street on his way to 150 and one result was a Yorkshire saying about him that rapidly became legend: 'He dab 'em but seldom, and when he do dab 'em he dab 'em for foor.' He was by no means finished; he and E.M. took all Yorkshire's wickets in their first innings, and he and G.F. eight in the second.

W.G. also travelled to Scotland for the first time. There was keen interest in cricket north of the border and even keener interest in seeing the English champion. His first biographer, W. Methven Brownlee, was Scottish. He wrote: 'A visit from the "All England Eleven" had been almost a yearly thing for several years, but we had never seen Grace, and how we had talked and dreamed about him.' The Scots finally got their opportunity in 1872 when he took a United South team to Glasgow to play a local XXII. The largest crowd ever to watch a cricket match in Scotland turned out to see the great man and had a big let-down when the United South were dismissed for 49, local hero Andrew McAllister taking 7–17, including W.G. In his customary fashion he made up for his failure by demolishing the bowling in the second innings with 114, including six sixes. He struck one out of the ground into a passing cab, and hit a young woman spectator on the arm with another thunderbolt. She moved to another part of the ground only to be targeted again by Grace, this time being hit in the chest by another boundary. When asked how he had got on in the second innings, McAllister replied ruefully: 'The ground wasn't big enough today', putting into words what many of Grace's victims must have felt before and since.

5 · MISSIONARY TO AMERICA

1872–1873

I N August 1872 W.G. set off on his biggest missionary journey
yet. He was invited by the MCC to take part in a tour to
Canada, where cricket was struggling to find its feet, and the
United States. The tour was the outcome of a visit to England
the previous year by two representatives of Canadian cricket, J.C.
Patteson, and Captain N. Wallace of the 60th Rifles (who later
went on to play for Grace's county, Gloucestershire). They visited
Lord's and explained to the MCC secretary, Robert Fitzgerald,
just how parlous was cricket's state in their native land. It had not
caught on in the same way as it had in Australia, possibly because
of the strong French influence in Quebec and the vagaries of the
weather. The Canadians were prepared to fund a tour by some
of England's finest with the aim of reviving interest among the
general public and giving the players a shot in the arm. Their
only stipulation was that one Englishman had to be in the party
– W.G. Grace, whose fame had crossed the Atlantic and who was
already the sport's outstanding figure.

There had been two previous tours of North America, the first
in 1859 led by George Parr and containing many fine cricketers
including John Wisden, the second in 1868 captained by Ned
Willsher.

Fitzgerald listened with sympathy and enthusiastically set about
assembling a team. As it was an MCC tour, all the players had to
be amateurs and Fitzgerald had considerable difficulty in finding

enough men who could spare the time to undertake a leisurely
tour of North America. Grace consented to travel but only three
days before the party was due to depart, the two Walker brothers
selected fell ill and were forced to withdraw. Panic ensued at
Lord's but after firing off a frantic series of telegrams and letters,
Fitzgerald came up with Alfred Lubbock's brother Edgar and
F.P.U. Pickering (Eton and Sussex). Fitzgerald – usually known
as 'Fitz' – was a colourful pipe-smoking figure with a beard even
longer than W.G.'s. He himself was tour manager and captain
while W.G. was undoubtedly the leading player in the party. The
other members were: the Hon George Harris (later Lord Harris,
the formidable Kent captain and MCC overlord), A.N. 'Monkey'
Hornby, the future Lancashire captain who was to share many a
long partnership with W.G., Edgar and Alfred Lubbock, W.M.
Rose, W.H. Hadow, C.J. Ottaway, C.K. Francis, who had just
come down from Oxford, A. Appleby, a left-arm fast bowler
from Lancashire, and Pickering. The batting looked strong but
the bowling was weak and a lot of work would fall on Appleby's
shoulders. As veterans of the Gentlemen against the Players, the
cricketers all knew each other well. The only professional they took
was Farrands of the Lord's ground staff – and then only to act as
their umpire. The party comprised only twelve men, leaving little
latitude in case of injury or illness. But if they stayed fit they were
all guaranteed plenty of cricket, unlike the professional tourists of
today who may go a month without playing.

W.G. was obliged to leave the Canterbury cricket week early
to travel to Liverpool from where the party sailed on 8 August
aboard the SS *Sarmantian* after a farewell lunch at the Adelphi
Hotel arranged by a group of local cricketers. The steamship
was the flagship of the Allen Line and at more than 4,000 tons
was considered to be the ultimate in sophistication. Among the
cricketers' fellow passengers were two hundred children, waifs and
strays plucked from the streets of London by the Brompton Home,
which was now sending them off to a new life in America. Once
past Ireland and out into the Atlantic, the ship ran into rough seas
and many of the tour party were badly seasick, particularly Harris
and W.G., who while usually the picture of robust health was never

much of a sailor. 'She takes a little playing this morning, George,' joked Alfred Lubbock to poor Harris, while Fitzgerald noted wryly of Grace: 'Gilbert the Great was bowled out very early and would have returned in an open boat from mid-Atlantic if such craft were in the habit of plying there.'

They encountered calmer waters after a couple of days so W.G. and company began to enjoy the voyage, especially the sight of whales and icebergs off Newfoundland, though Harris never found his sea legs and was confined to his cabin for the entire crossing.

They arrived in Quebec after nightfall on 17 August after an exceptionally fast crossing, the cricketers wasting no time in going ashore to sample the night life. They returned to spend the night on the boat. Fitzgerald dreamed 'that W.G. was not out, 1,000, he couldn't tell where but he awoke refreshed'. When they went ashore they found that no accommodation had been arranged for them and all the best hotels were fully booked. They were hurriedly found rooms in private houses.

Being great fishing enthusiasts, Fitzgerald and Grace could hardly wait to get to grips with the legendary Canadian trout streams. When the party undertoook an expedition to see the Falls of Montmorenci, the pair tried their hand in a nearby pool but the dozen or so fish they caught were of miserable size. 'The worms looked much more likely to swallow the fish than the fish to swallow the worms,' commented Fitzgerald. So after dinner with the Governor-General, Lord Dufferin, Fitzgerald and Grace and a couple of others who wanted to try the shooting returned upcountry in search of better sport. In a hair-raising fashion, they were taken through the night over rough roads in a coach and pair handled by a French-Canadian driver who spoke little English until they reached a stream above the Montmorenci Falls.

After breakfast in a log cabin belonging to an Irishman who was the greatest fishing expert in the area, W.G. and Fitzgerald settled down to a good morning's sport, pulling out 130 small trout until they got bored with the ease of it all. It was 5 p.m. before they and the others, who had gone shooting with a lot less luck, returned to Quebec. 'Before sundown we had a little cricket practice on the ramparts,' noted W.G. The only result was that Hadow put a finger out trying to catch a scorching drive by W.G., reducing the party to eleven fit men before the first match.

The affable chaos which seemed to surround most of their arrangements continued. Having carefully packed the best of the catch in ice for the journey to Montreal, they managed to leave it at the station in the rush to catch the night train. However a private sleeping car had been laid on for them by Captain Cumberland, managing director of the North Pacific Railroad. It contained a well-stocked bar and an affable barman, who, as Grace later commented, 'gave us . . . an introduction to the peculiar beverages which the Americans call "cock-tails", and of which they concoct an endless variety.'

Their first match was a three-day affair against a Montreal XXII starting on 22 August in stifling late-summer heat – 92° F in the shade. Inspecting it the day before the game, the Englishmen thought the ground in Catherine Street, in the shadow of a mountain and with a melon field on one side, primitive in the extreme and in very poor condition. It was three-cornered and looked like a cross between a rubbish dump and a quarry. They complained vociferously but conscious of their missionary status naturally had to play. In practice Francis was laid out by a ball which struck his head, forcing Fitzgerald, now down to ten fit men, to call a halt before anyone else was hurt. A thunderstorm from dawn to midday threatened the game but it started at 1 p.m. The visitors need not have worried: the opposition was as poor as the pitch. A disappointingly small crowd turned out to see Fitzgerald win the toss as he was to do in every one of the nine matches on the Canadian leg (eight of them so-called 'first-class'). He opted to bat, W.G. opening with Ottaway and getting the tour off to a good start with a century partnership. A local journalist described him:

W. Grace is a large-framed loose-jointed man, and you would say that his gait was a trifle peculiar, but when he goes into the field you see that he is quick-sighted, sure-handed, and light-footed as the rest. He always goes in first, and to see him tap the ball gently to the off for one, draw it to the on for two, pound it to the limits for four, drive it heaven knows where for six, looks as easy as rolling off a log.

He had made 81 in fine fashion with several mighty blows when he cut the ball hard into the stomach of a stout fielder named Benjamin at point, who clutched the ball as he doubled up in agony and was carried shoulder-high around the pitch by his jubilant team-mates for his historic act. The watching journalist was not so impressed: 'The nonchalance of the elegant Benjamin was a thin assumption,' he wrote. MCC were 130–3 at the close of the first day. Everywhere they went, the play was followed by a magnificent banquet in town. There were several speeches and to great glee W.G., who hated public speaking, was prevailed upon to reply to the toast to 'the Champion Batsman of cricketdom'. Grace got to his feet and spoke: 'Gentlemen, I beg to thank you for the honour you have done me. I never saw better bowling than I have seen today, and I hope to see as good wherever I go.' Fitzgerald commented: 'The speech took longer to deliver than you might imagine from its brevity, but it was greeted with applause from all who were in the proper position to hear it.' A running joke throughout the tour was that W.G. was invited to deliver a speech at various dinners around Canada and made the same one, substituting only 'batting', 'fielding', or on one daring occasion 'ladies' for 'bowling'. Indeed, the legend of his Canadian oratory was to follow him around for the rest of his life, and there was no doubt that he never enjoyed getting to his feet to make a speech. But he got better at it as he grew older, though he was never in any danger of subjecting his audience to a lengthy address.

Next day England totalled 255 and shot out the opposition, all twenty-two of them, for only 48 and 67 to win by an innings and 140 runs. Another local paper reported: 'If they hit a half volley, they were caught in the long field; if they left their ground they were stumped; if they stayed at home they were bowled or caught at point by Mr Grace.' It was as easy as catching trout for the seasoned Englishmen – and there were only ten of them. The day was rounded off by another dinner, at the St James's Club, pronounced by Fitzgerald to be quite as good as anything a London club could have laid on, down to the smallest detail. Each Englishman, for instance, found on the table a silk menu with his own name on one side and the names of his hosts on the other.

The Canadians' capacity for hospitality never ceased to amaze the party throughout the tour.

Then it was on to Ottawa by train and river steamer, the cricketers being impressed as they approached the city by the tang of sawdust in the air and the sight of thousands of logs being floated down the river Ottawa to the sawmills. On 27 August they embarked on their second match, against an Ottawa XXII, on a ground overlooked by the Governor-General's mansion, Rideau Hall. In contrast to Montreal, a huge crowd was present, the wicket had been well prepared and the outfield was well stocked with long grass, as well as grasshoppers and hundreds of large butterflies. It was 'a gay and animated sight', thought Fitzgerald. Grace was feeling below par because of a stomach upset but opened nevertheless and was soon in full flow. The spectators, clearly not well versed in the finer points of the game, kept thinking he was out caught when it was a bump ball. He was eventually out for 73, to a daisy-cutter from an underarm bowler named Boothroyd. The pattern of the game was very similar to that of Montreal: England made 201 and had little trouble in dismissing the locals for 43 and 49 to win by an innings and 110 runs.

It was becoming clear to the tourists that Canadian cricket had some decent enough bowlers and enthusiastic fielders but the batsmen had little clue and were never remotely a match for the English bowlers. They were excellent hosts, however, as they showed again with dinner in Ottawa's Parliament Square, featuring among other delicacies the hind leg of a bear, which the Englishmen found tough and unpalatable. In his speech, the chairman made a clumsy reference to The Three Graces which was so far above W.G.'s head that he thought he was referring to his sisters and was heard to comment that he was sorry they could not be there to reply for themselves.

On 30 August the party left Ottawa by train at 7 a.m. to travel up the St Lawrence towards Toronto. Again, Patteson's arrangements went awry. He had apparently fixed up a match in a town called Belleville but when the party reached the railhead at Prescott they could find no one who knew where Belleville was. It later emerged that hundreds of people had converged on Belleville to see 'The Unapproachable', as Fitzgerald dubbed W.G. and were sadly disappointed when neither he nor anyone else showed up. Instead, the Englishmen ended up at a country picnic at a place called Brookville where by the side of Lake Ontario they drank champagne, danced with the local ladies and gave an impromptu demonstration of cricket with a broom handle for a bat and a turnip for a ball.

They moved on to Toronto, the centre of cricket in Canada, where they spent a week. They drew large and appreciative crowds to the cricket ground; a temporary stand had been put up capable of seating two thousand people, and there were tents for the scorers and umpires. The Englishmen in their turn were appreciative of the better facilities, particularly the soap and towels they found in their changing room for the first time on the tour. On Monday 2 September they embarked on a match against a local XXII on a well-watered pitch, whose greenness stood out against the parched, brown outfield.

Grace's stomach upset in Ottawa had grown into something rather more serious in transmission across the Atlantic. *The Times* reported that he had cholera, to the alarm of his family in Gloucestershire. Unaware of this, W.G. opened the batting as usual with Ottaway, on a steaming hot day, and proceeded with caution until the fifth over when he opened his shoulders and struck a mighty six out of the ground. After that he was unstoppable. As in Ottawa, the crowd thought he was out caught but it was a bump ball and he was also dropped at point off a genuine chance but while wickets fell regularly at the other end he despatched the bowling all over the place. He proceeded to compile the first century of the tour, before John Brunel, the fielder who had dropped him earlier, held on to another chance to dismiss the great man for 142. It was 'a great performance and gave great pleasure to the spectators', noted Fitzgerald, who batted at number 12 and made 13 in three balls with two sixes and a single to take MCC's total to 319.

By then the match was into its second day but Toronto's batsmen were little better than their compatriots elsewhere. Before the day was out the XXII were dismissed for 97 and the match was over by 1 p.m. on Wednesday, with Toronto following on and making 104 to give MCC victory by an innings and 118.

During the game Fitzgerald had a taste of the brisk American way of doing business. He was approached by a man who wanted England to add a fixture in Chicago to their schedule. There was one drawback: no ground existed. 'By the time you get there I have no manner of doubt they will have made one,' he assured Fitzgerald. Another visitor was so taken with W.G. that he offered him two young bears to take back to England. 'I could not quite see to what use I could apply the creatures when I got them home,' commented Grace, 'so I declined the seductive offer.'

Later in the week, the Lieutenant-Governor and his wife, who watched every day of the cricket, gave a ball for the Englishmen, who were, not for the first time in Canada, much taken by the many attractive young ladies present. W.G. distinguished himself on the dance floor. According to a local paper, 'Mr Grace, who must now be known by sight to more people in England than Mr Gladstone himself, was especially noticeable for the skill and agility of his movements.' The ladies were much in evidence next day on an excursion to Lake Simcoe and the town of Couchiching on the North Pacific railroad, a massive and ambitious project still under construction destined to unite Canada's Atlantic and Pacific coasts.

At Port Banic, the party disembarked and took a short train journey to Allandale, where the locals had gone to enormous trouble to lay on a splendid open-air feast for their distinguished visitors. The station was decorated with a huge banner which left the stranger with no doubt as to the allegiance of the inhabitants of this far corner of the Empire: 'Welcome to the England Cricketers. God Save the Queen!' Mischievous reference was made at the banquet to the Englishmen's intentions towards the local ladies.

But there was a more serious side to such outings. The Canadian hosts saw the tour as important not only for encouraging cricket but for stimulating interest in emigration from Britain and assiduously exploited the chance to bang the drum about their country's glories. The tourists were impressed by the spirit of enterprise

Martha Grace, W.G.'s mother

The Chestnuts, Downend, where W.G. grew up and learned to play cricket on the lawn

The West Gloucestershire team, founded by W.G.'s father, Dr Henry Mills Grace, at Knowle Park, Almondsbury. This historic photograph contains Dr Grace and his five cricketing sons. Back row (L to R): Rev. H.W. Barber, Dr H.M. Grace, H. Gruning, Alfred Pocock (Uncle Pocock). Middle row: W.G. Grace, Henry Grace, E.M. Grace, Alfred Grace. Front row: F. Baker, W.J. Pocock, G.F. (Fred) Grace, R. Brotherhood

W.G.'s oldest brother, Henry

'The Coroner': E.M. Grace

W.G. as a young man

G.F. Grace, popular, brilliant and much-mourned

The Nonpareil: W.G. aged 25

W.G., when a whippy fast-medium bowler

E.M. at the wicket, dashing and unorthodox

W.G. with G.F. (right) and their cousin W.R. Gilbert, a talented cricketer whose career ended in disgrace

The MCC tour party to North America, 1872–3: (L to R): A. Lubbock, R.A. Fitzgerald (MCC secretary), A. Appleby, W.H. Hadow, C.J. Ottaway, W.G. Grace, W.M. Rose, A.N. Hornby, Hon G. (later Lord) Harris, F.P.U. Pickering, C.K. Francis, E. Lubbock

The MCC tour party to Australia, 1873–4:
Back row (L to R): J.A. Bush, W. Oscroft,
R. Humphrey, J. Southerton,
M. McIntyre, F.H. Boult, A. Greenwood,
W.R. Gilbert. Front row: James
Lillywhite, W.G. Grace, H. Jupp,
G.F. Grace

James Lillywhite's contract with W.G. for
the Australian tour 1873–4

Articles of Agreement made and entered into this day of September 1873 Between William Gilbert Grace of Downend in the County of Gloucester Gentleman of the one part and in the County of Cricketer (hereinafter called the said Cricketer) of the other part Witnesseth that the said William Gilbert Grace hereby engages the said to proceed to Australasia to play in 14 Cricket matches of three days each at such times and places as the said William Gilbert Grace shall from time to time direct for a period extending over about 100 days and returning on or about the 28th day of March 1874 And in consideration thereof the said William Gilbert Grace hereby agrees to pay the said James Lillywhite the sum of £150 at the times and in manner hereinafter mentioned and the said J. Lillywhite hereby agrees to and accepts the said engagement upon the following conditions that is to say

1 The said Cricketer is to report himself to the said William Gilbert Grace at Southampton on the 22nd day of October 1873 to embark on board the Peninsular and Oriental Steamer bound for Australia and announced to depart on the 23rd day of October 1873

2 The said Cricketer hereby agrees during such period as aforesaid to place himself under the entire disposal and directions of the said William Gilbert Grace and to obey all his orders and to play in each of the aforesaid 14 cricket matches if required by the said William Gilbert Grace so to do And the said Cricketer hereby agrees with the said William Gilbert Grace that he will not play in any other cricket match or cricket matches than those authorized by the said William Gilbert Grace or engage in any other pursuit without the consent in writing of the said William Gilbert Grace first obtained unless the further matches have been required

3 The said William Gilbert Grace hereby agrees to provide for the said Cricketer a free second class passage to Australia and back to England by one of the Peninsular and Oriental Steam Company's vessels and to provide Hotel accommodation and to pay all travelling and other expences during the said engagement except wines spirits and other liquors but hereby agrees to pay the said Cricketer the sum of £20 wines and his expences of wines spirits and other liquors

4 The said sums of £150 and £20 to be paid as follows £50 on the said Cricketer at Southampton

W.G. with W.L ('Billy') Murdoch, his great Australian opponent who became one of his firmest friends

Lord Sheffield's tour party to Australia 1891–2, led by W.G., in the botanical gardens, Adelaide

The Grace clan, photographed in the early 1890s: 1. W.G. Grace. 2. Alfie Grace (nephew).
3 George Grace (nephew). 4. Mrs E.M. Grace. 5. Mrs Page (neice). 6. Bessie Grace (daughter).
7. E.M. Grace. 8. Alfred Pocock. 9. W.G. Grace, junior. 10. Gerald Grace (nephew). 11. Mrs
Alice Bernard, W.G.'s sister. 12. Henry Grace. 13. Mrs Agnes Grace. 14. Dr Skelton (brother-
in-law). 15. Fanny Grace (W.G.'s sister). 16. Alfred Grace. 17. Rev. John Dann (W.G.'s brother-
in-law). 18. Henry Grace, W.G.'s second son. 19. Mrs Annie Skelton (W.G.'s sister). 20. Mrs
Henry Grace. 21. Mrs Blanche Dann (W.G.'s sister). 22. Charles Grace (W.G.'s youngest son).
23. Mrs Alfred Grace

"THE FIFTIETH YEAR OF GRACE."
NOT OUT.

W.G. at the crease, showing his distinctive stance, with the left foot pointing down the wicket

A Punch cartoon celebrating W.G.'s fiftieth birthday in 1898

W.G. as photographed by G.W. Beldam

they found all around them and the opportunities available to anyone willing to work hard to create a new life for themselves. 'Canada is not a country for the loafer,' observed Fitzgerald. 'But a loaf is at hand for as many as will ask, so that they are willing to put their strong shoulders to the common wheel.'

The cricketers were also struck by the democratic atmosphere. Coming from class-ridden Britain, and representing furthermore one of the most snobbish and patrician of its institutions, they were amazed at Canadians' relaxed and informal manner. Fitzgerald admitted: 'It was at first almost strange to us, Englishmen with our insular prejudices of caste or superior education, to be greeted, as we were, in the familiar, but not vulgar, manner of our brothers in Canada. It took us a week or two thoroughly to understand the relation in which man stands to man in the New World . . . . The hard crust of old English prejudice does not crumble without a struggle in the operation. But it did crumble ere we left the Dominion.'

The week in Toronto ended with a light-hearted twelve-a-side match between two mixed English-Canadian sides, one captained by Fitzgerald, the other by W.G., who won the toss on another hot day with hundreds of butterflies adorning the outfield. W.G. went in to bat with George Harris but to the crowd's disappointment he danced down the wicket to Rose's second ball and was stumped by Hornby for a duck. He was obviously a great hit with the local ladies, for he delayed his second innings at the specific request of a group of them with whom he was chatting. His compatriots in Fitzgerald's team were not so considerate. Indeed, they played an elaborate practical joke on the great man.

Batting at six, he had struck a whirlwind 27 in seven blows when a ball from Alfred Lubbock hit him on the pad. The whole field appealed and W.G. was given out, much to his disgust. Although like everyone else he claimed not to be taking the game too seriously, he left the field most reluctantly, muttering that the umpire had been bribed, much to the merriment of his friends. He had the last laugh, taking seven wickets in Fitzgerald's team's second innings as his side won by 178 runs. That evening the party went to the Lyceum Theatre and were greatly moved on entering when the band played 'Rule Britannia' and the rest of the audience rose to applaud them. Even the actors joined in.

So smitten were Appleby, Ottaway and Francis with the charms of the young ladies of Toronto that they asked permission to stay on and attend church with them on Sunday morning while the rest of the party went on to London, Ontario. Predictably, the trio failed to get to London for the start of the next match, on Monday 9 September, and those who were at the ground rather wished they were elsewhere too. They had already found the town a dismal place and their hotel primitive, the one consolation being that the streets were full of delectable young women.

The ground was small and badly tended. Fitzgerald remarked that they had walked across the wicket without realising it was there. The place had clearly been occupied at some stage by the military for there were rifle pits everywhere and they discovered that a line of wooden buildings on one side had formerly been a barracks, in such poor repair that the captain thought it must recently have been under siege. Inside, where lunch was served, it was even worse: 'Rats and vermin had long since left, as much too comfortless,' wrote Fitzgerald. But the local people made up for these shortcomings by turning out in their thousands to watch.

Without his usual opening partner, Grace opened with 'Monkey' Hornby and made 31, top score in MCC's 89 (the missing three players had finally arrived in the afternoon). That night he felt out of sorts and did not attend a dance laid on for the tourists but he was well enough next day to make 76 out of 161 all out. The London team fell to 55 and 65 and lost by 130 runs, displaying, thought Fitzgerald, 'the same unwillingness to open the shoulder, the same preconceived dread of the straight long hop' as the other Canadian teams the MCC had met.

Fitzgerald and Grace had one more sporting challenge: a game of croquet against the local lady champions (the women of London being sporty in every sense). The two bearded grandees eventually emerged victorious in a tight game. If the Englishmen were not being stretched on the field of play, they were getting plenty of exercise on the dance floor. The social whirl continued that night with another ball, hosted by the local ladies, young Canadian men being too busy, in Fitzgerald's judgment, for matters of the heart.

On by overnight train to Hamilton for their last game in Canada, the English players were impressed by the comfort of the sleeping cars but less so by the ban on smoking, which was strictly enforced by the conductors. It appears that the anti-smoking lobby was well to the fore in North America even in those days.

On another small ground, but in better condition than the previous venue, the match ended in scenes of low farce. MCC made 181 (Grace 17) and dismissed the Hamilton XXII for 86. They were anxious to finish the game in two days and thus have plenty of time next day to enjoy the splendours of nearby Niagara Falls. But the nights were closing in and by 6 p.m. it was almost dark but the Canadians in the second innings were only 43–10 (!). As the moon rose, MCC worked their way steadily through the batting and by 6.25 p.m. the score was 60–18, with the fielders crouching on the ground to try to follow the progress of the ball. The last pair hung on grimly but were finally undone by W.G. with an underarm delivery – 'skittles rather than cricket', thought Fitzgerald.

After a day at the Falls, the tourists held a ball of their own at the Clifton House Hotel, Niagara, to thank the Canadians for the welcome they had enjoyed. It was not easy to assemble a lot of people from such a huge country at short notice and the numbers were rather depleted. So invitations were despatched to the hotels on the American side of the Falls and a quorum was eventually assembled.

Had the mission to spread the cricket message been successful? A reader of the Toronto *Mail* who signed himself 'Vigilans' wrote to the newspaper from Ottawa to congratulate the visitors on the impact they had made. 'There is scarcely a vacant lot in the vicinity of our cities that has not of late been utilized by our schoolboys for cricketing purposes, and if the game grows more into favour with our youth a great end has been obtained . . . The ethics of muscular Christianity seem to have pervaded the community . . .' He was particularly impressed by cricket's moral side. 'There is an *esprit de corps* pervading every eleven of real cricketers which crowds out all selfish tendencies, while the quiet submission of individual opinion to the absolute rule of the umpire or captain often calls for the greatest self-control.' This might have raised a wry smile from W.G.'s closest acquaintances.

Fitzgerald certainly thought the tour had achieved its aim. He too wrote to the *Mail* to thank the Canadian people for their extraordinary hospitality. 'We leave the Dominion as if we were leaving a second home,' he wrote. 'I am confident that our expedition will establish a more enduring result than that of simply promoting our national game.' But, he added: 'Cricket was the primary object of our visit, and if we shall have helped to encourage a love for the game and to promote a generous cause of emulation amongst your young athletes, our efforts in the field will not have been in vain.'

Alas, as the history of cricket in Canada has shown, they were.

On 17 September they arrived in New York by steamer down the Hudson from Albany and enjoyed 'a dinner fit for the gods', feasting on oysters of a size they had never seen before. After the wide open spaces of Canada they were astonished by the hustle and bustle of New York. The ground on which they were to play a city XXII was in Hoboken, an area then being developed, and it was surrounded by unfinished streets and half-built houses. Fitzgerald lost the toss for the first time in North America and the Americans batted, but they were no better than the Canadians had been. Harry Wright, a baseball star from Boston, was heartily cheered as he aimed a few lusty blows but the New Yorkers were all out for 66 soon after lunch. Grace and Ottaway opened for MCC and proceeded to record a century partnership by stumps, the only blemish being a skyer by W.G. which fell to earth. He finished on 67 not out and a local journalist described him: 'A monarch in his might – of splendid physique, he at once won attention by the play of limb and easy exercise of muscle.' Of his team-mates, he was perhaps less impressed: 'John Bull's sons are generally fond of good cheer. They have a strange proclivity for taking their ease at an inn,' which shows, if nothing else, that cricketers on tour have not changed much over the last century and a quarter.

Two thousand spectators watched next day but saw little more of the Leviathan, who added only a single to his total. MCC were all out for 249 and shot the New Yorkers out for 44 in an embarrassing hour and twenty minutes. W.G. shared the bowling with Appleby, their respective figures being 11–26 and 9–18 (Appleby took 20 wickets in the match). At least the fielding was 'simply magnificent', thought Grace, 'as the fielding of all baseball players is.' How strange, then, that it took the English cricket establishment another 130 years or so before they thought of applying baseball throwing techniques to fielders, as happened with the England team in the mid-1990s.

The party decamped, perhaps reluctantly, to Philadelphia. Of New York, Fitzgerald observed: 'No town on earth presents better facilities either for acquiring money or spending it.' But the reception the tourists received in Philadelphia, historically the home of cricket in the United States, more than made up for any disappointment they might have felt at leaving New York so quickly. They were taken to the theatre, where the band struck up 'God Save The Queen' as they arrived to loud cheers from the rest of the audience. Posters abounded giving details of the three-day match to be played from 21–3 September against a Philadelphia XXII, who turned out to be the best side they faced in North America.

On the first day, a Saturday, the road to the German Town Cricket Club ground was packed with people on their way to the game. It 'might have been the road to the Epsom Downs on the morning of the Derby', wrote Fitzgerald. 'By 11.30 a.m. every bough had a boy on it, every hayrick a tenant.' A band played on the roof of the pavilion and lots of pretty ladies were to be seen. An elaborate programme had been printed, with Shakespearian quotations to illustrate every facet of the game. The ground looked a picture, with not a spare seat in the stand, as the Englishmen took the field.

The usual scenario unfolded, the hosts managing to get only 63 in all, although the last batsman, a young man called Welsh, enlivened things by giving Grace the charge with some success – 'giving him Yankee all round the shop' was Fitzgerald's amused description. W.G. was accorded a tremendous welcome from the seven thousand spectators estimated to be present but he found the going tough on a slow pitch against the best bowling he had faced on the tour plus agile fielding. He scratched 14 in an hour before one Charles Newhall clean bowled him. 'I have heard many a great shout go up in various parts of the globe at my dismissal,' he recalled much later, 'but I never remember anything quite equal to the wild roar that greeted my downfall on this occasion.'

MCC totalled only 105, the Philadelphians 74 in their second innings (W.G. 11–46), leaving MCC only 33 to win and a day to get them in. It did not seem too tall an order although the wicket was crumbling. The crowd came on the field at stumps and demanded that the English players appear on the balcony, a scene presaging the scenes after one-day internationals a century later, and in similar fashion to nowadays declined to disperse 'until they had been satisfied and given three cheers for Gloucestershire, for Grace and the British flag'.

That evening the players attended a massive dinner at the Union League Club, presided over by the commanding figure of General George G. Meade, a key figure in the American Civil War, who only nine years previously had led the Union army to victory over General Robert E. Lee's Confederate army at the battle of Gettysburg. His son was playing for Philadelphia: he bagged a pair but took six wickets. General Meade died only six weeks later.

When Grace looked at the pitch next morning he remarked that the 33 runs 'would take some getting' and he was right. The Americans were anything but cowed: in front of another big crowd they bowled like demons and Grace found the going even slower than in the first innings. When he departed for seven, made in an hour, the total was 18–4 and amid scenes of high excitement the score crawled up to 29–7. Appleby came to the wicket and not a run was scored for half an hour. A leg-bye broke the deadlock and then Appleby swung at the ball and managed to pierce the field for the winning boundary, to the Englishmen's huge relief. They raced for the Boston train, without stopping to say goodbye properly, which led to some criticism in the press next day, but still contrived to miss it.

They thus arrived in Boston on 26 September, later than

94

planned, and as their ship was to sail on the 28th from Quebec they had time only for a one-day match against another local XXII. Fitzgerald had business in Boston so W.G. took over the captaincy. The match should never have been played. Heavy rain had turned the ground into a sea of mud but the Englishmen felt obliged to do their best for their hosts. The whole field was given a liberal covering of sawdust but in many places the fielders were up to their ankles in slush.

The cricket must have been of a particularly low standard as four innings were managed in the day, both teams compiling 51 in their first innings. Grace was the only batsman who could handle the conditions, scoring 26 in a disciplined and patient manner. Despite the non-importance of the match, Fitzgerald, who turned up at the ground to find MCC 39–8, was scathing about the other batsmen's lack of application. Perhaps they had simply had enough after five weeks on tour. Set 44 to win, MCC were soon struggling as the light failed. Grace went for only 5 and with the score at 19–6 Fitzgerald decided to join in. He marched out to the wicket but any thoughts he might have had of showing his team how to conquer adversity soon evaporated when in near-total darkness a full toss which he never sighted hit him on the toe. At that, the umpires decided to call it a day. 'I am sure that we should have been beaten,' confessed Grace.

Harry Wright, the baseball player who had appeared against MCC in New York, also played in Boston, along with his brother George, also a distinguished baseball player. George presented each of the Englishmen with a baseball to take home as a memento, a gift which W.G. for one treasured for the rest of his life. Fitzgerald was under no illusions about Americans' preference for their own game. 'It will hold its own in America, and cricket can never expect to attain to its popularity.'

The party caught the train for Quebec, where they boarded the SS *Prussian* for the voyage home, arriving back in Liverpool on 8 October. It was a tour none of them would ever forget.

Fitzgerald was in no doubt as to who the star had been. 'Victory is of course largely due to the never-failing bat of W.G. Grace,' he wrote. Grace amassed 540 runs on the tour at an average of 49.1

(second best was Alfred Lubbock with 146) and took 66 wickets. Fitzgerald added: 'No Canadian is likely to become a second W.G. if he lives to be a hundred and plays till past four score.' The MCC secretary's delightful memoir of the tour *Wickets in the West, or The Twelve in America* came out the following year. The cover was embossed with a gold-coloured portrait of the Untouchable, and was signed, 'Yours Truly, W.G. Grace'.

6 · HONEYMOON IN AUSTRALIA

1873–1874

IN 1873 W.G., though still only twenty-five years old, completed his tenth year in first-class cricket. He returned from North America and after an understandably slow start re-emerged to dominate bowlers in much the same way as the previous seasons. His superiority was continually emphasised by a comparison of his performances with those playing alongside him. When he scored 145 for Gentlemen of the South v Players of the North at Prince's, it was out of a total of 237 and the next highest scorer was E.M. with 26. When he made 134 v Players of the South at the Oval, it was 12 more than the entire opposition combined. His – indeed, anybody's – highest score of the season was 192 not out for South v North, again on his happy hunting ground of The Oval, made out of a total of 311 against a strong attack, including Jemmy Shaw and Tom Emmett.

The match at Prince's, the charming little ground in Hans Place, long since submerged beneath the mansion blocks of Knightsbridge, was the result of press agitation to match the amateurs of the south against the professionals of the north. The weather on the first morning was very strange: oppressive heat, accompanied by a thick fog which made it hard for the occupants of the press box to discern what was happening in the middle. After the Players of the North had made 182, W.G. went in late on the first day and was 32 not out by stumps. The knowledge that he was at the crease drew a thousand spectators on Friday morning, despite the weather, and they were treated to a vintage Grace innings after a cautious start. The *Daily Telegraph* rhapsodised: 'There has been a good deal of talk lately about Mr Grace being out of form this season . . . but yesterday he came out in his true colours, showing all the wonderful command over the ball and great hitting power. After such a display we can confidently expect Mr Grace will give us many more innings as long and as brilliant as this latest performance.'

This forecast was amply borne out by events, particularly in the Gentlemen v Players fixtures. The first was at Lord's, where the pitch had at last been relaid in response to mounting criticism. It was never to be as bad again and W.G. celebrated by hitting 163 (including one drive for seven), surviving a catch at point off a Jemmy Shaw no-ball when 63, at which one watcher remarked, 'There's no getting the long'un out.' In the second match, at The Oval, he made 158 out of 320 in 195 minutes after playing Emmett's second ball hard on to his leg stump without dislodging the bails. He rubbed salt into the bowler's wound by hitting him for 25 runs off his next three overs. The *Telegraph* recorded: 'To say Mr W.G. Grace is far and away the best batsman that ever scored a run is to tell an old tale . . This week Mr Grace's star has been fast rising to the zenith.' The innings had been 'an extraordinary succession of grand hitting displays of which even he may well be proud'. He also took 7–65 in the match off thirty-four overs. The *Sporting Gazette* remarked, somewhat sourly: 'Mr W.G. Grace helped to spoil both matches . . . However, it would be idle to grumble. The majority of those who comprised the thousands who thronged both arenas have had their wish – they have seen Mr W.G. Grace bat, and that, to vast numbers of vague admirers of cricket is everything . . .'

There was a third Gentlemen v Players game, at Prince's, in which Grace scored 70 to make a total of 391 for twice out against the best professional bowling in England. Unlike the public, they must have been sick of the sight of him. To rub salt into the wound, the amateurs beat the professionals by an innings in two of the three matches, and by 48 runs in the other. One Surrey fielder certainly had enough of watching W.G. paste his colleagues all round the ground for Gloucestershire. Grace scored 83 at The Oval and a hard-hit 160 in the return at Clifton College. When W.G. reached his 150, the Surrey fielder remarked: 'We shall get him out soon, for his average against us cannot be more than 180.'

Another match against Surrey, for MCC, gave the brothers Grace the rare opportunity to play against each other, as Fred had been elected a member of the Surrey club. W.G. and G.F. had a marvellous relationship, much commented on by their playing colleagues, but they still relished the chance to better the other on the field. Fred got the better of the batting honours, contributing a fine 60 out of Surrey's second-innings total of 153, though he was finally stumped off his brother's bowling, 'which he had been knocking about pretty freely' commented W.G. With a target of only 55 to win, W.G. didn't bother to open but put himself at number 6. He soon found himself out at the middle, however, and so badly did MCC bat that he was still there with the totals tied and only one MCC wicket left. Fred Grace, who bowled at a brisk pace, had taken 5–24. In a final twist, W.G.'s last-wicket partner was dropped in the deep by, of all people, Fred, who was reckoned to be among the finest fielders in England, and the batsmen scampered the winning run.

W.G. had much the better of their next confrontation, when the XI who had toured Canada played an MCC XV at Lord's in late July. W.G. scored 152 and was particularly severe on Fred. 'The great batsman certainly had some luck in his long innings,' said the *Telegraph*, 'but his wonderfully free hitting and great command over the ball were as marvellous as ever.' It was so hot that poor Ottaway had to retire with sunstroke.

The heatwave came to W.G.'s rescue a couple of days later at The Oval playing for the South v North. On 42, he attempted to hit the ball to leg and managed only to sky it straight up in the air. But the fielder, Pinder, was blinded by the sun and made a hash of an easy chance. Grace took full advantage and went on to make a ruthless

192 not out. The *Sporting Gazette* reflected, ironically, that Grace has 'spoiled another good match', adding:

What is to be done with him? He is really ruining the cricket in first-class matches. He demoralises the fielders, and breaks the heart of the bowlers until his own display of batting is really the only feature of the match. And yet what can we do with him? No one else can draw gate money as he does, and unless he is doomed to play single wicket matches just to show his own batting, or unless any eleven which plays him be considered equal to a fifteen, we do not see how the matter is to be remedied.

It was W.G.'s finest all-round season to date, for he was credited with 2,139 first-class runs at an average of 71.30, and more than 100 first-class wickets for the first time (to be exact, 101 at 12.94), thus achieving his first 'double' of 1,000 runs and 100 wickets in a season. Modern research has downgraded games like the match against the MCC XV and revised W.G.'s tally but he still towered over everyone else. But nothing gave him greater satisfaction than Gloucestershire's progress in 1873. Although composed entirely of amateurs and in only their fourth season, they were joint winners of the (unofficial) county championship, with an unbeaten record (four victories, two draws). They were deemed to have shared the laurels with Nottinghamshire, who registered five wins and one defeat.

W.G. was, as usual, Gloucestershire's inspiration, averaging 62 with the bat and capturing 21 wickets. His sole century for his county came against Surrey at Clifton – a superlative unbeaten 160 in the second innings of a match which was drifting towards a draw. He had scored a brisk 48 in the first innings, including a magnificent pull over square leg which went out of the ground and exploded against the side of an adjacent house with such force that it almost rebounded into play. His century included several such shots out of the ground as he subjected the bowlers, with a wet ball on a greasy pitch, to a typical assault. 'How is to be expected for any ordinary – or average – county to make headway against scoring like that?' enquired the *Sporting Gazette*.

Grace's very presence – and of course that of G.F., reckoned to be the second-best all-rounder in England, and E.M. – counted for as much as his exploits with bat and ball. As Sydney Pardon, editor of *Wisden* from 1891 to 1925, put it: 'The fact of being on the same side with W.G. and his brothers made the other men play twenty per cent above their ordinary form.'

Just how much of an amateur was W.G.? The reality was that he made a better living from cricket than any professional. Until he qualified as a doctor in 1879, his main source of income was the United South XI, which took the game out to the provinces, and particularly to towns which rarely saw good-class cricket. He was paid a flat fee for each fixture, from which he had to pay the rest of the team, selected by him. A heavy penalty was payable if he himself did not play. The professionals he engaged for these games usually received a match fee of £5. Any surplus went into Grace's pocket. Throughout his long career Grace received a considerable annual income from cricket, topped up by generous public collections on his behalf, which led to periodic outbreaks of ill-feeling from professional players. They had a point – but the vast crowds who turned out whenever his presence was advertised were a continual reminder of the game's greatest attraction.

W.G.'s unprecedented popularity may have pulled in the crowds, but brought its own problems for that very reason. Nottinghamshire were keen to play Gloucestershire again at Trent Bridge but would not confirm the date unless W.G. was guaranteed to take part. On the date Notts proposed, he had agreed to play in a benefit match for Joseph Rowbotham, the Yorkshire captain, and having given his word that he would attend, declined to let the beneficiary down. Although E.M., who had become the Gloucestershire secretary, had suggested another date, the Gloucestershire committee would not hear of it, which led first to ructions within the committee, and then to a temporary break in relations with Nottinghamshire. The fixture was not resumed until 1875.

When W.G. took Gloucestershire to Sheffield to play Yorkshire for Rowbotham's benefit, twelve thousand spectators flooded into the ground and gave him a welcome he never forgot. He rewarded them with an innings of 79. What county treasurer in the 1990s would not happily settle for an attendance like that?

A writer in *Fun* magazine derived some heavy-handed humour from Grace's dominance. He suggested that a 'Society for the

Improvement of Things in General and the Diffusion of Perfect Equality' would submit the following:

That W.G. Grace shall owe a couple of hundred or so before batting –
  these to be reckoned against his side should he not wipe them off.
That his shoe spikes shall be turned inwards.
That he shall be declared out whenever the umpire likes.
That he shall always be the eleventh player.
That he shall not be allowed to play at all.

The Times was of similar opinion:

So deep is the apprehension entertained by every cricketer who is liable to find himself, in one or another match, ranged on the side to which Mr Grace does not belong, that grave propositions have been made in the higher councils of the craft . . . entreating that he will consent to play for the future either blindfolded or with his right arm behind his back.

Now it was Australia's turn to see this extraordinary man. In 1872 W.G. had received a cable from members of the other MCC – the Melbourne Cricket Club, the premier organiser of the game in Australia, where its popularity was growing fast, helped by the steady stream of migrants from the old country. The cable invited W.G. to put together a side to tour Australia, where his pre-eminence would undoubtedly pull in spectators by the thousand. There had been two previous English tours down under, but the last had been in 1863/64 (when the party had included E.M. Grace). In the interim, several unsuccessful attempts had been made by Melbourne clubs to induce W.G. to take teams out.

W.G. stated his terms: a personal fee of £1,500, plus expenses. The Australians were staggered by the size of his demand, which was far in excess of anything any other cricketer had demanded before, or indeed was to demand in the future. It would be in the region of, say, £100,000 in today's money, an incredible amount by any standard. But W.G. had a pretty shrewd idea of his own worth – and he knew there was no one else in the cricket world with anything like his pulling power. The Melbourne men did not proceed with the deal – for the time being.

Back they came in 1873, with a similar proposition. This time the Melbourne Cricket Club had joined forces with the East Melbourne and South Melbourne clubs. Although the clubs would not be financial guarantors of this latest venture, plenty of their wealthier members could see that an England tour party headed by W.G. Grace could be almost as lucrative a goldmine as the real things fuelling the country's development. The committee formed for the purpose by the three clubs agreed to W.G.'s fee of £1,500 and expenses, and £170 each for the other professionals he would recruit. Not surprisingly, this time he agreed.

As the invitation was to him personally and not to the MCC at Lord's, he was at liberty to pick both professionals and amateurs, and went after the best of both. He wanted both Alfred Shaw and Tom Emmett but neither fancied the prospect. From the amateur ranks William Yardley and Arthur Hornby agreed, only to withdraw at the eleventh hour, but Fred Grace was a natural choice. The eventual tour party, like that to North America the previous year, consisted of only twelve men, who were more or less guaranteed a game every time. The party was: W.G. Grace, G.F. Grace, their talented cousin W.R. Gilbert, the utterly reliable professional batsman Harry Jupp, Arthur Bush, the Gloucestershire wicket-keeper generally regarded as inferior to the professionals Pooley and Pinder, F.H. Boult, the Yorkshire batsman Andrew Greenwood, Richard Humphrey, James Lillywhite, Nottinghamshire's William Oscroft and Martin McIntyre, the pace bowler, and the Surrey slow round-arm bowler James Southerton.

As the game was still in its relative infancy in Australia, it was generally felt that the English were far superior. Accordingly, the Australians would put out twenty-two players against the touring XI or XII. When he had finally gathered his dozen, Grace wrote to his hosts: 'I am proud to say that I have succeeded in getting together a very strong team, and if we lose a single match, all I can say is that your teams of 22 must be a good deal stronger than we play in England.' Many Australians, however, were not convinced that they were seeing the cream of English cricket, apart from the Grace brothers. There were five amateurs and seven professionals in the party, although one of the amateurs was to earn nearly ten times as much from the tour as any professional. The division between amateurs and professionals was the principal reason for a frequently unhappy expedition.

Before the party left for the Antipodes, W.G. had personal business to address. On 9 October he was married to Agnes Nicholls Day, the daughter of his first cousin, William Day, a lithographer. Agnes was a quiet, attractive, dark-haired girl whom W.G. had met the previous year, presumably at a family function. The wedding took place in London, at St Matthias in West Brompton, as the bride's family lived at Clapham Common. W.G.'s brother-in-law, the Rev. John Dann, officiated, and the best man was Arthur Bush, W.G.'s burly county colleague who was shortly off to Australia with him. So indeed was the new Mrs Grace. She gallantly agreed to accompany her husband on tour, an unusual honeymoon in any age. It showed that W.G. knew how to pick a wife as well as a cricket team. Agnes developed an interest in cricket while never equalling her mother-in-law's passionate devotion to the sport. She was a model Victorian wife and the marriage was an exceptionally happy one.

A fortnight after the wedding the party left Southampton on board the P & O steamer *Mirzapore*. They nearly left Jupp behind, nursing a hangover. Charles Alcock, secretary of both Surrey and the Football Association, who had stayed aboard to say goodbye to his friends (chief of whom was W.G.), returned to shore in a small boat, found Jupp and put him in the tugboat taking mail out to the steamer. A sea passage to Australia in 1873 was no luxury cruise. For a poor sailor like W.G. the early stages, like the Bay of Biscay, were an ordeal and the *Mirzapore* had the added misfortune to encounter a bad storm in the Mediterranean. For the first and only time in his life, W.G. kept a diary, but he was no Pepys, alas. Its entries were terse in the extreme: 'Tremendous sea caught ship, and broke two or three hundred plates and saucers,' he recorded.

They were grateful for a few hours ashore at Malta, where they arrived on 1 November, and dined at the United Service Club where W.G. was prevailed upon to make a speech. Back on board, the cricketers played leapfrog and boxed: 'Nearly killed one of the team!' the diarist wrote. They were not impressed by Alexandria, where Grace declined the offer of a match by the British consul, Mr Stanley; he was apparently worried that some of his men might not make it back on board in time, although Stanley offered to lay on a special train to rejoin the boat at Suez. The cricketers were eager to see the Suez Canal, which had been open for only four years but in the event found it a let-down. The ship could move only during the day because searchlights were not used at that time, and the *Mirzapore* also ran into heavy fog. The captain insisted on proceeding regardless and managed only to run aground in the mud, which delayed the voyage still further.

Disembarking briefly at Point de Galle, Ceylon (now Sri Lanka), they transferred with some reluctance to a smaller and less well-appointed steamer, the *Nubia*, but crossed safely to Australia and landed at King George's Sound, Western Australia, on 8 December. The voyage had taken them forty-six days. According to reports reaching Australia, the Englishmen had started to get homesick halfway through their long journey but cheered up on finally reaching their destination.

The *Nubia* was met by a boat bearing a delegation who had made the journey from Melbourne to welcome the tourists. W.G. leapt nimbly over the side of the steamer on to the deck of the Australian boat, followed by the rest of the party. The tourists then went ashore for a few hours to stretch their legs and have some much-needed practice. To his great delight, McIntyre bowled Grace for the first time in his life. Local Aborigines gave them an exhibition of throwing the boomerang and W.G. could not resist trying his hand. After a few abortive efforts, he got the hang of it only too well and nearly took Gilbert's head off.

Then it was back aboard the *Nubia* for the final passage to Melbourne, where they arrived on 13 December, a Saturday morning. The steamer made such good progress that it arrived early and the dignitaries of Melbourne had to be rounded up in haste to get down to the railway pier from where they took a small boat to go out and greet the English party. Coming alongside the *Nubia* the Australians, who included the mayor of Melbourne, gave three cheers for the Englishmen, who, lined up on deck, returned the compliment.

The tourists disembarked at the town pier, to the disappointment of a large crowd who had gathered at the railway pier, and were taken by coach and four to the Port Philip Club, where another crowd had assembled to greet them. But even in the brave new world of Australia the divisions between amateurs and gentlemen persisted. The gentlemen were quartered at the Port Philip Club while the players were taken on to a hotel called the Old White Hart.

The Englishmen had their first taste of the vigorous Australian approach to sport that very afternoon. Mr and Mrs Grace in one carriage, the rest of the party in another, they had a tour of the city's three main grounds: the Melbourne Cricket Ground and the East and South Melbourne grounds. At the latter a cup final was being played in front of seven thousand spectators and the tourists stayed on to watch. With the match boiling up to a tight finish, one of the umpires gave a home batsman out, a decision to which the crowd took such exception that they invaded the pitch and the match had to be abandoned without a result. 'There are larrikins and larrikins, but the larrikins of South Melbourne are, without exception, the worst in Victoria,' complained the *Australasian* newspaper. 'The manner in which they hooted and yelled, and then broke over the ground was disgraceful.' W.G. was not impressed either.

After a day's rest on Sunday, the Englishmen practised at the Melbourne and East Melbourne grounds over the next ten days in front of large crowds, eager to get a glimpse of the world's most famous cricketer, the sessions being interrupted for the occasional champagne reception. The Englishmen graciously allowed some of the players who would be playing for Victoria in the first match, scheduled to start at the MCG on Boxing Day, to practise against them.

A great deal was expected of the visitors. 'Unless the Englishmen hit the ball out of the ground every time they won't satisfy a certain class of critics,' wrote one observer. 'By the cognoscenti, however, it has been found out that W.G. is the wonder he is described . . .

The bowling of the Graces I like greatly, it shows a constant variety of pitch, pace and flight, which, added to plenty of break and never-failing accuracy, must make it dangerous stuff.'

But not everybody was so impressed. There was some disappointment at the form shown by most of the England squad and the suspicion grew that they might not, after all, give the Australians the beatings that had been widely forecast until then. There was immense anticipation, none the less, at the prospect of seeing the Englishmen in action and in judging what progress Australian cricket had made in the decade since the last tour.

W.G. was astonished at the Australians' casual attitude towards preparing a pitch for the opening game. Seeing no sign of any work being done as the game approached, Grace enquired what was happening. The groundsman replied that he would pick a pitch on the morning of the game, roll it and all would be well. That was not good enough for Grace, who had no one like Robert Fitzgerald on the Canadian tour to help him out this time. He had to be captain and manager rolled into one. He immediately buttonholed the club authorities and persuaded them to start preparing and rolling a pitch. He believed his example caused a deep impression on the Australians who thenceforth took the whole business of pitch preparation much more seriously. It seems not to have occurred to them before that it mattered.

Fifteen thousand spectators were present at the MCG on Boxing Day to witness England's debut, Victoria feeling confident enough to put out an Eighteen rather than a Twenty-two. Among them were two opening bowlers, Francis Allan and Harry Boyle, who were to develop into two of Australia's finest bowlers of the century and regular destroyers of England's batting in some of the most historic matches played between the two countries. Also in the Victorian line-up was Bransby Cooper, the Old Rugbeian who had put on a record first-wicket stand of 283 with W.G. for Gentlemen of the South against Players of the South, and had since emigrated.

W.G. got down to his usual batting practice in the nets before the game. A young man stepped out of the crowd to join in the bowling, sent down a couple of looseners and then clean bowled the great man with a rocket which he never even saw. 'Who bowled that?' asked Grace indignantly but the bowler had slipped away. He was a rangy young man who had just celebrated his eighteenth birthday and he was to play against the tourists in Sydney in January. Grace would find out all about him in the years ahead. His name was Frederick Robert Spofforth, and he would shortly join Boyle and Allan in a devastating pace attack.

Australian confidence in their growing skills was amply justified by that game. There was some doubt whether Victoria's captain, G.P. Robertson, would be able to play because his father was seriously ill, but he turned up just before play was due to begin, won the toss and decided to bat. W.G. may have regretted the fuss he had made about the pitch because the Australians took full advantage of its good condition. The opening bowlers made little impression but W.G. took a wicket almost as soon as he brought himself on to bowl with the score on 77–2. Lunch was a splendid affair for a hundred people in a marquee with Grace sitting between the Governor and the Melbourne CC president and toasts being drunk to the Queen, the Governor and the teams. Perhaps it was no surprise after that that the Englishmen made heavy weather of bowling and fielding. The Victorians batted through the day to stand at 245–10 at close, Cooper having batted carefully and correctly for 84, seven of the wickets falling to the brothers Grace. There was a rumour that W.G. had sent telegrams back to his friends in London, from the MCG's new electric telegraph room, advising them to lay off bets they had placed on England to win the match.

The second day was 'a lovely morning, with a cool southerly breeze – the most perfect day for cricket that could be imagined'. Again, fifteen thousand people crammed into the ground, leaving not a spare inch. England managed to get Victoria out for 266, W.G. ending with 10–58, F.G. with 4–35. As W.G. and Jupp marched out to begin England's reply, the Victoria players gathered in the centre of the pitch to applaud them on. Against the bowling of the left-arm medium-pace Allan and Sam Cosstick, who was also to be a pain in their sides all tour, the Englishmen accumulated runs quietly until W.G. cut the ball to point and made off towards the pavilion, as if caught. The crowd cheered but the cheers turned to laughter when he returned to the wicket; he had been kidding them. It was one of his favourite party tricks, which never failed to bring the house down. However, when Boyle came on the bowler had the last laugh, knocking out Grace's leg stump and dismissing him for 33. It was England's top score; they were all out for 110 (Allan 6–33) and ignominiously asked to follow on.

The next day was Sunday, a rest day, which ended with a massive thunderstorm and heavy rain drenching the pitch. Despite the last day being Monday, and a working day, five thousand people turned out in the hope of seeing Victoria complete a historic victory. There was a dispute between the captains before the start. Grace considered the pitch to be dangerously bumpy and asked for it to be rolled. Displaying the determination not to give an inch to the old enemy which was to be a characteristic of Australian captains for the next hundred years and more, Robertson refused. The only way Grace could retaliate was to refuse Robertson's request for a substitute fielder as he was a man short.

Grace batted at five, entering with the score on 32–3 and proceeded to play both pitch and bowling with ease, but when two wickets went down, he again asked for the pitch to be rolled, and again Robertson declined. With Fred, he put on 50 for the sixth wicket, pausing only for a refreshing jug of champagne and soda water which was brought out to the middle. As Fred's and other wickets fell, W.G. stepped up the pace, snatching quick singles wherever he could to keep the strike and once smashing Boyle over the crowd's head and into the white fence behind them. 'Have another, old man!' one spectator was heard to shout. But England were all out for 135, losing by an innings and 21 runs.

'The crowd rushed the ground, and Mr W.G. Grace, the hero of the hour, walked up a lane of shouting beings, who cheered him to the echo. He carried his bat for 51 runs, made with an ease and power never seen equalled amongst us.' More champagne was drunk in the pavilion to celebrate Victoria's win and it was almost dark before the last excited spectator was ushered from the ground.

Opinions about the general health of English cricket were

swiftly revised. The general expectation had been that W.G. would slaughter everything put before him but even he had struggled in the first innings and had been unable to sustain the second all on his own. 'The great match is lost and won and what have we learnt?' wrote one observer. 'That colonial cricket is somewhat better than we deemed it, or English cricket somewhat worse. Which? A little of both . . . In batting and fielding we have advanced greatly, in bowling not so much. As to our opponents, I am greatly disappointed with their bowling . . . I fancy I know the secret of the long scores in England. I think Mr W.G. Grace a more dangerous trundler than any of them.'

The same writer provided a thoughtful description of W.G. as a batsman:

He was not all my fancy painted him, judging from the fulsome praises and accounts I had read of his wonderful skill. I could not recognise that 'remarkable facility for placing the ball' I had read so much about. Nor was cricket under his able hands reduced to billiards, as I had also read. Of course it was easy to see that his defence and hitting powers were far and away ahead of any we have ever seen before, but what I was most struck with was his truly splendid judgment, and herein, I imagine, lies the secret of his long scores. As a judge of a run, and for speed between wickets, he is unequalled in the world. He makes safe runs where we would not dream of even stealing them, and never seems bustled or in a hurry – always at the crease in time, with the wicketkeeper wondering how the deuce he got there. His innings on the Monday was worth all the rest of the match put together. Goldsmith ought to have been presented with a purse of sovereigns for missing him at long leg, and thereby giving us the treat he did. The ease and power with which the leviathan played the bowling – shooters and bumpers met equally coolly, no hitting the ball over the moon, but making runs simply and quietly, without apparent effort, showing, when opportunity offered, brilliant cutting and grand driving, defence impregnable – all this was as near perfection as it is possible for such to be.

However the Australian press was highly critical of the rest of his team. W.G. was furious and blamed the forty-day sea voyage for his side's lacklustre performance, omitting to mention the two-week acclimatisation period before the match, which ought to have been enough for anybody.

Now came a gruelling tour-within-a-tour upcountry, to a series of small isolated communities, linked by rough tracks. Travelling was frequently a hellish undertaking, which took its toll on the English cricketers. Agnes stayed behind in Melbourne with friends. She was already pregnant and may have been feeling unwell.

First stop, for a match which started on New Year's Day 1874, was Ballarat, reached after a long and tiring train journey. Victoria's great win had had the effect of increasing public interest in the game against a local XXII, which was just as well as there was severe competition from the biggest day in the Ballarat year: the Caledonian gathering, the Scottish exiles being more interested in celebrating the New Year than the arrival of an English cricket team, however distinguished.

Still, the cricket drew a crowd estimated at between six and seven thousand. The visitors were pleasantly surprised by the quality of the well-grassed ground and pitch at Ballarat's Eastern Oval. Before play got under way, the boundary scores were agreed: hits under the chain fence would be three, over it four, inside the outer fence counted five, and six would be awarded for hitting the ball right out of the ground.

The match got under way at noon, the locals being reinforced by Allan and Cosstick, two of the bowlers who had done so much damage in Melbourne. Winning the toss, Grace chose to bat and played with consummate ease, scoring 61 out of 94–1 by lunch, Jupp having gone for 23. When the slow bowlers came on after the interval, Grace flogged them all round the ground and sometimes right out of it. Cosstick was finally brought back to have the champion caught at mid-off for 126, made in four hours. He retired to a great ovation; it was the highest score made until then by an Englishman in Australia. When stumps were drawn, Fred Grace was still at the wicket and going well.

Next day, nearly as many spectators came to watch even though the main attraction had departed. The temperature reached 100 ° F in the shade and the wooden seats were too hot to sit on. 'It was about the hottest day in which I ever played cricket,' recalled W.G. much later. Fred made it even warmer for the fielders with another Grace century, scoring 112, and England's final total of 470 was the highest one-innings score made in Australia, which a local correspondent attributed partly to the smallness of the ground – 'the batsmen could all hit over the heads of the most distant fielders with ease' – and partly to the poor fielding. The locals did rather better with the bat, making a creditable 276 in their only innings and the match petered out in a draw. The *Australasian*'s correspondent concluded that while the English were strong in batting and fielding, the bowling was 'inferior', adding: 'W.G. Grace bowls chiefly for the field and generally succeeds in getting catches made, but at the expense of a good many runs'. This echoed the English opinion of him.

Back in Melbourne, someone at least was doing well out of the Grace connection. A young man claiming to be W.R. Gilbert, the Graces' cousin, was enjoying board and lodgings with a gullible clergyman, who was a cricket fan. The false Gilbert had a complicated story: he claimed he had bet W.G. £50 that he could stay on in Melbourne undetected while a substitute took his place in Ballarat. He greatly impressed the clergyman and his friends with what purported to be inside stories from the English dressing-room and was only exposed when the cleric proudly told a friend, who happened to be one of the tour promoters, about his distinguished guest. 'Why, my dear sir, I saw Gilbert and the rest of the team off to Ballarat by the seven o'clock train last evening,' said the promoter with a guffaw. How strange that the real Gilbert should be disgraced as a common criminal a dozen years later – and that he should end up an exile in the colonies.

After a depressing Sunday in Ballarat, ravaged by a dust storm, the party travelled through the bush to the small gold-mining community of Stawell, some 75 miles away, in an old coach over appalling tracks. Indeed, when they saw the vehicle in which they were expected to travel, several of the players at first declined to board it and eventually agreed to do so only with the greatest reluctance. Covered with white dust, a couple of them relieved the unpleasantness of the journey with potshots at parrots. As they approached Stawell, two brass bands struck up a welcome, terrifying the horses pulling one trap and causing them to bolt and destroy the carriage, though none of the party was hurt.

W.G. and his cousin spent an enjoyable day shooting in the bush and then it was back to cricket – after a fashion – against a local XXII, again boosted by some strong guests, including Cosstick and Cooper, the hero of Melbourne.

The pitch at the Botanical Reserve had been a ploughed field only three months previously and sown with grass a few days before. It was 'probably the worst the Englishmen will see in the colony', was one local reporter's verdict. 'A square piece of turf in the centre of the reserve had been in course of preparation for the last two months, but water being very scarce, it did not make a very desirable wicket. It was as hard as a board, and the bare soil was visible between the knots.' But as four thousand people, half the town's population, came along to watch, there was nothing for it but to play. 'The bumpiness and uncertainty of the wicket was apparent immediately the play began, and the Englishmen had evidently made up their minds for merry, if short, lives.'

Grace was emphatic: 'The cricket was shockingly poor and the match a ludicrous farce . . . one slow ball actually stuck in the dust and never reached the batsman.' His and Jupp's reaction was to hit out at everything. Grace managed one decent boundary, was dropped three times, including one enormous skyer, during which he ran two, and perished for 16, easily the highest score. England were all out in just over an hour for 43. The Stawell XXII amassed 71 and by the close England were 57–5 in their second innings. Thirty-six wickets fell in the day. There was even a swarm of flies to complete the Englishmen's misery. They struggled to 91 on the second day, setting Stawell 64 to win, which they managed for the loss of ten wickets, thus winning by ten wickets.

The pitch was not the only cause of England's defeat. The local hospitality played an equally deadly part, at least as far as the professionals were concerned. So freely did the liquor flow in their direction that it was little surprise, to the locals at least, that they performed so badly. The *Australasian* was in no doubt:

The two true causes of the defeat of the All England Eleven at Stawell were bad ground and good liquor – two experiences which the colonial cricketer meets with far more often than is good for him . . . The local papers spoke rather strongly and justly of the conduct of the 'pros' in accepting, while the match was going on, the indiscriminate hospitality that was offered them . . . They must remember that they are out here, and are paid to show us the best cricket they can; and it is their duty to resist the temptations which are certain to be held out to them everywhere they go, especially in such hard-drinking localities . . .

The division between the gentlemen and players was further accentuated when, to eke out proceedings for a third day, the six professionals played a single-wicket match against twelve of the locals, while the amateurs took the day off (W.G. went shooting). Understandably, the pros took it badly and made a nonsense of the extra day; they carried on drinking and managed a pathetic two runs between them, consisting of one hit by McIntyre – the archetypal beer match. The party retreated from Stawell in disgrace with a record of played three, drawn one, lost two. W.G. was forced to deliver a stern lecture to the professionals as to their future conduct, though whether they took any notice of him is another matter. This was not the all-conquering procession that had been forecast, and only the captain was exempt from a chorus of criticism from local observers.

'If we are to take this eleven as a sample . . . of the best English cricket then I say English cricket has certainly not improved since Parr's visit [in 1863/64]' declared a Melbourne cricket writer.

Grace himself is an extraordinary run-getter, a perfect wonder, and worth going miles to see every day in the week – and in eleven-a-side matches, to use a colonial phrase, 'a caution' to bowlers – but he is alone . . . He is a freak of nature, a phenomenon.

I fancy Mr Grace has by this time found out his mistake in not bringing out another first-class bowler, and no doubt he wished during that first match that he had had Shaw and Emmett or Freeman with him.

Grace himself is the only one the colonials have to fear; he must hit catches at times – his style of hitting cannot prevent him so doing.

Looking ahead to England's return engagement with a Victoria

XVIII, he wrote that if England were to win, 'Mr W.G. Grace must do it alone.'

Australians were as sensitive to slights as they are today. W.G. trod on a few toes by declaring to a visitor from Sydney that his team would easily defeat a New South Wales XVIII when they reached that city.

If the journey to Stawell had been bad, the next stage to Warrnambool, a pretty seaside village, was even worse. Heavy rain made the track almost impassable in places. Half of the party had to get out of the coach at Hexham because they were too heavy a load. 'Of all my travelling experiences, that coach ride . . . was the most unpleasant,' Grace recorded. 'The first thirty-one miles took five hours and a quarter.' The 91-mile journey took nineteen hours and the party finally arrived drenched and exhausted. W.G. was so fed up that he declined to attend a banquet laid on by the cricket club. When he finally got to bed and fell asleep, he was not best pleased to be awoken by a local reporter anxious to interview the distinguished visitor, an early example of the enterprise and persistence of Australian journalists, though this one departed without much of a story from his disgruntled interviewee.

The chief topic of interest among local aficionados was whether a popular sporting figure had died or not: this was an Aboriginal cricketer named Mullagh, who lived on a government station in the Wimmera district and of whom nothing had been heard for some time, giving rise to fears that he had expired. The authorities did not approve of Aboriginals playing cricket, 'believing that its pursuit leads them into temptation as regards drink', according to the local paper, which seems a fair enough assessment of the dangers of associating with cricketers for too long.

Although after their journey the Englishmen felt considerably below par they managed to put on a decent performance against the Warrnambool XXII on a better pitch and before another big crowd, estimated at around three thousand people, for whom such a visit would have been a welcome diversion. Grace was bowled by 'an easy full-pitched ball' for 18. 'The fall of the champion's wicket was signalised [sic] by the wildest shouts and congratulations on the part of the provincials, who screamed, leaped, rolled and turned somersaults, and hugged each other in their excess of joy,' wrote one reporter.

England won by nine wickets inside a day and a half, avoiding liquor and concentrating on the job in hand. They filled out the remainder of the scheduled three-day match with single-wicket games. On the third day the professionals again had to play while the amateurs went fishing and shooting. W.G. rode out with a group of stockmen in search of kangaroos, revelling in the day's sport. Then it was back to Melbourne, by boat, through rough seas on a small coastal steamer stinking of oil. 'Till then I had never spent so wretched a night on board ship,' lamented Grace, the bad sailor.

Pausing in Melbourne to pick up Agnes, W.G. and company sailed on to Sydney, through more stormy seas, arriving to a dockside packed with some five thousand cheering people. After a public breakfast at a hotel, there was a series of toasts, which, according to W.G., were 'carried to an extreme in Australia'. He was only too aware of the effect of too much socialising on his players.

Whether they had had a drink or not, the Englishmen's display against a New South Wales XVIII was little better than it had been in the first four games. Again there was a huge and expectant crowd, estimated at ten to twelve thousand on the first day and nine thousand on the second. Again victory went to the Australians, this time by eight wickets. There was a Grace family connection on the NSW side too in the person of the son of Uncle Pocock, who had so patiently coached the Grace boys on the lawn at Downend. But though young Pocock contributed to NSW's win, there was a more significant player in his side: Frederick Spofforth, who was to develop into the greatest Australian fast bowler of the century. Born at Balmain, then just outside Sydney, now a suburb of the city, he stood 6ft 3in tall and was raw but full of promise, taking 2–16 in England's second innings.

W.G. was out cheaply in both England's innings, each time in identical fashion, caught at slip by Lawrence off Coates, 'a coincidence which does not often happen' he remarked later. The crowd went mad at the sight of the great Englishman departing.

He had some sort of revenge with the ball, however, taking 18–82 in the match, including 7–13 in the second innings. The match barely lasted into the third day, so a single-wicket game was put on for the benefit of those spectators who had turned up. The NSW men scored 29, W.G. alone made 28 and with two byes the tourists won easily enough.

Next day the party was entertained to a picnic and boat trip around Sydney Harbour, a delightful day which stayed fresh in W.G.'s memory for decades. On the cricket front, the schedule was hastily changed when heavy rain submerged the pitch at Maitland, where the next match was due to be played. To the tourists' relief, it was called off, thus obviating another voyage through rough seas. Grace was of the opinion that the effects of so many sea journeys had contributed greatly to his team's poor performances. Instead, a game was arranged at Bathurst, 140 miles inland, which meant a spectacular and at times hairy train journey through the Blue Mountains to the terminus, five miles from their destination. A brass band and a large number of locals accompanied the party into town.

Fortunately for the visitors, the twenty-two local cricketers assembled to play on an indifferent and inadequately rolled pitch were not very good and the Englishmen dealt with them efficiently, winning by eight wickets (W.G. 27 and 16, G.F. 38 and 9 not out). A Bathurst resident wagered Mrs Grace a pair of gloves that her husband would not hit the ball out of the ground and won his bet, although W.G. did manage one hit over the scorebox. After a banquet and dance which went on into the small hours, and a morning's quail shooting for W.G., the party returned to Sydney for the most important match of the tour against a combined Victoria and NSW side, the Australians being so confident of their prospects that they fielded only fifteen instead of eighteen or twenty-two.

The game had split the Melbourne cricket community in two: the Melbourne Cricket Club committee thought that the six players invited to appear for the combination XV would do better to stay and play in some important inter-Melbourne matches, and at first forbade them from going on pain of suspension should they defy the order. Their stance was widely ridiculed and the committee forced to back down. The six proceeded to Sydney. One of them was the opening bowler Cosstick, who had played so well against the Englishmen in the first tour match. He soon proved troublesome again on the opening morning of the Sydney game, removing W.G.'s off stump when he had scored only 9, to the delight of the five thousand spectators present at the Albert ground.

Grace must have been disappointed not to have done better on a pitch described as 'hard as a rock and smooth as a billiard table'. With the temperature at 100° F in the shade, England scored 170, thanks to a spirited unbeaten 55 by McIntyre batting at number eleven. The combined XV were dismissed for 96 halfway through the second day. W.G. was given four 'lives' in his second knock but was still a class above everyone else on the pitch. At the end of the day he was on 56 not out and went on to 73 before being well caught on the leg-side boundary. 'His cricket has been a treat,' commented one observer. 'He placed many balls with an ease which must have irritated bowlers and fielders; and he ran, with Jupp and Greenwood, numerous "little ones" with a daring which would have been fatal to less excellent runners or inferior judges.'

Two incidents involving him and the English umpire, Boult, did not endear him to the Australian players, press or public. As the Combined XV's Gregory was about to bowl he noticed W.G., at the non-striker's end, out of his crease and whipped the bails off. Boult turned down his appeal, on the extraordinary ground that he had not broken the wicket 'from in front' and Grace was reprieved. 'Have the laws of cricket in England been altered to this effect?' queried the *Australasian*. 'Are they utterly disorganised? Or are they intact, but unstudied by this latest specimen of the amateur umpire?'

This was followed by an altogether more serious fracas on the third and final day when the Australians were set an impossible 309 to win in three hours. They understandably attempted to play out time and escape with a draw. The English bowlers started to winkle them out and, with six Australians already back in the pavilion, Boult, standing at square leg, gave Sam Cosstick out hit wicket. Cosstick walked off insisting he had not touched his wicket and there was vocal protest from the crowd. When he reached the pavilion, his team-mates told Cosstick he had been given out by the wrong umpire and he returned to the crease where, by this time, his replacement was already installed. Grace protested that three batsmen was one too many but Cosstick stood his ground, awaiting a ruling from the umpire at the bowler's end. He, however, said nobody had appealed to him and, with no movement from Cosstick, Grace marched his players off the field.

The authorities intervened and eventually managed to persuade Cosstick to depart. After that the Englishmen wrapped up the game just before the scheduled close and won by 218 runs, Lillywhite returning figures of 9–33. It was an emphatic victory over a strong side; Grace's men had at last shown the form of which they were capable. The crowd swarmed on to the pitch in front of the pavilion at the end of the match and insisted that all the England players parade one by one to be applauded, but the manner in which Grace had behaved was not to everyone's taste. There were plenty of Australians who were sensitive to any hint of arrogance by visiting Englishmen. One reporter wrote: 'Tonight we shall see the last of the English Eleven – at least such is the fervent hope of all in this city who care to see the game played in a courteous and manly spirit . . . In this colony, at least, we have an intense distaste for bumptious and overbearing captains.'

Back they went to Melbourne on the by-now familiar coastal steamer – two days of seasickness out of three – and then inland again to Sandhurst, another goldmining town, for a match against a local XXII which, for once, did not contain any reinforcements from outside. It was a dry and dusty place, the only green in sight being the cricket ground, which was surrounded by young trees. Opinions differed about the state of the pitch: W.G., who thought the Australians very backward and cavalier in their pitch preparation, described this one as dry, crumbling and dangerous; locals thought it 'carefully prepared'. Grace's reaction to a bad pitch was often to attack the bowling – to hit rather than be hit – and this was one such occasion. He scored 53 and 72 not out. England had an easy victory: *Lillywhite* for 1875 summarised it thus: 'Mr W.G. Grace won by seven wickets.'

There was great excitement at their next port of call, Castlemaine, until recently a mining boom town whose gold had run out and whose cricketers had beaten the first English touring side back in 1861/62, the only Victoria side to do so. The latest tourists were borne to the ground, three miles outside town, in a coach drawn by four cattle. The facilities were simple. The *Australasian* reported apologetically : 'The accommodation for dressing was not quite palatial, the place which "the greatest cricketer of all time" had to uncover his nether limbs in being merely a structure of branches enclosed on three sides only, a sort of enlarged gunyah, in fact – rather different to the pavilion at Lord's, or the dressing-room at Canterbury.' The pitch was, inevitably, just as primitive, the ball shooting around in highly menacing fashion.

The locals were shot out for 57 and when England replied, W.G. coped superbly. 'Mr Grace frequently played balls down that rose breast high in a way that surprised the countrymen, who were accustomed to see their own men bob their heads and let such go by.' His score of 30, out of 76 all out, was the highest of the match. It included one let-off when the president of the Castlemaine team caught him on the leg-side boundary but fell over the ropes as he did so. As a hit over the boundary counted five, the scorers did not know what to give Grace. According to Grace, he was granted only the single which he had run while the ball was in the air. 'As I had a keen suspicion that I ought to have been given out, I did not argue out the point,' he wrote later. Interestingly, the local newspaper reported him as being given the full five runs. Castlemaine were dismissed for 58 in their second innings and England made 40–5 to win by five wickets. Grace declined to open and, going in at seven, faced only one ball, to his great relief. As always, there were toasts and speeches during the luncheon interval. One reporter, referring to the controversies which had dogged the tour, stated that one speaker 'commented on the inhospitable way in which the [English] Eleven had been treated and spoken of elsewhere, and said that Castlemaine was determined to treat their guests as guests, and as the real good fellows they were'. He added: 'The Eleven were loudly cheered on leaving for Melbourne.'

There they played a return match against Victoria, who confidently reduced their numbers to fifteen but were weakened by late withdrawals, so much so that the match organisers had to scour the city for substitutes on the morning of the first day. The weather had turned cold and the attendance poor: no more than two thousand people. England won convincingly by seven wickets, though Grace, who had been averaging a respectable 42 on the tour thus far, failed this time, scoring only nine before a break-back surprised him into lifting the ball to cover.

He didn't bother to bat in the second innings, with only 50 to make, but as the match ended early on the third day, a Saturday, the promoters organised an exhibition match to see how only eleven Victorians would fare against the Englishmen. It gave the crowd the opportunity to see Grace in full flow; he rattled up a brisk 126.

'The exposition of batting given by Mr W.G. Grace . . . was a treat, the ease and power with which he put the bowling about for singles, doubles, trebles and quartettes, with only eleven in the field, being wonderful,' wrote one reporter. 'His placing past short leg and point was plainly noticeable, and his swiftness between the wickets was positively ludicrous when Jupp was his partner.' His *pièce de résistance* was a hit for five – 'picked clean off the toes, far and high out of the ground, pitching on the top of the marquee in the ladies' reserve, it fairly "brought down the house".'

The opposing team, pressed into bowling and fielding to this onslaught, were less than happy about it. One of the bowlers grew so frustrated that eventually he threw a delivery at Grace, to general embarrassment. And when there was a pause for refreshments to be brought on, two fielders left the field and did not return, causing a further delay while substitutes were found.

Next stop for the tourists was Tasmania, entailing a twenty-nine-hour voyage on the vessel *The Tamar*, at first in the rough waters with which the Englishmen were becoming wearyingly familiar and 'which left "The Eleven" with scarcely strength enough to return the cheers of welcome that greeted them at the little wharf' at Launceston. Next day W.G. and his cousin Gilbert went shooting while the rest of the team fished at a place called the Cataracts.

Their match against XXII of Launceston started next day. W.G. lost the toss and the locals batted. There was a crowd of around twelve hundred, including 'a strong muster of elegantly-dressed ladies' and the Earl of Donnoughmore, who happened to be passing through. A correspondent wrote scornfully: 'The Tasmanians were seized with a very bad fit of the "funks", going to the wickets but to be sent back again, declaring the bowling to be utter rubbish, and that they ought to have stayed in against it all day – but they didn't', a situation familiar to every cricketer who has ever played the game. They were all out for 90, the only innings of consequence coming from J.C. Lord, formerly of Hampshire, and E.H. Butler, who played one game for the Gentlemen v Players on a visit to England. In reply, W.G. and Jupp each made 33 against bowling so tight that Grace, unusually for him, managed not a single boundary. Fred Grace suffered no such inhibitions in a brisk 45 which a local observer called 'as fine an exhibition of cricket' as he had ever seen, 'hitting hard and clean, and defence perfect'. England made 247 and won by an innings and 32 runs.

For a change, a pleasant coach-ride along a well-made road took them to Hobart and a match against Twenty-Two of South Tasmania before a big crowd, including the Governor, the local judges and other dignitaries. Again Fred Grace was the star of the show, with a brilliant 154, the highest score to date by an Englishman in Australia and the highest ever registered in Tasmania. W.G. made 29 and England won by eight wickets. The match was followed by a dinner-dance and W.G. was able to fit in a rabbit shoot, in which 'a snake or two' was also bagged before the party returned to the mainland for the last three matches of an arduous tour.

Back in Melbourne, England faced a Victoria XVIII for the third and final game of their series. It was all-square and all to play for. Many realised that it might be their last chance to see the world's greatest batsman in action. 'It is quite possible that colonial players will never see Mr Grace in the brilliant form he is now,' wrote one journalist, 'for men are but mortal and cannot retain their best form for ever in the cricket-field, any more than can horses on a race-course.'

A heavy rainstorm the evening before, which continued well into the morning of the first day, left the pitch soft and difficult to bat on, but the sun came out and play started promptly at noon as scheduled. The Victorian XVIII voted who should be captain (Conway) and batted first in front of a small crowd of only some six hundred people, which grew to three thousand later, leaving plenty of gaps in the grandstand. Victoria batted first and Grace's main contribution on the first day was again to become embroiled in a row with an umpire. The English umpire, Humphrey, was unwell and replaced by a local man, Budd. The Victorian batsman Newing hit Lillywhite back over his head, the ball hitting the side of a running rink and rebounding into play. Budd signalled four, but Fred Grace claimed that he had stopped the ball, and only two runs had been scored. W.G. made no secret of his disgust at the umpire's decision and 'made use of expressions implying he considered Mr Budd impartial and unfair'. Budd promptly walked off the pitch, saying he was not standing for such behaviour. One commentator wrote: 'Mr Grace frequently shows a disposition to assist umpires in their decisions, which is, to say the least, undesirable, and ought to be discouraged.' Interestingly, Grace made no reference to the incident in his various volumes of memoirs.

Australians might take a dim view of his gamesmanship but they still wanted to see him bat. The knowledge that he would be at the crease on the second day attracted a bigger crowd, some five thousand, and they were not disappointed. Grace scored a chanceless 64 before he attempted to slog Billy Midwinter, who had just come on, and was bowled. Midwinter, a talented all-rounder, also bowled Fred. He was to play a big part in Grace's cricketing life in the years ahead, as he had been born in Gloucestershire but was taken to Australia as a small boy. He returned to England at Grace's invitation to play for Gloucestershire as a professional, the first such from overseas in English cricket although he was qualified by birth to play for his native county. The match in Victoria was washed out by a thunderstorm with England on the verge of an easy victory.

After the game, there was a grand farewell dinner for the Englishmen, which exposed the bitterness and division within the touring party. The cream of Australian cricket, the Grace brothers and the other three amateurs turned out – but the seven English professionals did not. When he stood up to respond to the hosts' toast, W.G. had to admit that he did not know why. He criticised the local press for what he called their hostile coverage of the tour, and proffered a grudging apology to umpire Budd.

If he thought he had defused the situation, he was mistaken. Next morning, the Melbourne papers were highly critical of him. 'Does Dr Grace expect us to lie down for him and never to utter a word of criticism?' asked one. A letter to the *Argus* explained the professionals' boycott. It was from James Lillywhite, who revealed their deep resentment at receiving inferior accommodation to the amateurs throughout the tour. Interestingly, he excused his captain from any blame. 'It has been stated that Mr W.G. Grace is the cause of this wretched second class business,' he wrote, 'but I am much deceived in the man if it is through him. Let the promoters send us home first class and the professionals will have at least one kindly recollection of them.'

There was nothing of the kind for the professionals – quite the reverse. For the penultimate match of the tour they had to endure in excess the elements that had made so much of it so gruelling: a dreadful journey followed by an even worse game of cricket, if it could be so described, and all because the promoters hoped to make a quick buck. They had fixed up one game in South Australia, where cricket was less developed than in Victoria and New South Wales. The obvious place was the state capital, Adelaide, but the promoters had a better offer from the remote little copper mining town of Kadina, on the Yorke Peninsula, where there was plenty of ready money and nothing much to spend it on in the way of entertainment.

First, there was another awful sea journey to be endured. It took seventy-four hours instead of the usual forty-eight to reach Port Adelaide on the steamer *Coorong* because of a violent storm, and the cricketers unanimously decided enough was enough: they were meant to make the whole journey by steamer but jumped ship and hired a coach to take them the last hundred miles, over rough roads which were still preferable to the sea. An Australian journalist accompanying the party described Kadina: 'It is a peculiar place, suiting a peculiar people. Like many other mining townships, it begins nowhere and finished anywhere.' Still, the town put on a good welcome for the Englishmen, a band playing as their coach drew up outside the Exchange Hotel.

But when the visitors travelled the three miles out of town to see the pitch that had been arranged for them, they could scarcely believe their eyes. The locals had done their best to prepare it for the biggest event in their history, putting up two grandstands and enclosing the ground with a seven-feet-high wire fence and the playing area with a lower one. The problem was the ground itself. It was, said the Australian reporter, 'beyond the efforts of men or money', being entirely covered with gravel. 'Providence never intended cricket to be played on the Peninsula,' he concluded. 'On the morning of the match a bushel of pebbles was swept up,' recalled Grace. The England bowler Southerton remarked: 'All over in two days and no side makes 100 runs.' Grace replied: 'Yes, and somebody killed.' A wicket was chosen, almost at random, as one spot was much like another, and marked out with some difficulty as there was no tape measure to be found. The wicket was so hard it had to be watered before the stumps could be driven in.

A crowd of around two thousand converged on the ground. A band played throughout the day, and mounted troopers in blue uniforms rode about the ground to keep order. Many of the miners were Cornishmen, and they turned out in force to see their compatriots, and to indulge in frequent fights and wrestling matches. The Kadina men won the toss and elected to bat. Although they were kitted out in new flannels and the latest equipment, it swiftly transpired that they had very little idea about how to play cricket.

'It is impossible to describe the play, for the simple reason that there was no play to describe,' wrote a baffled reporter.

Several batsmen appealed enthusiastically when they were bowled or caught. 'One man knocked his off stump kicking, nearly spoiling Bush's beauty for ever, and then wanted to know if he was out or not. Bush said, "Slightly!" but the umpire thought not, and he remained in . . . It seemed astonishing that men . . . should be so completely in the dark in regard to even the simplest rules of the game they were trying to play.' Grace did not share the general merriment, perhaps because when he held a difficult catch at point that too was ruled not out.

Lunch was taken at 3 pm, with the usual volley of toasts, and immediately afterwards the XXII were all out for 42. Grace and Jupp – 'the long and the short of it', said the Australian reporter – opened as usual. The opening bowler Arthur alternated between roundarm and underarm, one of which Grace, on 5, spooned to short leg. The local umpire's decisions grew increasingly eccentric, giving the bowlers up to seven balls an over (in those days there were four to the over). Grace received seven balls in one over, most of which fizzed over his head, after which he declined to face another and 'the umpire woke up and called "over" with great dignity'. Only Jupp and Greenwood reached double figures, the latter making top score of 22 before being given out by the local umpire 'off a ball which hit the ground twice ere it reached mid-on's hands'. All out for 64 just before 6 p.m., the Englishmen were taken back to their hotel in their coach, 'nearly carrying away the fence and wire gates'.

Next day there were two bands playing on the ground, simultaneously. W.G. led the way in repainting the creases and the locals fared even worse than on the previous day, amassing the mighty total of 13, including five extras. As the *Australasian*'s man put it: 'This deserves a place in "Lillywhite" and all other "Guides" or "Companions" as really a most extraordinary match, although on such a ground it can hardly be called cricket. It wasn't good enough for skittles.'

To keep the crowd – and particularly the boisterous Cornishmen – happy, the tourists agreed to play an exhibition innings, in which W.G. struck 54, 'doing some terrific hitting, to the great delight of the "cousin Jacks", as the Cornish miners are styled'. Two more exhibitions were mounted: a single-wicket match between the two batsmen who had top-scored against the English XI (they had tied on the mighty total of 7) for a a cup valued at 10 guineas. The bowler was W.G. and the field consisted of only two Englishmen. Despite this, the hapless locals were each dismissed twice by Grace without scoring. On his third attempt, one again made a duck but the other, whom the Englishmen found more congenial, at last managed to drive Grace back over his head for a single to claim the cup. Next day, there was yet another game, a friendly seventeen-a-side affair with the Englishmen divided among the locals and, to round off the delights of Kadina, a visit to the Wallaroo copper mine.

That was meant to be the last of the fourteen matches the England team played in Australia. But with Grace at the helm the script was always likely to be rewritten and so it was, the consequence being a legacy of bad feeling all round. Adelaide's cricketers were still smarting from the insult of being sidelined by the Kadina fixture. Several of them travelled to Kadina to invite Grace to play a last game in Adelaide on the way home, making him 'a liberal offer' to do so.

Grace was willing to accommodate them, as it would mean an unexpected cash bonus for him and his team. The problem was that the tour promoters had given an undertaking that the tourists would play one only match in South Australia, with the idea of attracting more people to the Kadina fixture (in the event, they lost money on it). They strenuously objected to the Adelaide fixture. But Grace shrewdly saw a loophole: he had been contracted by the promoters to play fourteen matches on tour and he had fulfilled his side of the contract. After that, he argued, he was free to do as he liked. Angry telegrams flew between Grace and the promoters whose representative, travelling with the team, also chipped in with his objections. Grace first called the Adelaide game merely 'an exhibition of skill' but the promoters still threatened an injunction to stop it.

Grace called their bluff and decamped from Kadina at short notice, bringing the dinner laid on by his hosts to a sudden and unexpected conclusion. He packed his players on to the coach and set off for Adelaide in the dark, with the result that the driver got lost out in the bush. Eventually they decided it would be best to stop and wait until daybreak rather than get even more lost. They finally reached Adelaide at 2 p.m. and, despite their weariness, were out on the famous Oval an hour later to face a South Australian XXII.

About a thousand spectators watched the locals batting almost as badly as their upcountry rivals had, to total only 64. Next day, five times as many people came to see 'the Champion', batting at 5. He disappointed, however, lofting the ball high to long-on where he was well caught right on the rope, having made only 6. The *Australasian*'s reporter commented: 'It was a moot point as to whether the catch was made over the line or not, but the umpire gave W.G. out on appeal.' On the final day, he did even worse after walking to the wicket to great applause for his last innings on the tour. He played on for only one run and 'retired, to the manifest disappointment of all'. The match finished with England victorious by seven wickets, and by 5 p.m. the same day the tourists were on board the SS *Nubia*, which left for England early the next morning, 29 March. Seven weeks later, seven months after they had left England, they landed at Southampton in the steamship *Khedive*, to which they had transferred *en route*.

'Our tour had, on the whole, been conspicuously successful,' recorded Grace, a great rewriter of history. The record was: played 15, won 10, drawn 2, lost 3. The Englishmen were still far superior to most Australian players, though standards were improving. But the Australian view was rather different. Although it was agreed that there was still a big gap between the best Australian and English players, Grace's Twelve had been notably deficient in batting and bowling. There had been one exception: Grace himself. He had, in effect, been the difference between the two countries. 'Leaving the captain out, a colonial eleven could have been found to play a good match, and most likely beat the rest of the (English) team,' wrote a correspondent in the *Australasian*. 'That Mr W.G. Grace himself was a wonderful player was soon discovered, and that the reports of his general skill as a cricketer, and extraordinary batting powers in particular, had not been exaggerated, was on all sides allowed.'

But his high-handed attitude had left a sour taste in some quarters. 'It is a thousand pities that want of tact and management on the part of the promoters and the Eleven, or rather their captain, has made them both unpopular,' went on the anonymous writer, going on to express the hope that Grace would not lead the next tour, by which time 'the hatchet of ill-will will no doubt have been buried'. It was to be nearly two decades before W.G. set foot in Australia again – and the hatchet of ill-will was soon disinterred.

7 · REWRITING THE RECORDS
1874–1877

W.G. returned from Australia with renewed vigour. Only four days after stepping off the ship, he and Fred were back on the cricket field and warming up for the first-class season in a local derby between Thornbury and Clifton. W.G. smote 259 in three hours, including ten sixes, for Thornbury and with Fred put on 296 for the second wicket, demonstrating that the brothers were on a different plane altogether from their West Country brethren. If he did not quite equal his performances of 1871 and 1873, that only emphasised how brilliant he had been then, for 1874 was still a procession of centuries – eleven all told, the highest he ever scored in a season and eight of them in first-class games. In fact, he scored twelve centuries that year if one includes his 126 at Ballarat on the Australian tour.

Three of them were made for Gloucestershire, who carried all before them to be undisputed unofficial county champions for the the first time in their short history. The first was 179 (out of 299) against Sussex at Brighton, the others in the two games against Yorkshire. The fixture at Sheffield in late July was regarded as the championship decider and thousands of Yorkshiremen attended to see the Grace brothers. W.G. did not disappoint them: he scored 67 before lunch on the opening day, with some fine drives on a good wicket. He went on to score exactly 100 more, well over half of Gloucestershire's 303. Then he destroyed Yorkshire with the ball, taking 4–60 in their first innings (including six successive maidens and twelve maidens out of thirteen), followed by 7–44 in the second to win the match. 'The northerners could not stand against him,' was the *Sporting Gazette*'s verdict.

In the return match at Clifton in mid-August, the atmosphere was rather different: some two or three thousand spectators (reckoned to be a good turn-out in inclement weather), including many ladies for whom the cricket week at Clifton was a great social occasion, taking their place in a grandstand especially erected in front of the college terrace. The result, though, was the same: this time W.G. scored 127 and the other Grace brothers weighed in too. W.G. put on 137 with E.M., who made 51, the champion eventually falling to a slip catch by Ulyett. W.G. took 5–44 and 5–77, G.F. 4–43 and 1–43, as well as making 81 with the bat. Gloucestershire's win was 'entirely and wholly due to the wonderful play of the brothers Grace', said the *Sporting Gazette*.

So it was against Surrey too at Cheltenham a few days later on a wicket which no one could handle. Gloucestershire shot Surrey out for 27 in their second innings, their lowest score ever until then, W.G. taking seven wickets in each innings. He also scored 27 by himself, the highest individual innings in the match. It finished so early that a jokey scratch game was arranged between Grace's XI and Frank Townsend's XI, in which Grace batted with a broomstick and still contrived to score 35, a score bettered by only one other batsman.

Another century came for a joint Kent-Gloucs XI v England at Canterbury, which replaced the South v North fixture (Gloucestershire were included purely so that Grace could play). Although his opening partner, I.D. Walker, was one of the fastest scorers in the game, he made only 37 to W.G.'s 102 in their partnership of 149 for MCC v Kent.

Grace finished the season with 1,664 first-class runs at an average of 52 but of greater significance was a huge improvement with the ball: he took 139 first-class wickets at 12.64 each. But of even greater significance was the birth of his first child, on 6 July, a boy to whom he gave exactly the same name as himself, and who would thereafter always be known as W.G. junior. He was to become a good enough cricketer to win his Blue for Cambridge and play for Gloucestershire, but never to be good enough to hope to match the father whose initials he bore.

W.G. senior continued spreading the gospel of the game, taking himself to Ireland for the first time with the United South troupe and a match against a Leinster XXII in July. He did not disappoint the thousands who made the pilgrimage to see him and Fred put on 200 together, W.G. contributing 153, to the pleasure of all save an Irishman who had travelled a hundred miles and left at 5 p.m. on the first day complaining that he would like to see someone else batting too.

There were other curiosities that summer. A team of baseball players from Boston and Philadelphia came over to try to tempt the English into adopting their game with exhibitions on various cricket grounds around the country. They did not succeed although their athleticism impressed the crowds. Curiously, they also played seven games of cricket against very inferior opposition as no one knew if they would be any good. The result was that they stayed unbeaten.

W.G. was invited to play in a match whose greatest claim to be remembered is that it boasted probably the longest billing ever afforded to a game of cricket: 'Gentlemen of England who had not been educated at the Universities v Gentlemen of the Universities, Past and Present', which might have been abbreviated to Brains v Brawn. The non-graduates, including W.G. and G.F., trounced the university men by an innings. The match was never staged again.

Yet another umpiring controversy dogged W.G., this time in the Gentlemen v Players match at Prince's. Again, Fred was at the other end, this time facing the bowling of John Lillywhite. Fred played the ball back to Lillywhite at a catchable height, only for W.G. to come between ball and bowler. Lillywhite and the fielders appealed vehemently for someone to be given out for obstructing the field but the umpires turned them down. The bad feeling persisted for some time, and W.G. did not help matters by taking his customary century off the professionals.

It happens to all great sportsmen at some time in their careers – the whisper that they are over the hill. The rumours that W.G.

was already past his best at the age of twenty-seven started to gain currency during the 1875 season and there was indeed statistical evidence to support the notion. His batting average plummeted to 32 but he himself had no doubt about the cause: unseasonal weather throughout the summer which gave the upper hand to the bowlers throughout. They, of course, included W.G., who cashed in for the biggest haul of first-class wickets he was to record in one season: 191 at 12.92 each, almost exactly the same as the previous year.

So long was W.G.'s career that he was to be written off at regular intervals over the next quarter of a century and he derived great satisfaction from proving the critics wrong time and time again. But another good reason for him to be out of form was that he had moved to London in February to continue his medical studies at St Bartholomew's Hospital. He and Agnes found an apartment in Earls Court, west London, possibly because it was convenient for Paddington Station and the trains for Bristol and the West Country.

However, he was in good form in non-first-class matches for the United South, with centuries against the likes of a Hastings XVIII, a North Kent XVIII and a Trinity College, Dublin XVIII. But his others were out of the top drawer, notably a typical 152 for the Gentlemen v Players at Lord's in early July when he and the promising twenty-year-old, A.J. Webbe, an Oxford undergraduate who burst on to the scene that summer, put on 203 for the first wicket in the second innings, the highest opening partnership recorded till then in the famous series. Webbe, who went on to captain Middlesex, remembered: 'How he used to run in those days; then there was no sign of stoutness in his figure.'

Webbe was able to acquire a batting education as he watched Grace from the non-striker's end. By lunch, he had scored just 12 to Grace's 45. After lunch Grace gave a hard chance to mid-on and then punished the Players with a whirlwind 55 in only twenty-five minutes to reach his century at 4.10 p.m. He was dropped again by Richard Daft at long-off and finally run out going for a sharp second. Of particular interest to his team-mates in the pavilion was the masterly way in which he dealt with shooters, which because of the pitch improvements at Lord's were never thereafter as common there. 'It was only by degrees that we detected what he was doing with the shooter,' recalled Edward Lyttelton. 'He brought down the bat with a curious dig, at such an angle that it not only went forcibly towards mid-on, but he positively placed it on each side of the field as he chose.' W.G. made his 152 in 205 minutes out of 242, 'his innings equal to any he has shown in late years, his batting as resolute and well-timed as ever', said the *Sportsman*. 'Nobody can wield the willow as he can,' was the respectful comment of the *Sporting Gazette*. 'It was the most titanic display of batting that I had ever seen,' wrote Lyttelton.

Three weeks later W.G. travelled to Sheffield with Gloucestershire to play Yorkshire. A huge crowd, estimated at nine thousand packed into Bramall Lane to watch cricket's biggest attraction and he did not let them down. As one observer put it, 'Mr Grace is always a safe sensation at Sheffield since he first astonished the natives of that district.' A total of twenty thousand was reckoned to have come through the gates in the three days of the match.

Grace won the toss, elected to bat, and was almost run out in the first over. Having given his fans such a nasty scare, he hit a fine on-drive for four in the second over and he was on his way. By lunch he had made 54, while his team-mates amassed only 32 and lost five wickets. He moved masterfully on to complete his century and was eventually stumped off Armitage for 111, made out of 174. 'Mr W.G. Grace was at the top of his tree with the bat, and he never played better in his life,' said the *Sporting Clipper*.

His third and final first-class century of 1875 came in a rain-interrupted match against Nottinghamshire at Clifton, played from 16–18 August, when he made 119 including a gigantic six off Oscroft which went over square leg and out of the ground, landing among the houses on the other side of the road which skirted the ground.

But if it was anyone's summer, it was Alfred Shaw's, for the great Nottinghamshire left-arm slow-medium bowler cleaned up wherever he went, notably against MCC at Lord's where he took 7–7 in the second innings. W.G. was one of his victims, though he did not give up his wicket without a struggle. He scored 35, at one stage adding only 10 in an hour on a difficult wicket against Shaw at his finest. Among all his centuries and double centuries, he remembered that innings as one of the best he ever played. W.G. admired Alfred Shaw enormously. 'Between 1870 and 1880 he was perhaps the best bowler in England,' he wrote later. He knew this from bitter experience, for Shaw had the distinction of clean bowling him in first-class cricket on twenty occasions, more than any other player.

Perhaps the doubters served only to inspire W.G., who was never one to ignore a challenge. The season of 1876 was the stage for his greatest feat of sustained batting, over eight days in August, and his highest score, 400 in a non-first-class match. He was slow to get going, for in the winter of 1875–6 he had started to put on weight for the first time, and by the time the cricket season opened he was no longer the svelte figure whom A.J. Webbe had marvelled at the previous summer. Perhaps because of the comforts of married life, his weight had ballooned to 15 stone and he had started to take on the imposing shape that has gone into cricket legend and which is the instant image we have of Grace today. But we should never forget that until he was twenty-seven he was a superb figure of a man, the epitome of athleticism.

His increasing weight and girth meant that he scored only 163 runs in May and 464 in June. By July he was back in form, as he showed with his annual fireworks displays in the Gentlemen v Players series. In the first match, at The Oval, he was bowled by Tom Emmett for a duck but took his revenge with 90 in the second innings. At Lord's he made 169, the third highest score at the ground until then. It was a devastating display against the best professional bowlers in the land: he made 110 before lunch out of 172, and continued in the same vein afterwards including a 'slashing drive' for six and a seven into the nursery garden. It was described as 'the finest innings played in London that season and his reception at the Pavilion at the finish great and enthusiastic'. The innings, said another commentator, 'went very far towards destroying whatever of interest might and must otherwise have been felt in the match'. He was also back to his best with the ball, taking 9–122 in the game and going one better in the third match at Prince's. The *Sporting Gazette* expressed contrition for having shared the doubts about the great man:

Many people, and those good judges of the game too, thought that Mr W.G. Grace's right hand had forgot its cunning this season; but they must, or ought to be convinced that they have formed an erroneous opinion concerning him. In past years we have grown so accustomed to read of or to see such tremendous scores from the bat of the 'champion' that we all expect to see the three figures attached to his name in whatsoever match he plays. That, up to this time, except when playing for his own county of Gloucestershire, he has failed in contributing his ordinary scores is true; but that his 169 at Lord's on Monday were obtained in a style to which none but W.G. Grace could attain is admitted on all hands by either cricketers or Cockneys who witnessed it. He had the best of bowling against him but he made actual mincemeat of it all until at last he was caught out at slip by Hill from Shaw's bowling with a very good catch low down.

Thus restored, W.G. took his United South team off to Grimsby for a match against a local XXII starting on 10 July. The Grimsby men made a bad tactical error before the game: they complained to W.G. that the team he had brought along was not up to the standard they had expected and presumably advertised around the town. Or perhaps they were just hoping for a rebate. As it was, W.G. made *them* pay – for thirteen and a half hours, the time he took to compile an epic quadruple century. To be fair, he did offer a chance when he was on 350.

The pitch was a good one but the grass in the outfield had been left uncut and many of W.G.'s strokes were slowed up before they could reach the boundary and he was forced to run 158 singles, which must have done his waistline some good. When the innings closed at 681, late on the third day, he was still unbeaten. He had faced fifteen different bowlers and, of course, twenty-two fielders. It was the only 400 of W.G.'s career, and 4 short of the highest score made until then. There was a rumour that the great man had in fact scored only 399 when he ran out of partners but asked the scorers to add the extra run. Nobody else was counting by then. 'It is the most extraordinary performance with the bat ever known,' said the *Sporting Clipper*. The Grimsby men were so shattered by the experience that they made only 88 in reply.

Charles Alcock was overcome with superlatives when he considered the innings in Lillywhite's *Annual*:

What can be written in praise of an innings against such odds, in which no chance was given until he had scored 350 and in which he had to contend against bowling, if not of the very best kind, still straight, and demanding from batsmen careful play?

Can one do aught but wonder at the masterly skill in placing the ball – the skill of the batsman – but admire the splendid physique that could alone accomplish such a feat? No paint can add to the beauty of the lily, nor will gilding improve refined gold. To extol W.G. Grace's merits as a cricketer would be superfluous. At the present time he is like Eclipse [the racehorse], first – and the rest nowhere . . . For the last ten years W.G. has stood alone as the most marvellous cricketer of his time.

One oddity was that non-members of the Grace family contributed only 72 to the United South's total: Fred Grace made 60 and W.R. Gilbert 116. The Grace family grew by one during the game: on the second day, news arrived from Downend of the birth of W.G.'s second son, Henry Edgar, whose arrival was toasted in champagne by the proud father that evening.

A fixture he would not have missed for anything was Richard Daft's benefit at Trent Bridge. W.G. and Daft had fought some epic battles for South v North, Gloucs v Notts and Gentlemen v Players (Daft was first an amateur, who became a professional in 1859 and reverted to the amateur ranks in 1877, towards the end of his career). They held each other in the highest regard. 'He was the most finished and graceful batsman in England for a great many years,' wrote Grace. 'I was just as thankful to see his back to the wicket as he was to see mine.' The public gave generously to Daft: £160 on the first day, £180 on the second, and £92 on the third. Grace chipped in with a typical unbeaten 114, though he was as much a beneficiary as Daft, who dropped him when he was on 29.

This was a mere curtain-raiser for the events of August. Grace's first stop was Hull, where he took his United South team to play a powerful United North side – too powerful for Grace's team, who made 28 between them, but not for W.G. who hit 126 in 150 minutes, including several balls despatched into the grounds of an adjacent lunatic asylum and another which was borne away by a passing goods train. In the second innings he contributed 82 out of his side's total of 194.

Then it was down to Canterbury and the by now regular fixture between the combined Kent-Gloucs team and the Rest of England, the main attraction of the Festival week. England's captain was the young and inexperienced A.J. Webbe, who lost the toss and found himself in the field with a man short. The wily pro Alfred Shaw advised him to place a man between slip and third man to cover both positions and went there himself. To their amusement, W.G. sliced a catch to him and was out for only nine, marching off in some disgruntlement with the remark, 'He was in no position at all.' Inevitably he made up for it in the second innings with 91. The match ended in farce, with wickets tumbling so quickly that Fred Grace, who had changed out of his whites, had to rush to the wicket in his ordinary clothes and hold out for a draw. High comedy was the order of the day during that game: when the august figure of Lord Harris walked out to bat, the scoreboard operator inadvertently left out the first letter of his surname on the board, which reduced the crowd, many of whom had been drinking, to fits of laughter until the mistake was spotted and corrected.

The next day, Grace switched sides, as it were, and turned out for MCC v Kent in a twelve-a-side game. Faced with a Kent total of 473 (Lord 'Arris 154), MCC were shot out for 144 and followed on. W.G. went out to open the batting with no thought of batting to save the day: that was never his way. So he hit out to entertain the crowd, hoping and expecting to be on the train home to Bristol the following day, which would enable him to get a good day's rest before Gloucestershire confronted Nottinghamshire. But as often happens in such circumstances, the reverse occurred: 'I risked a little more than usual, helped myself more freely than I would have done under different circumstances, and everything came off.' Helped by short boundaries and a good wicket, MCC had 100 on the board in forty-five minutes. By the close of play, W.G. had rattled up a whirlwind 133 not out, reaching his century with the second of two big hits for four on to the booths beyond long-on.

His friend C.C. Clarke described it as 'the most attractive contribution I ever saw either from him or any other cricketer. It did not matter where George Harris placed the field, whether point was forward or set back, nor how the men in the deep were set, with clean cuts and strong pushes he was sending ball after ball past them'. And that was with a bat which, Grace confided to Clarke that evening, had something wrong with it. So after dinner they 'tinkered up' another bat, 'making the handle bigger by splicing an old white glove round it'.

The next day was a Saturday and the usual bumper Festival crowd was treated to an extraordinary exhibition by Grace, the like of which had never been seen before on a cricket field. The general expectation was that Kent would still win, but Grace had other ideas. He batted for most of a blazing hot day, fuelled by champagne and soda water at the tea interval. He showed an uncharacteristic nerviness as he approached his double century but once that was passed he resumed normal service. When he reached 279, out of 451, he finally achieved a long-held ambition by creating a new record for the highest first-class individual innings, previously set by William Ward in 1820 with 278. Grace had gone close in 1871; now the record was gathered in. On he went to his triple century. When MCC's score reached 500, he was on 315, and Kent had tried ten bowlers against him without success. He was eventually caught low down at mid-off for 344, in 380 minutes. The press were unanimous in their superlatives: 'A sensational innings . . . the greatest batting exhibition yet recorded,' said the *Sporting Gazette*. 'Ordinary words of praise would seem absurd when applied to such a stupendous achievement,' agreed the *Daily Telegraph*. 'That he should have made all those runs without a chance must add still more to the surprising character of the performance, which must be classed as by far the most remarkable event in the annals of cricket,' purred the *Sportsman*. 'After Mr Grace's retirement the game became singularly uneventful.'

There was just one complaint, from the *Sporting Clipper*, and it was aimed at the meanness of the Canterbury authorities: 'Although the management took something like 200 pounds more than ever known before, they did not present Mr Grace with a prize bat to commemorate such a great performance.' Needless to say, the match was saved. But as it turned out, Grace's mighty achievement was only the first part of an amazing sequence.

He took the train to Bristol on Sunday and next day, another hot one, was ready to take on the men of Nottinghamshire at Clifton College. The visitors were late and the start was delayed until 1 p.m. Winning the toss, W.G. opened the innings and swiftly showed that, far from being drained by his efforts at Canterbury, he had brought his form with him. Nottinghamshire boasted a formidable opening attack, Alfred Shaw and Fred Morley, but Grace treated them like novices. In Shaw's first over he drove and cut him for successive fours. E.M. held firm at the other end, while W.G. cut loose, hitting Tye so fiercely to square leg, where there was no boundary, that he ran seven for it. At one stage he hit four successive fours and when lunch was taken at 2.30 p.m., he had made 83 not out out of 122. After lunch he struck a six over the road, and lofted another drive into the grandstand where Fred Grace rose and caught it, to the delight of the ladies gathered there, 'in order that it might not spoil the features of a Clifton villa', according to one report. To add to the fun, W.G. made as if to leave the wicket and walk back to the pavilion.

He hit an all-run six, which was his undoing, for in attempting to repeat the shot he was caught at long-on off the bowling of John Selby, the England batsman who had only been brought on in desperation after the front-line attack had been hit all over the ground. (It was one of only five first-class wickets he took in his life.) Grace had made 177 in 190 minutes. Notts were forced to follow on but after a good start were undone by W.G. with 8–69. He was not called on again with the bat, as Gloucs were left with only 31 to win on the third day, which Fred and E.M. knocked off in 25 minutes.

The match also contained a row, when the Notts player Tolley took what the Gloucestershire team considered to be an unnecessarily long time putting on his pads before going out to bat. 'Mr

W.G. Grace was very wroth,' wrote one observer. 'This is nothing new in a Clifton match.'

On their way back home, the Nottinghamshire squad met the Yorkshire team travelling south for their own match against Grace and Co. The Midlanders warned them that W.G. was in top form but the Yorkshiremen were unimpressed. Tom Emmett is said to have retorted: 'The big'un has exhausted himself and cannot do the century trick three times in succession.' If he did, he added he'd personally shoot him, and anticipated the approval of his fellow pros. He ought to have packed his gun.

The match was played at Cheltenham. 'A fresh breeze from the hills tempered the blazing heat, and the beautiful College ground had seldom appeared to greater advantage,' wrote one scribe. W.G. reckoned the pitch was as good as he had ever played on and Gloucestershire had first use of it. With 521 runs under his belt in the previous six days, he carried on where he had left off against Notts. 'Though the bowling continued very good, all was of no avail against the skill of the great batsman,' reported the *Sportman*'s correspondent. Grace batted untroubled throughout the first day, reaching his century soon after lunch with a blow over square leg off Tom Emmett on to the gymnasium roof, and hitting more sixes into the grandstand and on the main tent. At 5.30 p.m. he reached another double century and finished the day on 216 not out. The next morning it rained and play could not start until 1 p.m., giving Grace a rest. In the afternoon he added another century, running out of partners, to carry his bat for 318 out of a total of 528. 'Goodness knows how many more he would have made had any of his side lived to keep him company,' commented the *Sporting Gazette*.

So total was his dominance that the Yorkshire bowlers fell out with one another. At one stage Allen Hill refused point-blank to be brought back by his captain Ephraim Lockwood. Emmett told Lockwood to insist that Hill bowled, upon which Hill turned on Emmett and growled: 'Why don't you bowl yourself? You're frightened.' The infuriated Emmett grabbed the ball – and bowled three wides in succession. (To be fair, Grace once noted that Emmett never seemed to know where he was bowling and could surprise the batsman with a straight one after spraying the ball all over the place.) So Grace had racked up 839 runs in eight days, a performance never equalled before or since, and between 3 and 19 August made 1,164. 'C'est magnifique, mais ce n'est pas la guerre! might well Mr Grace's opponents declare,' wrote one journalist, 'for when he once gets set no bowling at present to be had can get rid of him. Indeed it is growing to be a common opinion among spectators, that "Grace can get a score whenever he likes".'

His total for the month was 1,389, greater than any other batsman managed in the whole of the 1876 season. Grace's aggregates that year were 2,622 first-class runs, average 62.42, 3,908 runs in all cricket, and 130 first-class wickets at 18.90 each. Just as important for him, Gloucestershire were county champions again.

In the autumn of 1876, R.A. Fitzgerald, Grace's comrade-in-arms in Canada, resigned through ill health from his post as secretary of MCC after a stint of thirteen years, and James Lillywhite led the fourth English tour of Australia, an entirely professional affair. It was most notable for Australia's first victory over England, at Melbourne in March 1877.

Nobody, not even W.G., could have equalled his achievements of 1876 and the summer of 1877 was bound to be something of an anticlimax. The figures tell it all: in thirty-seven first-class innings he made 1,474 runs at an average of only 39.83, though he was still comfortably the highest scorer in England. But his bowling more than compensated for his relatively lacklustre performances with the bat. It was a wet summer and accordingly the bowlers had the upper hand. W.G. finished with 179 wickets, which was to be the second highest of his long career, at an average of only 12.81.

There was no doubt about his finest batting display in 1877: a superb 261 for the South v the North, a benefit match for the Cricketers' Fund played between 31 May and 2 June at the Prince's ground. It was one of the last big innings to be played there. It had formerly been Middlesex's home ground but they had now decamped to Lord's, and Prince's, situated on a prime piece of building land at Hans Place, just off Sloane Street, was soon to fall to the developers; indeed, they were already nibbling away at the corners and reducing the size of the field of play. Grace's double century was the highest individual score of the first-class season.

He soon lost his opening partner, his cousin, W.R. Gilbert, run out for seven with the score on 27, and was joined at the wicket by Joseph Cotterill of Sussex, a brilliant batsman whose career (unlike Grace's) was curtailed by the demands of medicine. Grace punished the North's attack of Morley, Tye and Clayton to the tune of 90 out of 119–1 by lunch. At 3.20 p.m. he reached his century and carried on ruthlessly flogging the ball to all corners of the ground. *Bell's Life in London* recorded: 'The bowling was now fairly collared, the Champion apparently doing as he liked.' Grace brought up his double century with an on-drive for three off Morley and then lost Cotterill, whose share of a stand of 281 was 88. At stumps, W.G. was undefeated on 252 out of 385–2, (Fred Grace 34 not out) but did not last much longer on Friday, a day affected by rain and wind, hitting a catch to mid-on. Fred went on to make 54 in the South's 459 all out.

Mrs Grace had made the journey to London to watch her sons play. She was sitting with a Dutch friend when an elderly clergyman sat himself down next to them and, assuming the two women, knew nothing about cricket or cricketers proceeded to deliver a running commentary on the match (the sort of neighbour with whom all cricket lovers will be familiar). Mrs Grace managed to conceal her identity even when the parson started to tell her all about her own son. Alas, his reaction when W.G. came over to greet his mother is not recorded.

Meanwhile Gloucestershire were carrying all before them. It was their best season yet, winning seven out of eight matches and drawing the other, and for the second consecutive season they topped the unofficial county championship. They had an interesting new recruit: Billy Midwinter, the Victoria all-rounder whom Grace had got to know when he toured Australia four years previously. But by birth he was a Gloucestershire man: he had been born in 1851 in St Briavels, Gloucestershire, and was taken to Australia as a child. Now he was recruited by Gloucestershire and became, in a manner of speaking, the first overseas player in the county game, and the first professional to play for Gloucestershire. He was a hard-hitting batsman, a steady and effective medium-pace bowler, and a brilliant fielder.

The county game was rapidly gaining in popularity with the public, who could identify with their own sides. It meant that the end was drawing near for the professional circuses, such as the United South and All England XI: the latter played their last game in 1877 and the writing was on the wall for the United South although they survived for a few seasons more. But cricket promoters still put together strange combinations to attract an audience, such as a Gloucestershire-Yorkshire XI which played the Rest of England at Lord's on 17 and 18 July. W.G. hit 52 in the first innings and to mark his twenty-ninth birthday made a memorable century (110) in the second, including a six struck out of the ground into J.H. Dark's garden (Dark was the former administrator of the ground).

Gloucestershire's finest moment came with a game arranged against a strong England side, a signal honour to be accorded to a county. Gloucestershire showed how much they deserved it by winning by five wickets. Grace took seven wickets in the game but perhaps his finest-ever performance with the ball came in his county's game against Nottinghamshire at Cheltenham, the first time the Midlanders had played there. His match figures were 76–36–89–17 (9–55 and 8–34) and in Notts' second innings he took seven wickets in seventeen balls without conceding a run, including three in one over, 'entitling him to a new hat' according to the local newspaper. But it was as much the manner in which he lured the opposition out that had affected the figures, startling though they were. He placed his brother Fred and cousin W.R. Gilbert as twin long-legs, and batsman after batsman contrived to hit the ball down their throats. The Notts captain, Richard Daft, berated his batsmen for falling for the Grace leg-trap in such a fashion, only to do exactly the same himself second ball. 'Mr W.G. Grace's performance with the ball was quite of an exceptional character,' said the *Bristol Evening News*. 'He took as many wickets as he

scored runs.' Therein may have lain his determination to do well
with the ball for he had been given out in dubious circumstances,
playing a ball from Morley to cover-point where Selby claimed the
catch and W.G. was given out, 'a decision which was questioned
by several who declared the ball struck the ground before it
reached him'.

The next day W.G. laid waste Yorkshire at Clifton in similar
manner, with a spell of 6–6 and a total of eight wickets in
the innings. All season he skittled the opposition: in the South
v North match at Lord's he took 8–36 in the North's second
innings, for Gloucs v Surrey at Clifton, 5–26, and for MCC v
Kent at Canterbury his figures were 6–19.

The end of the 1877 season was a watershed not only for Grace
but for English cricket. For more than a decade he had been a
full-time cricketer during the season. Now belatedly he was to
embark on the final, and most serious, lap of the much-prolonged
studies that would at long last qualify him as a doctor. He was
almost thirty and, in common with most sportsmen, his very
greatest achievements were behind him, although he still had
one truly astonishing season well ahead of him. Physically he
had changed from the lithe young man of his late teens and
early twenties. He was now assuming the girth and persona of
grand old man of cricket, the image of him which prevails to the
present day.

His cricketing career was very nearly ended by a shooting
accident in September 1877. Lord Westmoreland had invited him
up to Apethorpe in Northamptonshire to play for the village side
against Lord Exeter's XI, a match the two peers took very seriously
indeed. After the previous year's defeat had been avenged thanks
mainly to a century by W.G., a day's shooting of partridge and
hare followed. In the afternoon, W.G. unwisely moved ahead of
the line of guns, unseen by the others. When the partridges were
put up, he was right in the line of fire and was hit in the eye.
Fortunately Fred Grace, a medical student, was on hand to take
charge and bandage his brother, who was led away amid fears that
the damage could be permanent. It was not. It is interesting to
think of the number of great cricketers who suffered eye injuries,

from shooting or traffic accidents, and whose game was never the same again – Ranji, the Nawab of Pataudi, Colin Milburn – and to ponder the fact that the great W.G. was only a whisker away from joining them.

8 · GRACE THE CRICKETER

WHAT was W.G. *like* as a batsman, bowler, fielder, captain? This is the most frustrating question that can be asked of all the great players of the pre-cinematic and pre-television age. Nowadays we are all experts (or we think we are) about every cricketer. We see them continually on television: we know that Greg Chappell and David Gower were the personification of elegance, that Viv Richards had such a superb eye that he could hit across the line and get away with it, that Brian Lara had both eye and elegance, that Denis Lillee's and Michael Holding's bowling actions were poetry in motion. The image most of us have of Ian Botham's all-round brilliance actually *depends* on television, for most of us see far more cricket on TV than we can possibly do in the flesh. Going back to the 1930s and 1940s, there is enough cinema footage to get a good idea of Bradman's footwork and remorseless accumulation of runs, of Hutton's grace and poise, of Compton's effervescence and brilliant unorthodoxy.

THE BATSMAN

There is some film footage of W.G. but it affords only a tantalising glimpse of him practising in late middle age. There is none of him in action out in the middle against real bowling. So we have to rely on the eyewitness accounts of those he played against. Fortunately, there exist enough of those to build up a good picture of the Doctor at the crease.

First, his stance. No more detailed portrait has been presented than by Sir Arthur Conan Doyle, who was a keen club cricketer, played against Grace (like him, a doctor) and indeed once claimed his wicket. This was in the later stages of Grace's career but many of Conan Doyle's observations echoed earlier descriptions of Grace in his prime – and were worthy of Sherlock Holmes in the closeness of their scrutiny. Remember that Grace stood six ft 2 ½ in tall and from his mid-thirties onwards presented a vast bulk to the bowler.

I do not know if he took the centre or the leg guard, or the point between them, but he actually stood very clear of his wicket, bending his huge shoulders and presenting a very broad face of the bat towards the bowler.

It was not surprising that Conan Doyle was unsure about Grace's guard. The great man was dismissive about the question: 'It makes very little difference what guard you take,' he once wrote. What mattered to him was that the batsman should stand 'as near as you possibly can in the line of the wickets without getting your feet in front – in fact, your toes must be just clear of a line drawn from wicket to wicket.' Contrary to Conan Doyle's memory, he advocated positioning the back foot well inside the crease. He used to mark the line he had chosen with one of the bails.

The novelist went on to describe Grace's most characteristic movement, a defiant cocking of the left foot as the bowler approached the wicket. He 'would slowly raise himself up to his height and draw back the blade of his bat, while his left toe would go upwards until only the heel of the foot remained upon the ground'. W.G. himself described the remarkable position of his left leg: 'I prefer to place (it) about twelve inches in front of *and nearly at right angles* [my italics] to my other leg.' It signalled aggression from the first.

This posture is well captured in some brief film footage of Grace practising at Brighton, presumably around the turn of the century, as Ranji was filmed too. Wearing a round-topped straw hat, his flannels held up by a belt, W.G. is shown playing six shots, in front of a single stump and, just behind it, a seated row of appreciative men and small boys, all much more smartly dressed than would be the case today. There does not appear to be a net protecting them. W.G. plays two on-drives, an off-drive off the back foot straight at the cameraman, a couple of characteristic pushes to leg, also off the back foot, and a final rather ungainly back-foot off-side prod.

In the first on-drive, his cocking of the left foot is most evident. Perhaps the most interesting feature of his stance revealed by the camera is a double take-back of the bat before the ball has been bowled, which is displayed in every shot. First, he picks it up to a position about level with his knee, holds it there momentarily, then takes the bat back as high as his shoulder before bringing it down for the shot. This double pick-up is not referred to in any literature but is clearly automatic. It contrasts strongly with Ranji's pick-up, when the Jam Sahib is shown in the next frames, practising a couple of shots in front of the same stump. Unlike W.G. he does not bother with pads or gloves, and has not even removed his blazer. He picks the bat up with one flowing movement before unleashing a wristy off-drive and then a corking square cut. It is a fascinating glimpse of his lordly technique, while the overall impression W.G. leaves is one of workman-like efficiency.

Conan Doyle went on:

He gauged the pitch of the ball in an instant, and if it were doubtful played back rather than forward.

R.A.H. Mitchell, who played with W.G. for the Gentlemen in the 1860s and went on to become a master at Eton, was quoted as saying that W.G. 'never made great use of the back-stroke, which has been perfected since his time', and Grace himself was of the 'when in doubt, play forward' school. But he was in fact the first batsman to combine both forward and back play with equal ease. In this respect, he invented modern batting, as C.L.R. James put it.

Ranji (or possibly his 'ghost', C.B. Fry) was in no doubt about this:

W.G . . . revolutionised batting. He turned it from an accomplishment into a science . . . Before W.G. there were two kinds – a batsman played a forward game or he played a back game. Each player, too, seems to have made a speciality of some particular stroke . . . It was bad cricket to hit a straight ball; as for pulling a slow long-hop, it was regarded as immoral. What W.G. did was to unite in his mighty self all the good points of all the good players . . . He founded the modern theory of batting by making forward and back-play of equal importance, relying neither on the one nor on the other, but on both . . . I hold him to be, not only the finest player born or unborn, but the maker of modern batting. He turned an old one-stringed instrument into a many-chorded lyre. And, in addition, he made his execution equal his invention. All of us now have the instrument, but we lack his execution. It is not that we do not know, but that we cannot perform.

Ranji was certainly being unduly modest, for no one played more beautiful music with the instrument he was bequeathed by W.G. Then he changed the metaphor:

Before W.G., batsmen did not know what could be made of batting. The development of bowling has been natural and gradual; each great bowler has added his quota. W.G. discovered batting; he turned its narrow straight channels into one great winding river . . . The theory of modern batting is in all essentials the results of W.G.'s thinking and working on the game.

Perhaps the most striking feature of his contemporaries' recollections is the common consent that Grace was not a graceful batsman. Ranji defined it as elegantly as one of his cover drives: 'What W.G. did was . . . to make utility the criterion of style.' Canon Edward Lyttleton, a notably stylish batsman himself and captain of the 1878 Cambridge side which beat the Australians by an innings and 72 runs at Lord's, agreed: 'He was strangely lacking in attractiveness of style . . . The style was unattractive, not because it was laborious, but because the movements were ungainly.'

Charles Francis, who played with Grace for the Gentlemen and toured North America with him, wrote in similar vein: 'There was nothing very attractive in his style, which was quite different from that of anyone else. There was none of the finished and graceful wrist-play of an Alfred Lubbock or Alfred Lyttleton or Charlie Buller.' These views were echoed by A.G. Powell, who watched him play for Gloucestershire many times and wrote an engaging little biography of the Grace brothers published in 1948: 'There was . . . nothing about W.G.'s batting that you could describe as distinctive, save that he managed somehow to get nearly every ball in the middle of the bat, and you could no more associate a lucky snick through the slips or to leg with his batting than you could visualise Mendelssohn writing jazz.'

Stylish he may not have been but all agree that Grace somehow dominated from the very beginning of an innings. According to Lord Hawke, he liked to get off the mark as quickly as possible, just as Bradman was to do. His philosophy was simple ('No one ever had a more unanalytic brain,' remarked Edward Lyttelton): to put bat to ball, not the other way round. 'There has never been any show about his play,' wrote Richard Daft, who played with and against him for the best part of three decades. W.G. seldom, if ever, left the ball alone, a custom he abhorred. If it was a good ball, he would defend against it. If it was a bad one, it was there to be despatched.

He always sought to hit the ball hard but he never seemed to over-exert himself, combining strength and timing to perfection. Charles Francis noted: 'He was never what I should call a big hitter . . . I have seen him hit a ball out of Lord's . . . but it was not very often that he opened his huge shoulders in that way.' Francis reflected: 'What always struck me about his own peculiar style was that he made batting look so ludicrously easy, the ball always seemed to hit the middle of his bat, his timing was so exact, he was never too soon or too late.' P.J. de Paravicini made almost exactly the same observations: 'The biggest hit never seemed the slightest effort. He did not appear to put out any greater strength for a huge drive than for a mere block.'

Like all the greats, he played straight, at least until middle-age. He claimed to abhor the pull to leg of the ball pitched just outside the off stump. When it was put to him that he himself played that stroke successfully, he retorted, 'But I never pulled a ball until I was forty years of age.' And, as all great batsmen, he had an uncanny ability to place the ball between the fielders rather than straight at them – it must be remembered that he often had to contend with twenty-two. Daft described this gift as 'truly marvellous'.

Another difference with the game of today is that boundaries were only gradually introduced during W.G.'s career, so that many of his greatest innings consisted almost entirely of singles, which entailed an extraordinary amount of running between the wickets. Despite appearances, in later life at least, he was superbly fit. Many noticed how he never seemed to tire, but even after reaching a century would proceed relentlessly on. 'His astounding feats with the bat,' wrote Daft, 'could have been accomplished by no man, however good a player, who was not possessed of great physical advantages, and iron constitution, and who did not live temperately . . . In my opinion, the two great secrets of his success have been his great self-denial and his constant practise [sic].'

W.G. agreed wholeheartedly. 'Temperance in food and drink, regular sleep and exercise, I have laid down as the golden rule from my earliest cricketing days . . . The capacity for making long scores is not a thing of a day's growth . . . Great scores at cricket, like great work of any kind, are, as a rule, the results of years of careful and judicious training and not accidental occurrences.'

Which modern batsman resembles him most? I believe the nearest we have seen is Graham Gooch, who has many of W.G.'s characteristics: a formidable physical presence, devotion to fitness, not particularly stylish but highly effective, a ruthless accumulator of runs who never tired of batting and was still as good as anyone else in the country in his mid-forties.

W.G. was also patient, a discipline he had learned young. 'He was not in the strict sense a quick-scoring batsman, for he was content over after over to treat each ball on its merits,' wrote Gilbert Jessop, who joined W.G.'s Gloucestershire side when the great man was in his late forties. 'At the same time his mastery of all the strokes made run-getting appear a supremely easy matter.'

He could dig in and defend when the occasion demanded. Indeed, there are many instances of him being the only batsman in his side with the skill and determination to stay in on a bad wicket. The fact that he was reared in an era when pitches were poor, unreliable and often downright dangerous was a big factor in his make-up. He learned as a boy how to keep out 'grubbers' and it was not until he was approaching the age of thirty that pitches generally started to improve in quality. He therefore amassed some of his greatest innings on various dubious surfaces. A legacy of that period, thought Conan Doyle, was a habit of dragging the bat across the surface of the pitch as he played forward, presumably acquired in days when the ball was as likely to shoot along the ground as to bounce. Edward Lyttelton, too, remarked on W.G.'s 'unique play of the shooter' in this case the one aimed at leg stump: 'He brought down the bat with a curious dig, at such an angle that it not only went forcibly towards mid-on, but he positively placed it on each side of the field as he chose.'

Conan Doyle thought his greatest strength was his mastery of off-side play. Facing that most uncontrollable of all balls, the good-length ball outside the off stump, 'he did not flinch from it as a foe, but rather welcomed it as a friend, and stepping across the wicket while bending his great shoulders he watched it closely as it rose, and patted it with an easy tap through the slips'. Conan Doyle also admired the unflinching manner in which he faced up to the quickest bowling even when approaching the age of sixty. But then he always loved fast bowling. He had no weaknesses of technique or character but if he did have an Achilles' heel it was thought to be slow bowling. He could play the quick men all day but was more vulnerable when the pace dropped.

Charles Thornton, another Etonian, former captain of Cambridge University and one of the finest hitters the game has ever seen, noted: 'Slows bothered Grace most.' Jessop agreed, up to a point: 'Though slowness of foot did make him appear uncomfortable against leg-breaks, yet he rarely succumbed to them.' It may have been that he preferred the ball to come on to the bat and was always liable to 'have a go' at the slows and thereby be lured into an indiscreet shot. He was once expatiating, perhaps over a drink, one evening on how to hit one lob bowler: 'The way to play him is to hit him out of the ground,' he explained. Next morning he was quickly dismissed by his intended victim.

Grace retained masterly footwork until late in his career, when his increasing girth and bulk got the better of it. His nimbleness was all the more remarkable when one remembers that he had massive feet. (One damp morning, he and E.M. walked up and down a sodden Gloucestershire pitch for several hours with the same effect as a heavy roller and enabled the match to start on time.) All the greatest batsmen have had magical footwork; Len Hutton marvelled that Bradman's tiny feet were 'like Fred Astaire's'. But there is a parallel with Grace.

Several of W.G.'s contemporaries commented on his ability and panache as a dancer, remarking how he carried his mighty frame lightly across the floor, and he was always in great demand among the ladies at balls. There is a delightful story of Grace, on one such evening, inviting a younger team-mate to step outside and admire the night sky, which the young man duly did, only to turn around and see Grace waltzing off with his partner. That sort of footwork translated easily to the cricket pitch.

How heavy did he like his bat to be? There is conflicting evidence on this. In his book *Cricketing Reminiscences* he stated categorically: 'Personally I play with a bat weighing about 2lb 5oz, which, I think, is heavy enough for anybody.' But Alfred Lubbock recounted how W.G. boasted of wielding a bat weighing 2lb 9oz, heavier than anyone else's.

He was once asked how a certain delivery should be played. He thought for a momemt and then replied, 'I should say you ought to put the bat against the ball.' Like the greatest athletes, he didn't really think there was anything very extraordinary about what he did. It was only to ordinary people that it seemed so – and still seems so to this day.

THE BOWLER

As a young man, Grace was a brisk round-arm fast-medium-pacer, whose pace slowed down as his girth expanded. It is often forgotten that he was first selected for the Gentlemen in 1865 as a bowler, and his youthful action was described as attractive and 'slinging'. He appears to to have been a pretty straightforward sort of bowler who 'had not then acquired any of his subsequent craftiness with the ball'. He always had the knack of moving it away from the right-handed bat off the pitch – even in his fast days – which he developed when he reduced his speed. He could also produce the occasional slower ball, with the general idea of tempting the batsman into lofting a catch to long-leg, where Fred Grace, a brilliant fielder, was frequently the grateful recipient. It was a successful gambit, if an expensive one.

W.G. generally bowled from round the wicket, still wearing his red and yellow MCC cap, and his tall bearded figure must have presented a formidable aspect as he raced in to bowl. He tended to move swiftly across to the off side, a manoeuvre which he would not have been allowed to get away with these days for fear of roughing up the wicket, but in the mid- to late-1860s the wickets were so bad that even Grace's massive boots could not have made them much worse. It also brought him a lot of catches off his own bowling. What struck everybody was that he always bowled a good length; no one could ever recall a long-hop, which speaks of long hours of practice. He was always a perfectionist.

But it is his later style of bowling, adopted in the mid-1870s, that is of more interest. Once he had slowed down, his principal delivery was a gentle leg-break and his continuing success with it baffled most people. He looked utterly innocuous, from close up and from the pavilion, yet he lured batsmen out by the sackful, albeit expensively. Lord Hawke put it thus:

His obstinate persistence in invariably bowling one leg ball in every over must have cost thousands of runs, but when he did get a man caught by his leg-trap his glee was delightful. His bowling looked very easy from the pavilion, but it was a great mistake to underrate its artfulness, for he put just a little more or less work on his ball which was often deceptive.

Gilbert Jessop, who played under Grace for the first five seasons of his first-class career and the last five of W.G.'s, wrote in similar terms: 'Why such simple-looking, round-arm slow "stuff" should cause any uneasiness except perhaps among the tail-enders must have constantly puzzled thousands of spectators in their day.' Jessop, of course, refused to allow any bowler to dictate terms to him: he hit them all over the shop, regardless of reputation, but his own explanation was that W.G.'s secret weapon was the top-spinner, which surprised the batsman expecting the leg-break.

E.H.D. Sewell, who played under W.G. for London County Cricket Club when he was well into his fifties, went further: he believed the old man imparted not only top-spin but a sort of googly, that is, he could certainly move the ball into the batsman when he thought it was going the other way, and that while he propelled the ball slowly through the air, it came off the pitch much more quickly than the batsman expected.

W.G. believed that the most dangerous ball was one that broke only a little off the pitch. 'One of the great mistakes a bowler can make is to break too much,' he once wrote. 'If a bowler can only manage to make a ball break about three inches, and to do that quickly and imperceptibly, and at the same time hit the wicket if it gets past the batsman, he has learned the great secret of successful breaking.'

But W.G. thought that there was more to bowling than mere technical mastery. 'True skill in bowling involves head work – a good bowler bowls with his brain more than his arm . . . It is by the machinations of the slow bowler who uses his head that batsmen are most frequently tempted into the indiscretions which cost them their wickets.' This was an accurate description of his own *modus operandi*.

THE FIELDER

It is rare for a great batsman not to be a fine fielder too. The requirements are the same: a good eye and hands, quick feet, fast reflexes: W.G. had all these in abundance, and consequently was one of the best fielders and catchers of his time. There was a family tradition to keep up: E.M. was acknowledged to be the finest fielder in England, lurking with intent at point, which was also W.G.'s favourite position. Early in his career, while E.M. fielded at point, he would be stationed at mid-off or mid-on where his superb athleticism could be shown to good advantage. Then along came G.F., who was without doubt the best outfielder of his generation, a wonderful sight racing round the boundary to hold on to catches that no one else would have even got close to. When W.G. fielded at point, just as E.M. did, he gave the impression of snatching the ball off the face of the bat, so close did he crouch, the ball disappearing into those huge hands 'like a pea in a jar' as one contemporary put it. He took 875 first-class catches and countless others in club cricket.

W.G. had the priceless gifts for the fielder of stamina and concentration – and a keenness that no one could equal, even in his fifties, when his massive bulk made it difficult for him to bend down and reach the ball. But for thirty years he was as dominant in the field as with bat or ball. As a young man he was a magnificent thrower of a cricket ball. In a contest at Eastbourne he threw the ball 122 yards. On another occasion he threw it 109 yards in one direction and 105 the other way. As he aged, he preferred to bowl the ball in from the long field, recalled Lord Harris, who also remembered that he was always on the look-out to catch a batsman out of his ground.

You would see him occasionally face as if about to return the ball to the bowler, and instead send it underarm to the wicket-keeper, but I never saw him get anyone out that way.

He also loved to take the opportunity of keeping wicket and did so once in a Test match at The Oval in 1884. He was credited with five first-class stumpings. His enthusiasm caused the immortal remark to be made: 'That fellow would like to keep wicket to his own bowling.'

THE CAPTAIN

W.G. was captain more often than not, of Gloucestershire, the Gentlemen, London County, and the United South, although oddly enough he did not captain England until 1888, the year he turned forty. He was a natural, if rather unimaginative, leader, who led from the front, and his very presence in a team was a terrific morale-booster. He knew the value of encouragement. He was very good with young players, with a pat on the back and a gruff 'well played young 'un' for anybody who tried, even if he had failed. But he was no tactician. Lord Hawke, who knew a thing or two about captaincy, was dismissive: 'He was a remarkably good and encouraging judge of the cricket of others but one would scarcely say a good captain. Sometimes he would do strange things when in command.' He would often appear to have lost all interest in what was going on. Hawke remembered him allowing the same two bowlers to operate at Hastings while the batsmen put on 200 runs.

When it came to setting a field, W.G. took great care when he himself was bowling, but tended to be less bothered when anybody else was. If the bowler had no firm opinions, he would allow the fielders to spread themselves around in the traditional places, for he was no innovator. He did think deeply about the game but he did not react to changes in the game as it developed in the last two decades of the nineteenth century, spearheaded by the Australians, who brought in the notion of different fields for different bowlers. Grace was a traditionalist to the end.

The greatest criticism of him was that he overbowled himself, and there is little doubt that the accusation was justified. 'His little weakness was a desire to be always bowling,' was how Lord Hawke put it. He just could not bear to be out of the game, and could rarely accept that anybody else might be more capable of breaking a big partnership. Gilbert Jessop, for one, considered the criticism unfair: 'Though he loved bowling himself, it was very difficult in my time to get him to bowl enough,' he wrote, but that was towards the end of W.G.'s career – and Jessop was a very charitable man.

9 · DR GRACE

ON 27 October 1868, W.G. Grace was admitted to Bristol Medical School, continuing in the footsteps of his father and three older brothers. He must have been an awe-inspiring figure to his young contemporaries, for as a 1917 history of Bristol Royal Infirmary put it, 'he was in his twenty-first year and was already one of the most famous men in England'. However, he probably inspired less awe among his teachers. Students were required to pursue their studies for four years before presenting themselves for their final examination. It took W.G. more than a decade, constantly interrupted by the demands of his cricketing career, to qualify as a doctor. In the jargon of the era, he was a 'chronic', a permanent student, and the seemingly endless nature of his studies gave rise to a great deal of amused comment in the cricket world.

His time at the BMS coincided with a turbulent period in the institution's history. It came into being in 1826, the brainchild of an inspirational doctor named Henry Clark, who made space in his own home in King Square for lecture and demonstration rooms. It was given official recognition in 1828 and opened fully in 1833.

Some distinguished figures, and one or two eccentric ones, graced its staff. Among the former was William Budd, a pioneer of epidemiology and the first man to realise that tuberculosis was spread by microbes, a notion that he said suddenly occurred to him one morning as he walked on Durdham Down, where Henry Grace senior, a friend of his, had once practised cricket with his fellow medical students.

Among the eccentrics was Samuel Rootsey, a botany lecturer in the 1840s and 1850s, who had a chemist's shop in the city but preferred to wander the countryside studying rocks and plants and was several times imprisoned for debt. Undaunted by his own pecuniary problems, he confided in one prison visitor his plan for paying off the national debt – it involved planting the ocean with floating seaweed on which corn and other crops could be harvested. His lectures were notorious for their disorderliness because he was inclined to wander off the subject at the least excuse. Nor was erratic behaviour confined to the lecture halls. A surgeon at the Bristol Royal Infirmary in the 1850s and 1860s he once inflicted such a severe injury to his own nose with a long knife used for amputations, as he drew it back prior to use, that he required emergency treatment from his colleagues before he could proceed with the operation.

There were intimate links between the Medical School and the Royal Infirmary, where the students acquired the practical side of their profession. Grace entered as a pupil of Mr Robert Tibbitts, a fiery character who was only five years older than Grace and had been elected surgeon earlier that year. He was a bristling, impatient man of a reforming, radical cast of mind, with a quick temper. He was a strong advocate of the most modern techniques in antiseptic surgery and was always happy to demonstrate his undoubted ability as a surgeon to his students, to whom he was known as 'Slasher'.

His enthusiasm for higher standards of cleanliness in the operating theatre was understandable. In those days Bristol surgeons performed minor operations in their ordinary clothes. For major operations they would put on an old black cloth coat, rows of which hung in the consultation rooms ready for use. 'They must have been so full of germs that it is a wonder septic troubles were not even commoner than they were,' observed the BRI's historian, Dr G. Munro Smith. 'As late as 1895 I have seen a former member of the Infirmary staff, when operating in private, stick the needles he was to use for sewing up the wound in the bed curtains, "to be handy" as he expressed it.' Some of the dressers (the surgeons' assistants) carried their instruments in their waistbands in the theatre. One burly, bearded student 'represented a terrific aspect in the operation room, with saws, forceps and knives stuck into his belt, looking very much like a comic bandit'. (Could it have been W.G.?)

The physicians and surgeons did their ward rounds attired in silk top hats, while their students went bareheaded. It was a student's greatest ambition to 'pass the College' and be entitled to wear a topper himself. The custom slowly died out in the 1870s when one or two surgeons abandoned their hats, and the rest of the staff and students gradually followed suit.

Grace became an Assistant Pupil in December 1870 and a Physician's Pupil, under Dr Frederick Britan, in January 1872. He had entered the Medical School at a period of decline and crisis. Many lecturers had lost control of their students, who preferred to read newspapers rather than listen to their tutors. Lectures were often rowdy occasions, punctuated by practical jokes. Students in the dissecting rooms were left to their own devices. Indeed, at times the place seemed to be run by an elderly Irishman named William Fitzpatrick. 'His official capacity was that of porter but he usurped charge over everything, including lecturers and students,' wrote Munro Smith. 'He took the liberties of an indulged, eccentric servant and talked as if he had the management of the establishment. When I obtained one of the prizes at the school, he called and told my family that "he and the lecturers thought I deserved it".' In such a lax atmosphere, it is easier to understand how Grace managed to take as long he did to complete his studies. Anywhere else, he might have been invited to pursue his sporting career and forget about medicine.

Some of the senior staff at the Royal Infirmary were so concerned at the poor results of the medical school students in the Royal College of Surgeons' examinations that they demanded reforms and even proposed setting up a rival school. Tibbitts was active in the reform group, and the controversy reached the pages of the *Lancet*.

Finally a solution was reached. In 1876 the medical school affiliated with University College, Bristol, later to become the University of Bristol. Tibbitts died, aged only thirty-seven, only two months after the vital meeting that sanctioned the affiliation. The medical school moved into a new building, universally derided for its ugliness, in 1879, the year that W.G. finally qualified as a doctor, via two years at St Bartholomew's and Westminster Hospitals in London, becoming a Licentiate of the Royal College of Physicians at Edinburgh, and a Member of the Royal College of Surgeons. He was said to have owed his success in his final examinations to intensive coaching from Professor Howard Marsh at Bart's.

With the proceeds of the MCC's testimonial that summer, Dr and Mrs Grace were able to move into a house in Stapleton Road, Bristol, which included a surgery. W.G. settled down to the life of a general practitioner during the autumn and winter, plus some summer weekends, and cricket during most of the spring and summer. In 1880, the Gloucestershire committee agreed to pay him £20 to employ a locum for the summer months while he was away from his practice. But before the 1882 season began W.G. was complaining that the sum was not sufficient and the committee 'resolved that as Dr W.G. Grace was not satisfied at his allowance for expenses out of pocket last year he shall be allowed the sum of £6.1.0 towards paying his assistant in addition to the £20 already paid'. That obviously was not enough either. The following October, his allowance was increased to £36.15.0.

Grace's official title was surgeon, medical officer and public vaccinator to the Barton Hill district. It was a mixed practice, with patients of all classes who appear to have appreciated their famous doctor's services. W.G. administered to their health for twenty years, even though he and Agnes eventually moved out of the area. They first moved to Thrissel House, which was not far from Stapleton Road and had a garden just big enough to accommodate the cricket net W.G. found indispensable. The Graces then bought a bigger house in Victoria Square, Clifton, several miles away, but W.G. thought nothing of walking to and from his surgery, and of doing his rounds on foot. This constant exercise, which he had maintained since childhood, should not be underestimated when considering his tremendous fitness, which lasted into his sixties, apart from bad knees and other sporting injuries. The Graces' last residence in the area was another large house at Ashley Grange, not far from the county ground, which had been opened in 1889.

A great deal of attention was being paid to public health in Bristol as Dr Grace embarked on his professional practice. The Medical Officer of Health to the City and County produced his first annual report in 1886. It showed the city's population had grown from 202,950 in 1877 to 220,915, and steady progress was being made in reducing the death rate for children and adults. The infant mortality figure for 1877 had been 153.5 per 1,000 births; by 1886, this had come down to 149.1. In a study of death rates for the eight largest cities in England and Wales, Bristol's was the lowest. The main killers were tuberculosis, which was rampant in the 1880s, diarrhoea, measles, whooping cough, scarlet fever and diptheria. In 1875 an epidemic of scarlet fever had killed 408 people; by 1886 the disease's victims had been cut to 89 by improving sanitary conditions. Typhoid was an ever-present danger too: indeed, it killed W.G.'s only daughter, Bessie, in February 1899.

Dr Grace probably did more good for his patients by dispensing common sense rather than sophisticated medicine, and by virtue of his huge personality. For example, he was also medical officer to the Pennymills Collieries, five of whose workers were badly burnt in an explosion. They were taken to Bristol Royal Infirmary, and asked for W.G. to come and see them. Their faces were largely covered by dressings, but when he arrived he knew them all by name and raised their spirits merely by his presence and his sympathetic words.

There were many such stories, for instance of the old woman whom Grace was summoned to see, and who exclaimed when he arrived, 'Oh, it does me good just to see his face!'

There was a certain amount of evidence from the cricket field of Grace's abilities as a doctor. In 1887, he saved the life of his Gloucestershire team-mate A.C.M. Croome, who was involved in a horrific accident during a match against Lancashire at Old Trafford. Trying to cut off a four, Croome ran headlong into the railings in front of the pavilion and tore his neck so badly that he would have bled to death had not Grace rushed over and held the wound together for a full half-hour before a surgical needle and thread were found and the gash was stitched.

The Kent amateur C.J.M. Fox was also able to thank W.G. for his medical expertise, when he dislocated his shoulder while fielding against Gloucestershire. W.G. lumbered out of the pavilion and, while E.M. held on to Fox, manipulated the limb back into place with his huge hands. The same thing happened to Fox a couple of years later, as often happens when there is a weakness in the shoulder, but incredibly, it was once again in the Gloucestershire match. This time, E.M. put it back without the assistance of W.G., who was not playing.

As these incidents show, Grace's virtues as a doctor were largely that he was an intensely practical man although he had one interesting faculty that was highly prized by his medical colleagues: he was said to be able to smell smallpox as soon as he entered a sickroom. But H.R. (later Sir Henry) Leveson-Gower, for one, had his doubts about his medical abilities. When Leveson-Gower suffered a badly-bruised thumb while fielding at mid-off one day, he asked W.G. for an immediate opinion. 'He looked at it, gave it a pull, and I certainly felt much worse,' wrote Leveson-Gower. 'I said, "I shan't pay you for this treatment, Doctor – I shall want some money *from* you!" But he only laughed.'

As so often with W.G.'s cricketing career, there were a host of stories about his medical life that were probably apocryphal. For instance, he was said to have been asked to examine an old gentleman who was displaying signs of madness, with a view to certifying him. Dr Grace asked him several questions, one of which was: 'Have you a canary that talks?'

'No,' replied the old man, 'but I have seen you bowled for a duck.' W.G. certified him.

That one bears all the signs of fiction, but there were others that may have had more connection with reality. There were plenty of instances of him staying up all night attending to a sick patient or a sick infant and then going straight to the cricket ground to resume a match. In 1885 he was up all night helping a woman in childbirth, then went to the Clifton College ground to score 221 not out against Middlesex. He also took ten wickets in the match and Gloucestershire won by an innings.

In the 1930s the (now defunct) *Bristol Evening World* had the inspired idea of asking its readers to send in their own personal stories of W.G. It was already nearly half a century since he had left the city for ever but dozens of ordinary Bristolians contributed their memories. There were many of Dr Grace at work. Mrs G. Langbridge recalled her brother walking along Stapleton Road late one evening during an influenza epidemic and seeing a man knocking on W.G.'s closed surgery door. At length, an upstairs window was thrown open and the familiar bearded face appeared to ask what was wrong. The man shouted up that his wife was ill again, and could the doctor visit her right away? W.G. was disinclined to oblige. 'Warm half a pint of old beer and give her that,' was his prescription. 'I'll see her in the morning. She'll be all right.'

The local chimney-sweep, who liked a drink, once called in at the surgery and asked for a pick-me-up. 'Mary,' W.G. shouted up to the maid at the top of the stairs, 'throw down those boxing gloves.' Turning to the chimney-sweep, he said, 'You want exercise, not medicine.' The man fled, shouting to a friend in the street, 'The big blackguard wants to fight me.'

But there was no doubt that W.G. had a soft heart and a deep concern for his poorer patients' welfare. One winter day, he called on a sick woman in a slum house and was appalled to see that there was no fire, despite the bitter cold. Told that the woman's husband was out trying to earn a few pence to buy fuel, W.G. told her to send him round to the surgery for her medicine, which he would doubtless have given him for nothing. As he left, he gave her little boy what he thought was a penny – but it was half-a-crown. When her husband came back, his wife insisted he take the coin to the surgery and tell the doctor about his mistake. When he did so, W.G. told him to keep the money, added another half-a-crown, and later helped the man to find a job.

In March 1888, the district was flooded, and to reach a patient W.G. had to commandeer a water-police patrol boat to make the risky crossing through the raging waters by the Monkland Bridge. Immune to physical fear, he did not turn a hair.

On the cricket field, he may have preferred public schoolboys to mere artisans, but in his neighbourhood he had no pretensions to social superiority. One reader remembered, as a boy, playing snowballs in the street when W.G. appeared on the way to see a patient.

He joined in the game with us and quite a crowd gathered, women throwing at him and he pelting them. I can see him now stooping down and picking up the snow and roaring with laughter. He seemed to be the youngest boy there.

W.G. could never resist snow. On another winter's day, he was standing in his surgery door watching four boys playing snowballs when a man wearing a top hat came round the corner. The temptation was too much for W.G. He fashioned a snowball and hurled it at the man with the accuracy of the fine fielder he was, knocking off his topper. Then he disappeared back into his surgery while the man berated the boys. When he had gone, W.G. reappeared, hugely amused, and gave the boys half-a-crown.

Out on his rounds, he was walking past Lawford's Gate Prison on a winter afternoon when the schools closed for the day. Out poured the children, some of whom started bombarding W.G. with snowballs, aiming particularly at his silk hat. He stopped, made himself a pile of snowballs and bombarded his attackers in return. Then he strolled off, doubtless delighted with his day's sport.

Visiting a sick man one evening, W.G. arrived just as his wife was putting out the supper. 'That smells nice,' said W.G. 'Would you like some?' asked the woman, to which he replied he would like 'a snack' if it could be spared. She served him a plate of steak and fried onions which he polished off appreciatively. 'That was lovely,' he said. As the provider of the story commented: 'He was a good gentleman, with no pride whatever.'

He was less pleased at another patient's house to which he had been called to attend to a sick baby. The mother was making a roly-poly pudding when he knocked. She hastily put the board with the dough on a chair before opening the door. W.G. attended to the baby, then sat down to write a prescription – on the chair with the dough-board.

His medical career came to an abrupt end in 1899, when the Poor Law Unions in Bristol were amalgamated. He and several other doctors resigned in protest at the way their own practices would be affected. But unlike the others, W.G. had plenty to fall back on: he had just received the proceeds of a national testimonial worth about £250,000 in today's money, and had been offered the job of running the London County Cricket Club at Crystal Palace in south-east London. So the decision may not have been a difficult one, although, at fifty-one, he might have thought there was at least a decade of doctoring left in him. He may not have been a great loss to medicine, but his patients mourned his departure for years.

10 · ENTER THE DEMON
1878–1879

W.G.'s concentration on his medical studies meant that he missed the early part of the 1878 season. In May he became a father for the third time, when his daughter Bessie was born.

The year marked another watershed, not for one man but for the whole of English cricket. English sides had toured Australia four times but the visit had never been reciprocated. Now for the first time an Australian party arrived to tour England and the impact they made on the domestic game was profound. By winning 18 and drawing 12 matches out of a gruelling programme of 37 games with a party of only twelve men, they well and truly exploded the myth of English invincibility. But they also imported new playing habits and practices which helped to transform the game in England.

Led by David Gregory, whose nephews Sydney and J.M. were to be Test stars of the next century, they impressed with their teamwork, preparation and general slickness. Their batting was moderate; it was their bowling which time and again devastated the English club and county sides, led by the quartet of Allan, Boyle, Garrett and, above all, Spofforth, whom Grace had no hesitation in designating as the world's finest. (It was the beginning of a long tradition of Antipodean teams taking sports invented by the English to new levels with an injection of fresh ideas and a much higher standard of fitness and athleticism. In the 1930s and 1940s Don Bradman led a succession of teams that dominated the cricket world. The Australian rugby league tourists of 1988 carried all before them but, more than that, created a new standard of speed and mobility by which all subsequent British sides were to be judged. Not long after that, the Australian rugby union team that won the 1991 World Cup did much the same.)

After a low-key start (losing to Notts at Trent Bridge), the Australians exploded on to the national scene in the legendary match against MCC, containing the cream of English cricket, at Lord's on 27 May. It was to all intents and purposes a Test match. Scheduled to be a normal three-day game, it was all over in a single, unforgettable day. By then, W.G. was playing again and despite his lack of match practice he was an automatic choice. It had been a wet May which had not done the Lord's track any good and it rained again on the morning of what was meant to be the first day. This incidentally kept the crowd down to a mere five hundred or so, who were treated to a quite extraordinary day. The sun then came out and dried the pitch to the perfect 'sticky dog' and then went in again, for Spofforth remembered the Australians shivering in the field in their silk shirts, 'not one of the team having a sweater'.

MCC batted first, W.G. opening with A.N. 'Monkey' Hornby. Australia's attack was opened by the slow-medium left-armer Allan. W.G. struck his opening delivery to the leg boundary for four but that was MCC's first and last opportunity to celebrate. Fielding at square leg was Gloucestershire's new recruit Billy Midwinter. Grace pushed Allan's second delivery in the same direction as the first but this time he was easily caught by his new county colleague. Spofforth called it 'a shocking bad stroke' and MCC never recovered. They were shot out for 33 in an hour and five minutes largely though a savage spell by Spofforth, bowling first change, of six wickets for only 4 runs in 5.3 overs. The Australians fared little better, totalling only 41.

Thus by mid-afternoon, when the crowd had grown tenfold as word spread of the amazing turn of events, MCC embarked on their second innings and contrived to fare even worse. Having been dropped at the wicket by Murdoch off the first ball he faced, W.G. again went second ball, clean bowled for a duck by Spofforth. The bowler recalled: 'The . . . ball knocked his leg bail thirty yards, and I screamed out "Bowled".'

The crowd greeted the wicket 'with extravagant delight', according to the *Sportsman*. W.G. did go out to the middle once more, to act as runner for Hornby, but was not called upon to expend much energy. MCC were all out for the derisory total of 19 (Boyle 6–3, Spofforth 4–16), leaving Australia 12 to win, which they duly did by nine wickets. The humiliation of MCC and of W.G. was complete. Spofforth's performance earned him the sobriquet 'Demon' by which he would always be known.

Spofforth had a good record against W.G. You can almost hear the laconic Australian accent in his comment: 'I never had any particular difficulty in getting him out. I clean bowled him seven times.' Spofforth reckoned most bowlers were so in awe of Grace that they held back against him (and therefore presumably enabled him to plunder them even more easily). 'Never in my case,' he added. He was not averse to a bit of psychological warfare against W.G. He always posted a silly mid-on for him, which he claimed worried him, and in addition would wrap his fingers around the ball in a strange fashion because he knew Grace would be scrutinising him carefully. Indeed, he claimed to have dismissed him at least once by persuading him to play for a non-existent off-cutter which carried straight on and had him leg before. It appears that Spofforth was more than a match for Grace in the mental game at which the Englishman generally excelled.

Grace played twice more against the Australians that summer. He appeared for Gentlemen of England at Prince's, where the playing area had shrunk still further because of building developments on the perimeter, and made a handy contribution to the Gentlemen's innings and one run victory, scoring 25 and taking 6–52 in the match. But the Australians had their revenge when they took on Gloucestershire at Bristol, inflicting the county's first-ever home defeat by a crushing 10-wicket margin. Spofforth was again the bogeyman, taking 12–90 in the match and rubbing salt in the wound with a top score of 44. He took particular pleasure in hammering the bowling of Grace, who incurred some criticism for keeping himself on too long. Perhaps he was determined to get his own back on Spofforth but, if he was, the plan misfired badly.

The Australian tour provoked one extraordinary incident involving W.G. It concerned Midwinter, who was contracted to play for both Gloucestershire and the tourists. According to Grace, Midwinter had promised him he would turn out for the county in all its matches but when the West Country men arrived at The Oval to play Surrey, they were told that Midwinter was unavailable as he was appearing for the Australians at Lord's.

This was too much for W.G. Accompanied by E.M. or the burly wicketkeeper Arthur Bush, and by one account both of them, he hailed a cab and headed for St John's Wood in high dudgeon. Back at Kennington, the start of play was delayed because of the the sudden absence of the Gloucestershire captain. At Lord's, W.G. marched in, confronted Midwinter and somehow persuaded him to desert his compatriots and return with him to The Oval, where E.M. had finally tossed, in his brother's continuing absence, and put Surrey in, Gloucestershire taking the field with three substitutes.

W.G. never explained how he pulled off what amounted to a kidnapping. One can only surmise that he appealed more to Midwinter's wallet than his better nature. He was immediately pressed into service with the ball, taking 1–36 off 27 overs, while W.G., doubtless invigorated by his successful raid, returned the highly economical figures of 43.3–21–43–4.

The Australians were furious and mounted an unsuccessful expedition to attempt to recover their man from the clutches of the enemy. They were not content to let the matter rest, for Midwinter was now ineligible to play for them any more on the tour, having appeared for a county. Their manager, Conway, bombarded Gloucestershire's secretary, E.M., with protest letters. The affair was finally settled when W.G. climbed down and sent an abject letter of apology in July, particularly for his 'use of unparliamentary language to Mr Conway. I can do no more but assure you that you will meet a hearty welcome and a good ground at Clifton'.

When the Australians arrived at Clifton in September, Midwinter sat the game out with an injured thumb, which was perhaps just as well. The tourists extracted a measure of revenge by beating the county comprehensively, dismissing W.G. for 22 and 5 in the course of a ten-wicket victory wrapped up in less than two days. Spofforth not only took 12–90 in the match but was top-scorer too, with 44. It was the first time Gloucestershire had lost at home.

There were few other excitements in 1878. Grace scored only one first-class century, for his county against Nottinghamshire at Trent Bridge. The Midlanders had one of the strongest attacks in the country and Grace's second-innings 116 was an example of him at his most patient and watchful: it took him five hours and twenty-five minutes, although he should have been stumped on 85. Eventually he 'fluked a ball up to point, and retired amid deafening cheers'.

W.G.'s next best score, but his finest display of the season, was a sparkling 90 for the Gentlemen v Players at Lord's, terminated only by a brilliant one-handed catch by Alfred Shaw. In the first Gentlemen v Players game at The Oval in early July he opened the innings as usual and was last man out, having ground out a dogged 40 while his team-mates amassed only 36 between them. Fred Grace, with 10, was the only other batsman to reach double figures. Facing a deficit of 46, the Gentlemen were struggling on 45–3 when Fred came in to join W.G. and transform the situation. In the liveliest batting seen so far in the game, the brothers put on 89 before W.G. was given out lbw to Barlow for 63. 'I don't fear the bowlers but I do fear the umpires,' he gruffly observed back in the dressing-room, but Fred went on to make 35. The Gentlemen totalled 202, and dismissed the Players for 101 (W.G. 3–20) to run out convincing winners by 56 runs. For the South v North in the Whit weekend fixture at Lord's, before a crowd of more than ten thousand holidaymakers, he scored 45 and 77 and took nine wickets.

There was an even bigger crowd at Old Trafford to watch Gloucestershire's first match against Lancashire, where some eighteen thousand people were estimated to have squeezed into the ground, a couple of thousand of them scrambling over the walls after losing patience with the long queues at the gates. This is the match that inspired the most famous poem about cricket, by the Lancastrian Francis Thompson (1859–1907), although its title 'At Lord's' is liable to mislead. The refrain at the end of the first and last stanzas has achieved immortality but the references to the Graces are less well known.

It is little I repair to the matches of the Southron folk,
　　Though my own red roses there may blow;
It is little I repair to the matches of the Southron folk,
　　Though the red roses crest the caps, I know.
For the field is full of shades as I near the shadowy coast,
And a ghostly batsman plays to the bowling of a ghost,
And I look through my tears on a soundless-clapping host
　　As the runs-stealers flicker to and fro,
　　To and fro:
O my Hornby and my Barlow long ago!

It is Glo'ster coming North, the irresistible,
　　The Shire of the Graces, long ago!
It is Gloucestershire up North, the irresistible,
　　And newly-risen Lancashire the foe!
A Shire so young that has scarce impressed its traces,
Ah how shall it stand before all-resistless Graces?
O, little red rose, their bats are as maces
　　To beat thee down, this summer long ago!

This day of seventy-eight they are come up North against thee,
　　This day of seventy-eight, long ago!
The champion of the centuries, he cometh up against thee,
　　With his brethren, every one a famous foe!
The long-whiskered Doctor, that laugheth rules to scorn,
While the bowler, pitched against him, bans the day that he was
　　born;
And G.F. with his science makes the fairest length forlorn;
　　They are come from the West to work thee woe!

It is little I repair to the matches of the Southron folk,
　　Though my own red roses there may blow;
It is little I repair to the matches of the Southron folk,
　　Though the red roses crest the caps, I know.
For the field is full of shades as I near the shadowy coast,
And a ghostly batsman plays to the bowling of a ghost,

And I look through my tears on a soundless-clapping host
  As the runs-stealers flicker to and fro,
  To and fro:
O my Hornby and my Barlow long ago!

Many will have read this poem and mistakenly assumed that 'the long-whiskered Doctor, that laugheth rules to scorn' was W.G. It was a perfectly accurate description of him, but Thompson was referring to E.M., to whom it also applied one hundred per cent. W.G. did not qualify as a doctor until the following year. Before that he was often described in the Press as 'Mr Gilbert Grace', while E.M. was 'the doctor'. Once W.G. had qualified, he took over the appellation of 'doctor' while E.M. was promoted to 'the coroner'.

It may not have been a vintage season but W.G. was still one of only two batsmen to exceed 1,000 first-class runs, and he finished second in the aggregate table, with 1,151. He also collected 152 wickets.

The following season – 1879 – was even more restricted for W.G. as it was his final year at medical school. He missed the whole of May but perhaps it was just as well. The winter of 1878–9 was particularly severe, the snow lasting in places until the early spring and it was followed by the wettest summer in living memory and a thoroughly gloomy one for cricket. When play was possible W.G. produced his best form for Gloucestershire, hitting centuries against Surrey, Notts, and Somerset. Against Surrey at The Oval he made 123 and Fred 57 in a total of 239, and took nine wickets in setting up a ten-wicket victory.

At Trent Bridge, he delighted the largest crowd of the season with a vintage 102 in a total of only 197, as well as taking 4–54 off 54 overs in Notts' first innings. When Somerset arrived for the start of the Clifton Fortnight, they found W.G. at the top of his form. On the first day alone, he took 6–30 while Somerset struggled to 126, then marched out to plunder 113 out of Gloucestershire's 200–3 by close of play, including one gigantic pull for six out of the ground and into the road.

Against Middlesex, the next visitors to Clifton, he made a masterly 85 in the first innings (sharing a partnership of 160

with W.R. Gilbert) and 81 not out in the second on a tricky
wicket to save the game and Gloucestershire's proud record of
never having lost at home to another county. The following match
in the Clifton Fortnight was against Lancashire and was a benefit
for Billy Midwinter. Grace produced yet another extraordinary
all-round display, first taking 7–37 as the northerners were skittled
for 53 on a drying wicket, then making 75 not out by stumps
out of 123–7, showing again how his technique placed him head
and shoulders above anyone else then playing. (Unluckily for
Midwinter, the match had to be abandoned as a draw without a
further ball being bowled next day because of heavy rain.) In the
return against Surrey at Cirencester, W.G. took fifteen wickets in
the match.

But his finest hour had nothing to do with his performances on
the field. In the summer he passed his final medical examinations
and qualified to practise as a doctor. Two years previously the
MCC committee had agreed an unprecedented honour for W.G.
proposed by its president, the Duke of Beaufort, and treasurer,
Lord Fitzhardinge – a national collection in recognition of his
'extraordinary play' and 'great services to cricket'. A subscription
list was opened and all the counties and clubs circulated. The
response from wealthy individuals and ordinary members of the
public was generous. The MCC chipped in with 100 guineas, the
Surrey, Kent and Yorkshire clubs each gave £50, and the Prince of
Wales, who resembled Grace somewhat in figure if not athleticism,
contributed £5. A special benefit match, Over Thirties v Under
Thirties, was arranged for 21–23 July at Lord's.

Grace would not hear of the proceeds going to himself. In a
gesture of extraordinary generosity, he insisted that all the receipts
should go to his great adversary (on the field, that is) Alfred Shaw,
whose own benefit earlier in the season had been ruined by rain.
For a professional like Shaw, his benefit was crucial to his future
financial well-being, and unlike today there were no secondary
activities to generate money. Now thanks to Grace he had a second
chance, though this was at risk from the weather too. The omens
were not good; it had rained heavily in previous days, the first day
dawned overcast and the drenched ground was not really fit for

cricket. But play was started in front of a disappointingly small crowd at 1.20 p.m., the under-thirties batting. W.G. was cheered as he stepped on to the field accompanied by E.M. The fielders could hardly stand, let alone chase the ball. The youngest Grace, Fred, was naturally enough playing for the under-thirties. W.G. dropped him at short leg and he was undefeated on 35 when the innings closed at 111 (W.G. 3–54) after an interruption for more rain. On his big day, W.G. did not even receive the easy ball for a single which it later became the custom to deliver to a beneficiary. He was bowled by Morley of Notts third ball for a duck.

At lunchtime on the second day there was a presentation, in front of the pavilion by Lord Fitzhardinge, to W.G. of a clock (worth £40), bronze and marble obelisks, and a cheque for £1,458, £770 of it raised in Gloucestershire alone, the rest by MCC. Because of the overcast weather and sparse crowd, both in the pavilion and round the ground, the occasion lacked the atmosphere it deserved, but those present made as much noise as they could. Fitzhardinge told them that before the previous Christmas the trustees of the Gloucestershire collection, who included the Duke of Beaufort, had at first thought of buying Grace a doctor's practice but he had not passed his final examination at that stage so they decided to hang on to the money for the time being. Now that Grace had qualified, they thought him 'old enough and strong enough' to buy his own practice, so it had been decided to amalgamate the county and MCC collections and present Grace with the money.

Grace made a brief but touching reply. He was not a speech-maker, he said, and wished he could find words to express his gratitude. The testimonial had far exceeded his expectations. Typically, he switched the emphasis to Alfred Shaw, regretting that both his benefit matches had been spoiled by rain and hoping that MCC would consider granting him a third, if not this year, then another. 'He was deeply sensible of the kindness he had received from cricketers,' the *Sportsman* reported him as saying, 'and he should never look at the clock to see the time without thinking of this happy occasion.'

Lord Charles Russell, one of MCC's most distinguished members, spoke eloquently and movingly of W.G.'s unique contribution to the game (as well as promising to make the money up to £1,500, which he felt a more suitable figure than £1,458). He even felt able to tease the great man before launching into praise:

I agree with some friends that we have seen better bowling than we see now. You must not be surprised then to hear me say that I have seen better bowlers than Mr Grace, but I can say with a clear conscience that I have never seen anyone approach him as a batter, that I have never seen a better field. But he might be the good bowler that he is, the fine field, and the grand batter, without being a thorough cricketer; more than usual dexterity and agility of limb are required to play cricket – the game must be played with head and heart, and in that respect Mr Grace is very prominent. I have often seen an England Eleven playing an uphill game steadily and well; a sudden change had placed the game in their favour, and a change came over the field, such as there would be were the sun now to break out over our heads. Looking at Mr Grace playing, I have never been able to tell whether he was playing a losing or a winning game. I have never seen the slightest lukewarmness or inertness in him in the field. Should anyone want to know how he plays cricket let him look at him playing one ball. You all know the miserably tame effect of the ball hitting the bat instead of the bat hitting the ball, but whether acting on the defensive or offensive, in playing a ball Mr Grace puts every muscle into it, from the sole of his foot to the crown of his head; and just as he played one ball so he played the game – he was heart.

When considering this encomium, it is worth remembering that W.G. was still a week short of his thirty-first birthday.

But as with almost everything in which the Graces were involved, the testimonial was not without controversy. The net receipts of the Gloucestershire v Yorkshire match at Clifton College were designated as part of the county's contribution to the fund-raising exercise. Without consulting the county committee, E.M. announced that the entrance charge for the match would be a shilling, double the usual rate. Several members of the committee were outraged and five resigned in protest, but after a series of acrimonious meetings E.M. got his way, as the Graces usually did. But the combination of the high-mindedness that W.G. had shown towards Shaw and the mercenary ruthlessness that E.M. exercised for his brother's benefit was somehow rather typical of the family.

II · A DEATH IN THE FAMILY
1880–1884

THE 1880s saw several important developments in cricket: the rapid rise in popularity of the county game, a new era of professional players, particularly batsmen, and the swift progress of the game in Australia, including several tours of England which confirmed that the gap in standards between the two countries had narrowed and ultimately disappeared. As the game in England grew in popularity, standards improved at every level, from batting and bowling to the quality of pitches.

In the 1870s W.G. had been top of the first-class batting averages every year but one (1875, when he still scored most runs). He topped the averages in 1880 but thereafter never again although he was often the heaviest scorer. In the first few years of the 1880s he was diverted by his new professional responsibilities, attending to his medical practice in Bristol and usually starting the first-class season late.

So in 1880 he played club cricket in Gloucestershire during May and June, scoring heavily, as might have been expected, for the likes of Thornbury, Lansdown and Bristol Medicals. For the Gentlemen v Players on a damp and deadly Lord's pitch he compiled a monumentally patient 49 in 160 minutes, another exemplary display of coping with the shooter. Returning to HQ, he scored a much more typically brisk 51 and 49 for the Over-Thirties v the Under-Thirties.

It was not until August that he really hit top form, with a

series of excellent scores for Gloucestershire. Against Yorkshire at Clifton he made 89 and 57 not out to win the match against the clock, of which the *Bristol Evening News* commented: 'The captain was evidently on his mettle and hit out in rattling style . . . W.G. carried out his bat . . . in quite his old style.' Other good performances were against Middlesex at Lord's (69), Surrey at Cheltenham (67, 31 not out and 7–65), and Lancashire at Clifton (106) at the end of the month.

This was his first first-class century of the season, and he made it out of 223, having put himself down the batting order at number seven. Lancashire had made 186 (W.G. 4–53) and at 58–5 Gloucs were in danger of following on, but W.G. at seven and E.M. at eight (what a pair to have coming in as lower-order batsmen) stopped the rot and turned the match. W.G. dislocated the Lancashire bowler Barlow's finger with a stinging cut but he returned to the field and with the first ball of a new spell had E.M. given out caught at the wicket, 'the decision being loudly disputed by W.G.'

When he was out, caught at slip, he had been at the crease for 175 minutes. 'He went in at a most critical stage of the innings, and throughout he played in the vigorous style that has characterised his performance during the past fortnight,' said the *Sportsman*. 'In all-round play he has again shown himself the foremost cricketer of his time, and his present contribution . . . was in the very best form of his younger days.' The result was that Gloucestershire won by seven wickets.

The match against Surrey gave rise to one of the great Grace stories, involving the three brothers. Both sides had made high first-innings totals (Surrey 285, Gloucs 351) and it was only after lunch on the third and final day that Surrey went in again. A draw looked the likeliest outcome and at the luncheon interval Fred Grace, in high spirits, laid odds of either 100–1 or 5–1 (depending on the authority) on that result. Both W.G. and the Surrey player L.A. Shuter, a friend of Fred's, swiftly accepted the bet.

Surrey were dismissed for 117, leaving Gloucestershire 52 to win in forty-five minutes. Being the quickest scorer in the team, E.M. assumed he would open and show Fred what a bad judge he was, but as he was strapping on the pads saw his other brother striding out to the middle with W.R. Gilbert. 'There they go,' growled the Coroner, 'the slowest pair of run-getters in England.' They knocked off the runs in twenty-five minutes and Fred had to pay up.

Another Grace brother, Henry, who was usually to be found watching Gloucestershire's home matches, played a shrewd part in events: before Surrey batted again, he took W.G. and Midwinter, Gloucestershire's most effective bowlers, into the refreshment tent and bought them a pint of champagne each. Thus restored, the two skittled Surrey out, W.G. taking seven wickets. Perhaps the formula should be tried out on England's bowlers today.

All this was a mere prelude to the big event of the cricketing year, the first Test Match in England, against Australia. When one considers its significance, it is strange to realise that it was nearly not played at all. After the pioneering work done by several England tours of Australia, including Grace's of 1873/74, and the successful venture to England by the Australian team of 1878, relations between the two cricketing communities had cooled sharply as a result of a riot at Sydney during Lord Harris's team's tour in 1878/79, when thousands of angry spectators invaded the pitch intent on lynching the umpire and possibly a few Englishmen as well.

The Australians were due to tour England in 1880 but it was not until late spring that this was confirmed, by which time the county fixture list was in place. The Australians duly arrived to find they had nobody decent to play. All they could muster was a series of meaningless games against club sides far below their own standard. They were even reduced to advertising for opponents. Yorkshire contrived to play them twice, unofficially, but for most of the season it looked as if there would be no game against an England side. Grace tried to fix one up, the proceeds to go to the Cricketers' Fund, but failed.

Only at the end of August did Lord Harris, Grace and C.W. Alcock manage to arrange a three-day match at The Oval for 6–8 September. It was very late in the season, and most of the leading amateurs had to be summoned from their shooting on the moors, a telling indication of the social climate of the day. Grace was no exception; he was at Kingsclere in Hampshire for a few days' shooting and thought he might be out of practice for the big match.

The fixture caught the public imagination, which perhaps demonstrates how out of touch the cricket authorities were with popular demand. Fifty thousand people were estimated to have watched over the three days. The atmosphere on the first morning was electric. As the *Sportsman* reported:

From an early hour amateur cricketers by the thousand streamed into the ground and took up positions to see the game with a perseverance and a skill which were both alike admirable. Stands improvised from water-carts and steps from office-stools and Windsor-chairs, from old orange boxes, from little Plevnas [Plevna was a Bulgarian town taken by Russia from the Turks in 1877 after a siege lasting 143 days] of dirt which were hastily thrown up, and had to be stoutly defended against attack – stands, in fact, of all kinds and sizes were the general order of the day.

The roofs, balconies and windows of the houses which overlooked The Oval were packed; some even got on to the top of the famous gas-holder. 'Men of an aspiring turn of mind swarmed the large tree which grows near one of the entrances of The Oval, and this leafy monarch of all it surveyed bore about as dense a crop of human fruit as was ever seen looking proudly over the heads of the rest of creation.' When the Australians were recognised they were given hearty cheers. The crowd grew throughout the day so that after lunch (i.e. 2.45 p.m.) 'The Oval was literally packed, and anyone who could have bought it for export with its various adjuncts would have been able to send abroad a fairly representative slice of English life'. The official total of paying customers was 20,736 'and a more orderly crowd has never been seen on a cricket field'.

The three Grace brothers had all been selected for this historic fixture. Lord Harris won the toss and W.G. and E.M. walked out to open the batting to more cheers and applause. The wicket was in perfect condition and the weather had cooled after a heatwave that had gripped London in the previous weeks. The Graces

were doubtless cheered by the news that the great Spofforth had
withdrawn on the eve of the match because of an injury to his right
hand. The Australian attack, deprived of its most potent weapon,
did not trouble the Graces. The 50 came up in forty-five minutes,
60 in an hour, and 'a splendid cut for four by W.G. brought down
the house' and brought up 80. At 91 E.M. holed out to mid-off
for 36, but W.G. sailed serenely on and when the luncheon bell
rang at 2 p.m., the score was 167–1, Grace on 82 and the crowd
in raptures.

After lunch, Grace, partnered by A.P. Lucas, began to score
even faster and soon reached his century, to loud cheers. He was
dropped in front of the pavilion on 134 and finally bowled by
Palmer for 152, made out of 281, with ten fours. 'The general
satisfaction felt at the splendid cricket he had shown was proved
by the universal applause showered on him.'

England's total was 420, Australia's only 149, so they followed
on 271 behind and at the end of the second day looked down and out
on 170–6. Then came one of cricket's great rearguard actions, with
Australia's captain Billy Murdoch batting doggedly on through the
morning of the third day to top Grace's total by one run and help
add 140 for the last two wickets. Although George Giffen was later
labelled 'the Australian W.G.' for his all-round ability, Murdoch
was a nearer equivalent, a big, imposing but good-humoured man
who captained his country in six series against England and, like
W.G., loved to accumulate big scores, including the first Test
double century at The Oval in 1884. It was not surprising that he
and W.G. should become firm friends. Faced with only 57 to win,
England nearly bungled it, losing five for 20, before W.G. came
out and, with Frank Penn, steered his country to victory without
further loss of wickets.

Of the Graces, only Fred failed with the bat, suffering the
indignity of a 'pair' but, ever the superb athlete in the field, he
redeemed himself with probably the most famous catch in the
history of the game. Bonnor, who stood 6ft 6in tall, sent up such
a mighty hit that the batsmen had crossed for two before Fred,
racing round the boundary, clutched it safely to his chest. The
distance from wicket to where he caught it was measured by the

A rare photograph of W.G. horsing around, at the Hastings Festival. The pipe-smoker is the Kent all-rounder Jack Mason. On the left is Lord Hawke

In the rough-and-ready changing room at Cumberland Lodge, Windsor, with A.J. Webbe (centre) and Jack Mason, for the match between Albert, Duke of Schleswig-Holstein's XI v Charterhouse, in 1911

Life outside cricket: Practising his drive (BBC Hulton Picture Library)

With his wife Agnes. She was rarely photographed

With David Munro at the Mid-Surrey Golf Club, September 1893 (*MCC Library*)

Playing bowls at Crystal Palace

With the Worcester Park beagles, 1908

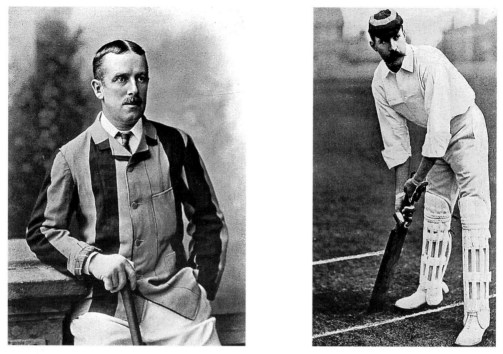

Four of W.G.'s key contemporaries: Albert 'Monkey' Hornby of Lancashire and England, frequently his opening partner; Andrew Stoddart of Middlesex and England, a great batsman and friend whom W.G. claimed to have invented as a bowler

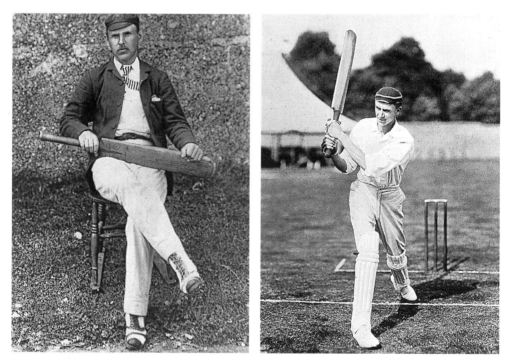

Arthur Shrewsbury of Nottinghamshire and England, his favourite batsman; and Charles Townsend of Gloucestershire and England, whom W.G. picked for the county at the age of sixteen

Two fast men who between them caused W.G. no end of trouble at the crease.
Frederick Spofforth, 'The Demon' from Australia who destroyed MCC – including Grace – at Lord's on one epic day in 1878; and Charles Kortright of Essex who angered W.G. just before his Jubilee match in 1898 and then partnered him in a memorable last-wicket stand

With his sons W.G. junior (left) and Charles Butler Grace

A disgruntled W.G. leaves the crease, Crystal Palace in the background

Still playing vigorously for Eltham at Gravesend in 1913

W.G.'s last game, Eltham v Grove Park in July 1914. He scored 69 not out

Contributing to a collection for Belgian refugees at a charity match, Catford Bridge, 1915

One of the last photographs of W.G., outside the front door of his home, Fairmount, Mottingham, where he died in October 1915

groundsman and found to be 115 yards. Little did the cheering crowd, or anyone else on the ground, know that they would never see Fred again.

From The Oval the youngest Grace went straight to Stroud, Gloucestershire, to play in a three-day match for the United South against a local XXII lasting from Thursday 9 September to Saturday 11 September. It rained heavily on Thursday and again on Saturday and Fred got wet on both occasions. Although he was not feeling well, he managed to score 44 in one innings, and arrived home at Downend on the Sunday. He had a cold and a cough, which he was thought to have acquired at Stroud, although he also mentioned he had slept in damp sheets somewhere. He stayed at home until Tuesday, when he set off for Basingstoke, *en route* to a benefit match at Winchester starting on Wednesday, although his family did not think him well enough to travel. He, however, said he felt well enough to go and stayed at the Red Lion Hotel in Basingstoke on Tuesday night.

Next morning he was about to leave for Winchester when a friend, Dr Frere Webb, became concerned about his health and ordered him to return to bed. Next day Dr Webb found that Fred's right lung was affected and wrote to his eldest brother, Henry, a surgeon at Kingswood, Gloucestershire, asking him to come urgently. Meanwhile W.R. Gilbert arrived to look after his cousin. Henry arrived on Saturday and, finding Fred improving, departed that evening. He returned on Monday, when Fred still appeared to be on the mend. Early on Wednesday morning, however, he took a sudden turn for the worse and Webb and Gilbert sent telegrams to Henry and W.G. Henry had gone off to Bradford and W.G. headed there to tell him personally that he was needed in Basingstoke. Meanwhile their sister, Mrs Dann, and her husband, rushed to Basingstoke but were too late: Fred died at about noon on Wednesday 22 September 1880 the infection having spread to both lungs. W.G. and Henry received the news as they were about to leave Bradford.

It was a terrible blow for the whole family, the youngest child being the first to die. It was all the more difficult to bear because Fred had always been in such good health. More than that, he was

185

a captivating character and popular in all the circles in which he moved.

As a cricketer, he was in the next category beneath his incomparable older brother, a batsman who loved to attack, a good quick bowler and a fielder without equal in England. The news of his death, coming so soon after he appeared among the world's finest players at The Oval, shocked the cricketing world. The *Sportsman*'s obituary recorded: 'Right up to the day of his death, he upheld his reputation as a thoroughly representative cricketer. His fast round-arm bowling was the terror of his opponents, and the style in which he defied fatigue was little short of a marvel.'

The *County Gentleman*'s Cricket Notes commented: 'It is not too much to say that the lamented young gentleman was all but idolised in the county of his birth, and amongst almost all classes, not only in England, but in our most distant colonies, was a universal favourite.'

The same newspaper's leader writer added: 'Wherever this thoroughly English game is played, the deepest regret will be experienced at so talented a cricketer being cut off in the very prime of life . . . There were few finer specimens of the British athlete than the late Mr G.F. Grace, and his untimely end is a sad instance of how liable the strongest man is to the insidious attacks of disease, mainly through overrating his own strength.'

The *Bristol Evening News*, the Graces' local paper, noted that G.F. had played in every single Gloucestershire match since the county club was founded in 1870, more even than W.G., who had missed some by being in Australia in 1873–4. 'Popular everywhere for his genial manner and good humour, and for his skill as a cricketer, he will be deeply and sincerely mourned.'

The players in the match between the Australians and the Players of England at Crystal Palace wore bows or bands of black crepe as a mark of mourning. Like all the Graces, Fred had loved riding, shooting and fishing and like his three brothers was set on a medical career. He had studied at Bristol Medical School and St Bartholomew's Hospital, London, passed his preliminary examinations in anatomy and physiology and was expected to pass his finals the following winter.

A massive cortege, estimated at three thousand people, attended his funeral in Downend on 28 September. The Australian team sent a telegram of condolence, and many cricketers who could not be present sent wreaths. Among them was Richard Humphrey, to whose benefit Fred had been on his way. It was a more than usually sombre scene. In almost every house, the blinds were drawn as a mark of respect, for young Fred had been a popular figure in the village. Because of the short distance between The Chestnuts and the Downend church, the mourners followed the coffin, covered with a plain back cloth, on foot. There was just one carriage, bearing Fred's mother and his fiancée, Miss Robinson. After the church service, the crush in the churchyard was so intense that the family had difficulty in getting through to the graveside. Fred's brother-in-law, the Rev. J.W. Dann, gave a short but moving address, speaking of the great affection in which Fred had been held and of the disbelief that the young man who had left the house a fortnight earlier would never return. Then Dann broke down in tears. It is a fair assumption that W.G. did not allow himself a similar public show of emotion, but no one felt Fred's loss more. Miss Robinson, at least, found consolation in the arms of E.M., whose second wife she became, bearing him five children.

The years 1881–2 were subdued ones for W.G. in the cricketing sense. In 1881 his main preoccupation was his new medical practice and he played comparatively few first-class matches: he had only 21 innings, in which he scored 792 at an average of 37. There were still two sparkling centuries: 100 for the Gentlemen v Players at Lord's, which was said to be as good as any innings he ever played (he also took 7–61 in the Players' second innings), and 182 for Gloucs v Notts at Trent Bridge, the highest in a county match on that ground until then, and the highest innings of that county season. It followed 51 in the first innings. In his second innings, he was dropped at slip on 3, but was untroubled thereafter. Like all great batsmen, he hated getting out, however many he had scored, and this was a good example. He was finally given out for obstructing the field, and left, grumbling vociferously, although he had taken Gloucestershire's total to 440.

He was also severe on Middlesex in Gloucestershire's two

matches against them. At Lord's he made 64 and took 7–30, to secure victory by six wickets, and in the return, at Clifton, made 80 out of 102 while he was at the wicket. He contrived to run himself out, a most unusual occurrence for him, but he was run out twice more that summer, perhaps a reflection of his increasing girth and weight.

The following season started badly for him. He caught mumps, was sidelined for several weeks, and did not get going properly until towards the end of the summer. Perhaps family pressures played their part: in March, Agnes gave birth to their fourth child, and third son, Charles Butler Grace, completing their family. With the demands of a busy medical practice and a family of four children under the age of eight, W.G. had plenty on his plate. For the first time in his long career, he failed to score a first-class century, although he registered his usual clutch of them in West Country club games, and once again fell short of 1,000 first-class runs, making 975 at the abysmal average, for him, of 26.

What little good form Grace showed in 1882 he reserved for the right opponents: the legendary Australian touring side, which he and other good judges of the era rated as the strongest ever to come to England.

Australian cricket had made huge strides in the eight years since Grace took his side down under. Their batting had improved greatly – the captain, Murdoch, was rated the world's best batsman after Grace – and the bowlers were the best group ever collected in one team until then, led again by Spofforth at the height of his powers, backed by Boyle, Garrett and Palmer.

Grace pitted himself against them several times, first for Gentlemen of England at The Oval on 22–4 June, when he weighed in with 61 and 32. Gloucestershire had two matches against the tourists in August, both at Clifton. In the first Grace scored 77, in the second he took 12–152 in the match.

The latter was the immediate precursor to perhaps the most historic Test match of all time between England and Australia, which took place at The Oval on 28–30 August. Before a capacity fifteen-thousand crowd and on a damp pitch, the all-conquering Australians were put out for 63, but struck back to restrict England to 101, Grace yorked by Spofforth for 4. In appallingly wet conditions, Australia managed 122 in their second innings (Sammy Jones run out by Grace in controversial circumstances when he wandered out of his crease thinking the ball was dead), leaving England 85 to win. When Australia cleared off the arrears, wrote H.S. Altham, 'at point the Champion was seen to be pulling anxiously at his beard'. Perhaps he had a premonition of what was to come. His great antagonist Spofforth told his team-mates in the pavilion, 'This thing can be done' and so it could. At 15–2, England were in deep trouble. The Yorkshireman Ulyett joined W.G. at the crease and after Grace had survived a chance to Bannerman, fielding close in at silly mid-on, the pair took the score to 51, at which point England looked sure to win. But Spofforth bowled Ulyett and at 53 came the critical blow: Grace drove at Boyle but succeeded only in giving a catch to Bannerman at mid-off for 32, and with him went England's last chance.

In a desperately tense finale – one spectator died of a heart attack and another one gnawed anxiously through his umbrella handle – Australia winkled the last man out at 77 to win by seven runs. Spofforth took fourteen wickets in the match and was carried shoulder-high from the pitch.

This was the match which prompted the newspaper obituary notice lamenting the death of English cricket, the body to be cremated and the Ashes taken to Australia. It is one of the great might-have-beens of sport. If Grace had not fatally lifted that drive, surely England would have won, their supporters would have been satisfied, and the Ashes would never have been invented. But, as Grace gruffly reflected: 'I left six men to get 32 runs, and they couldn't get 'em.'

There was a growing feeling that it was not only English cricket that was washed up. So too was its champion. In 1883 Grace was thirty-five years old, perceptibly thicker round the waist, a portly paterfamilias rather than the lean, tigerish figure of his twenties, streaks of grey in the once jet-black beard, his hair thinning on top, noticeably less agile in the field and between the wickets, bowling more slowly than before and with less menace, still dangerous with the bat but less often.

To offset his increasing physical difficulties, pitches were at last improving in quality, which made life easier for batsmen. In 1883 W.G. made just one first-class century, 112 against Lancashire at Clifton, described as 'a grand display of cricket', and the other highlights were few and far between: a bright 89 and 12 wickets against Middlesex at Lord's, exactly half of the South's 128 against the North, also at Lord's. He still managed to amass 1,352 first-class runs, the third highest aggregate, and took 94 wickets, a respectable figure if at the expensive average of 22 (perhaps partly attributable to those improved wickets). However, for the first time in sixteen years, he missed the Gentlemen v Players game at The Oval because of his medical duties. (It managed quite well without him, ending in a dramatic tie.) Many thought the writing was on the wall and the Leviathan was at last laid low.

At the beginning of the 1884 season it seemed as if the critics were right. Grace found time to play first-class cricket throughout May but he managed only 70 runs in his first seven innings and had many low scores throughout the summer, but he balanced them with some innings which showed him back to his best, and he reserved most of them for the Australian visitors to England.

The Australians had settled into an English tour every two years, and many of the triumphant 1882 party were back. They had a much tougher itinerary and a fine record, but were rated as not quite up to the standard of their immediate predecessors. They brought with them a slow bowler in whom they invested great hopes, W.H. Cooper. In one of W.G.'s blandly-ghosted autobiographies, notable for their lack of revelation and insight, W.G. remarked that the tourists were 'hampered by the failure of . . . Cooper, who had to stand out from most of their matches'. He entirely neglected to mention that it was because of his own demolition of Cooper's bowling in his first match on English soil, v MCC Club & Ground at Lord's in late May, that the poor man was dropped and never recovered.

'Everybody was eager to see what he [Cooper] would do,' wrote Lord Harris, 'but never will [I] forget how W.G. pulverized him. Before lunch the bowling of the new-comer was virtually finished . . .' Grace went on to make a superb 101,

Cooper to take only seven wickets on the entire tour, at 46 each.

Next month Grace made his second century of the summer against the Australians, 107 for Gentlemen of England at The Oval, and his third, 116 not out, for Gloucestershire at Clifton in August. In brilliant sunshine, he made an uncertain start, treating 'some of the earlier balls in rather queer form', according to the *Bristol Evening News*, before he opened his shoulders to play 'several magnificent strokes'. It was a patient, chanceless innings, lasting three-and-a-quarter hours. When Australia batted, replying to Gloucestershire's 301, Woof bowled eighty-three overs, taking 6–82, and W.G. fifty-three overs, for figures of 2–96. No one else bowled more than sixteen overs. When the great hitter George Bonnor came in, 'W.G. tried [him] with the usual bait but three consecutive boundaries outside the ropes was the result'.

W.G. was not so commanding with the bat in the Tests. The first Test, at Old Trafford, 10–12 July, was abandoned because of rain. England were dismissed for only 95 in their first innings, but W.G. scored an invaluable 31 as England reached 180–9 and safety after Australia had made 182. England won the second Test at Lord's, thanks largely to a sterling 148 by A.G. Steel. One oddity was that Australia's first-innings top scorer 'Tup' Scott was caught for 75 by his own captain, Billy Murdoch, on the field as substitute for W.G., who had injured a finger.

The third match at The Oval, featuring Murdoch's double century, was drawn, to give England the rubber 1–0. W.G.'s most notable contribution was to take over the wicket-keeper's gloves – which he loved to do – during Australia's mammoth first innings of 551 to enable the Hon. Alfred Lyttelton to bowl under-arm lobs, with which he contrived to bag four wickets. To his huge delight – and that of the crowd – W.G. caught Midwinter in Lyttelton's first over, the makeshift bowler and wicket-keeper shaking hands in mid-wicket to celebrate the event. The hotelier and sporting man-about-town, Harry Preston, who eighteen years later gave W.G. his first ride in a motor-car, was a spectator and described how W.G. fielded in every position while the Australians flogged the English bowlers all over the ground. All eleven England players had a turn with the ball.

W.G. returned to Old Trafford later in July for Gloucestershire's match against Lancashire. Twenty minutes after lunch on the second day, he was at the crease, having just embarked on his second innings (he was 1 not out, having made 53 out of 119 in the first innings) when news arrived that his mother had died unexpectedly. 'Monkey' Hornby, the Lancashire captain, immediately offered to abandon the game so that W.G. and E.M. could return to Downend, an invitation they gratefully accepted. It remains the only first-class match to be abandoned for such a reason, which is faithfully recorded in the Gloucestershire scorebook in the immaculate handwriting of the county scorer, J.J. Smith: 'Drawn owing to the death of Mrs Grace – the Mother of the famous cricketers.' The *Bristol Evening News* reported: 'The utmost sympathy was expressed both in the pavilion and amongst the crowd.' The funeral took place on 29 July, in much the same fashion as poor Fred's four years earlier, but with less of a crush. Most of the village turned out to follow the cortege from The Chestnuts to the churchyard, where Mrs Grace was laid to rest beside her husband and son, from whose death she had never really recovered. She remains the only woman whose details are recorded in the 'Births and Deaths of Cricketers' section of *Wisden*.

W.G. made a few other good scores that summer – a big-hitting 66 in the first Gentlemen v Players game, 89 in the return, and 94 v Middlesex at Lord's. He ended with 1,361 runs, at 34.1, and was second in the averages to A.G. Steel, with whom he had put on an attractive 137 partnership in the first Gentlemen v Players game. But again the rumour surfaced that he was on the point of retiring from the first-class game. In consequence, the *Pall Mall Gazette* sent a journalist, M.H. Spielmann, to Lord's – where Grace was playing in a jokey end-of-season game between Smokers and Non-Smokers – to find out if it were true. (W.G. played for the Non-Smokers although he assured his inquisitor, 'In moderation, tobacco certainly does no harm.' Although he is normally described as a lifelong abstainer from tobacco, there is a certain amount of anecdotal evidence that he enjoyed the occasional good cigar.)

Spielmann set the scene:

All the time he was talking his head was turned towards where the cricket was going forward. His love for the game is intense. His enthusiasm is still like that of a schoolboy, and his happy delight when his side is winning is a pleasure to see. Gunn . . . fielding on the other side of the ground, effected a marvellous catch which dismissed Mr Christopherson. 'Was that really out, Christopherson?' Dr Grace cried, as that batsman came in. 'It's the most wonderful catch I've ever seen in my life – there's not another man in England could do it!'

Spielmann enquired whether he thought he was playing as well as ever.

My defence is as good, but I can't punish the bowling as I used to, and, besides, as you get older you lose your activity and can't field as well. I shall only play for the county next year, as my professional duties will keep me at home. I really mean it this time. I shall only take about three weeks' holiday next year.

Did cricket interfere with his medical practice?

A great deal; patients don't like an assistant, never mind how good he is. You see, I have a good practice which increases every winter when I am at home, and decreases in the summer when I am away from home. This is the real reason I shall not play much away from home next season.

12 · QUEEN AND COUNTRY
1885–1889

I N 1885, at the age of thirty-seven, W.G. confounded the
critics and rediscovered his best form, being the only English
cricketer to do the double of 1,000 runs and 100 wickets. It
was no flash in the pan either. He batted in his old dominant style
for the following three seasons too, in each of them topping the
first-class aggregates and producing some spectacular individual
innings. This wave of good form ebbed, as it was bound to do,
and the end of the decade and the early 1890s resembled the
early 1880s. Even then he was not done.

Let us return to 1885. Perhaps the key to his revival was that he
felt more at ease with his medical duties, despite the misgivings
he had expressed the previous autumn to the *Pall Mall Gazette*.
He may have restricted his appearances outside county cricket
but when he played for Gloucestershire he displayed much of
his old form, as he showed in his finest innings that summer
– his best, indeed, for many years. On 24 August, while the
newspapers debated a suitable memorial to General Gordon, cut
down in Khartoum at the beginning of the year, Gloucestershire
entertained Middlesex at Clifton. Grace won the toss and batted.
He was irresistible, toying with the bowling all day, although he
was becalmed for a while in the nineties until he reached his
century with a delicate late-cut for 3. He ended the day on 163
not out and next day continued in the same vein until he ran out
of partners, to finish on 221 not out made out of 348 in six and a

half hours, his first double century since 1877. His only chance was an easy catch dropped by third man as he took the total past 300. His first biographer, W. Methven Brownlee, was present at the College ground. He described it as a

. . . wonderful innings, in which timing, placement, and clean, powerful hitting were so prominent, but all through admiration for the phenomenal endurance of the man was greater than love of the dazzling scientific display . . . His hitting at the end [was] as clean, severe, and dashing as at the beginning, looking as if he could stay for the week if somebody were strong enough and patient enough to keep him company.

The reason for Brownlee's praise was that either on the previous evening or between the first and second days of the match (contemporary accounts differ) Grace was called away to a difficult confinement and stayed up all night trying to save the mother and her baby. He went straight to the Clifton ground and, legend has it, reported on his night's work: 'The child died and the mother died, but I saved the father.' W.G. rounded off his astonishing performance by taking 11–120 in the match, and never once showed the slightest sign of fatigue, despite being on the field of play for the whole match. He was still a physical phenomenon, despite appearances to the contrary.

His form continued when he moved on to Scarborough for the Festival, a week he loved, and the Gentlemen v Players. He hit 174 out of 247 while he was at the wicket, a display which revived memories of his greatest days. Brownlee called it 'a magnificent innings, scientifically played and cleanly hit'.

He also made two centuries for Gloucestershire, helping his county's fortunes revive somewhat after a lean spell – 132 v Yorkshire at Bradford in late July, and 104 v Surrey at Cheltenham in late August, which set him up for his double century a few days later. His most dashing feat of the summer, however, was reserved for the game between an England XI and the team led by Alfred Shaw (which had returned from a tour of Australia in the spring) at Harrogate in September: he raced to 51 out of 53, with two sixes out of the ground.

His season's total was 1,688 runs at 43.28, an aggregate bettered only by Surrey's Walter Read (1,880), and took 117 wickets at 18.79 each. Lillywhite's *Annual* recorded reverentially: 'He is still, after nearly a quarter-of-a-century's hard work, the noblest Roman of them all.'

The following season, 1886, he continued to rule the game as surely as any Roman emperor his dominion. The students of Oxford University thought the only way to dethrone him was by getting him drunk, so arranged a dinner at Oxford after the first day of their match against MCC in June, which W.G. ended on 50 not out. At dinner, they plied him with champagne and looked forward to dismissing him early the following day. Practising in the nets before play began, he was bowled by a fizzing leg-break by an undergraduate named E.A. Nepean, who was to make a name for himself in the first-class game. Thinking their ploy was working, the students took the field in excellent spirits, which were somewhat deflated when W.G., showing no sign of a hangover, proceeded to a chanceless century, then took all ten Oxford wickets in MCC's innings victory.

Another Australian tour party arrived, of distinctly inferior standard to their two immediate predecessors. They had one thing in common, however: they frequently felt the lash of W.G. at his finest. He repeated his achievement of three centuries against them, but was not at his best in the three Test matches until the final one at The Oval. In the first, at Old Trafford, he was out cheaply (8 and 4) in both innings, but England still managed to win by four wickets. In the second Test, at Lord's, W.G. and everyone else on either side was overshadowed by Arthur Shrewsbury. England won the toss and batted first, but W.G. again failed to make an impact, being caught at slip for 18. Shrewsbury more than compensated with a magnificent 164, the highest score recorded until then against Australia in England, taking the distinction away from W.G.'s 152 in 1880. Thanks largely to Briggs's bowling (he took 11–74 in the match), the Australian batting collapsed again, England won by an innings and 106 runs, and took the rubber.

Shrewsbury's record stood for less than a month. When the teams reassembled at The Oval in mid-August, W.G. made up for his two earlier failures with 170, the highest score he ever made against Australia. Indeed, it was the highest score by an Englishman in a home Test match until Phil Mead's 182 not out against Australia in 1921. W.G. was a little fortunate in that his great adversary Spofforth injured his bowling hand early in the tour, had missed a month, and never quite recaptured his form of old, but it was none the less a determined display, if not by any means chanceless. In fact, he was dropped five times: at slip when he had scored only 6, by Giffen off his own bowling on 23, at long-off – another easy one – when 60, in the slips again off Giffen on 93, and finally another return catch just before Blackham finally held on to a catch, off the persevering Spofforth.

Unusually for him, W.G. was the soul of caution early on, perhaps influenced by his opening partner, William Scotton, the Nottinghamshire left-hander who was a byword for slow play. Here Scotton excelled himself, taking eighteen overs to get off the mark, and remaining on 24 for sixty-seven minutes, while W.G. added 63 at the other end. Of their opening partnership of 170, Scotton's share was 34 in three and three-quarter hours ('a fine defensive innings', *The Times* called it). W.G.'s innings was oddly uneven – his first 50 took 130 minutes, an eternity by his standards and on a blameless pitch, his second 50 came up in only forty-five minutes, and the third in seventy. He certainly dominated the day – when he departed for 170, the score was only 216–2. *The Times* was moved to consider the day's play in its leader columns and clearly did not think the Champion had attained his (and its) usual Olympian levels:

W.G. fell to a magnificent catch which ended a performance which was a great deal longer than it should have been and in which fortune and skill may claim about an equal share.

Having dealt with him, the paper went on to loftier things:

Cricket, Lord Hawke is reputed to have said, is doing more to consolidate the Empire than any other influence. This may be an over-statement of a good case, but it is at least certain that cricket is doing something to promote mutual respect and good will between England and her chief colony.

Whether the Australians felt the same way after being thrashed by an innings and 217 runs a couple of days later must have been open to question.

W.G.'s other centuries against them were even more memorable. For Gentlemen of England, also at The Oval, in mid-June, his performance could not have been more dissimilar. There was no Spofforth to discomfit him and he and his fellow amateurs took full advantage, making 350 on the first day, of which Grace's contribution was a blistering 148 on a fast and helpful track, his cutting being especially eye-catching. He was finally caught at cover point by Trumble off Garrett. 'The Champion, it is almost superfluous to record, met with a most enthusiastic reception on returning to the pavilion,' went one report, 'umpires and Colonists alike sharing in applauding a contribution that proves that though close upon forty his power with the willow is still indisputable.'

Making 110 for Gloucestershire at Clifton, he was particularly severe on the bowling of George Giffen, who had been the star turn thus far of the ill-starred tour. He nearly had a fourth century against the tourists, falling on 92 for Lord Londesborough's XI during the Scarborough Festival in September. For the first time since 1879, he scored more first-class runs than anyone, his 1,846 pipping Read by 21.

For a decade and a half, W.G. had played cricket alongside his cousin Walter Raleigh Gilbert, who had been a regular member of the Gloucestershire team since 1876 and toured Australia with him in 1873/74. W.R. Gilbert was a short, stocky all-rounder in the Grace mould – a fine batsman, with a first-class double century to his credit, a useful slow bowler and an excellent deep fielder. He also played a couple of seasons for Middlesex. Nothing had prepared the cricket world for what was to happen in 1886.

At the beginning of the season, Gilbert, then thirty-two years old, announced that he was turning professional, which is perhaps evidence that he was short of money. He was due to play for Gloucestershire v Sussex at Hove in June but did not appear. For a couple of days previously, he was observed stealing money from a coat hanging in the pavilion at Cheltenham, where he played as professional for East Gloucestershire. He was sentenced to twenty-eight days' hard labour and was then despatched to Canada, where he lived for the rest of his life. His employers, family and friends suppressed the story, and Gilbert vanished from the English scene as if he had never existed. In his various books of memoirs, W.G. made no mention of his cousin's disgrace. That wasn't the Victorian way of doing things.

W.G.'s return to form was no temporary comeback: he did the same for the next three seasons and in 1887 topped 2,000 runs in a season for the first time since his *annus mirabilis* eleven years earlier. He missed the double by only three wickets. His 2,062 runs placed him more than 400 clear of his nearest rival, Arthur Shrewsbury, who, however, made the highest individual total of the year, 267 for Notts v Middlesex. Grace's own highest score was 183 not out, against Yorkshire at Gloucester, to earn an unexpected draw. After 92 in the first innings, it made a total of 275 for once out in the match.

He was in similarly unforgiving mood when Kent visited Clifton for the first time in late August. With E.M. he put on 126 for the first wicket, the older brother outscoring him to reach 70 before, as the local paper, put it, 'Martin, attacking uphill, upset the coroner's pegs'. W.G. went on to his century with his favourite late cut, and was stumped next ball for 101. In Gloucestershire's second innings, he repeated the feat, reaching his century off the penultimate ball of the game, to end with 103 not out, amid scenes of high excitement. Small wonder, for it was only the third time the feat had been accomplished in the first-class game. Only Grace himself had done it in modern times and that was back in 1868 (he was to do it again in 1888). Here he was, at the age of thirty-nine, dominating the scene once again. He himself attributed his success in the match to the slow, dry wicket, which he said he preferred by now to the fast, dry wickets he had relished when younger. 'The first day the wicket was perfect of its kind,' he recalled, 'every ball coming easy and with very little break, travelling quickly when hit, as the outside ground was much harder than the pitch, which had been watered.'

It was a year of anniversaries: Queen Victoria's jubilee and the MCC's centenary. As if by arrangement with the gods, the summer was a long and hot one. The greatest sportsman of the Victorian age and the finest cricketer ever to sport the MCC's colours took full advantage of the hard-baked pitches to compile a further series of big scores to commemorate both institutions. This was highly appropriate, for W.G. ruled cricket as majestically as Victoria her empire, and was just as well known and respected by the public. If anyone epitomised her reign, it surely was Grace, even though she had been on the throne eleven years before he was born.

Two Centenary matches were held at Lord's in June, one serious, one light-hearted. The serious one was between England and MCC, captained by W.G. 'It is probable,' recorded *The Times*, 'that two teams never entered the field so skilful at all points', adding that they included W.G., 'the greatest cricketer of his, and in the opinion of most people, any other day.' They were indeed the flower of a game coming to full bloom. The other MCC players were Hawke, Hornby, A.J. Webbe, J.G. Walker, Barnes, Gunn, Flowers, G.G. Hearne, Rawlin and Sherwin. But the England team looked even stronger: W.W. Read, Stoddart, Barlow, Bates, Briggs, Hall, Pilling, Maurice Read, Lohmann and Ulyett. Some eight thousand people crammed into Lord's on the opening day, including a host of peers in the pavilion.

Winning the toss, W.G. opened with Hornby but was soon dismissed for 5. All out for 175, MCC then had to endure a massive opening partnership of 266 between Arthur Shrewsbury (152) and Andrew Stoddart, whose 151 was his first century at Lord's. The only consolation W.G. could derive was that they narrowly failed to break the first-wicket record at the ground (283) that he and B.B. Cooper had set in 1869. No wonder that when he was asked who would be the first player he would pick for any of his sides, W.G. replied, 'Give me Arthur.' England compiled 514, and although W.G. did a little better in the second innings than he had in the first, with 45, MCC were all out for 222, to be crushed by an innings and 117 runs.

That evening, three hundred dined in the tennis court, and

listened to a dozen speakers, including W.G. and the Liberal politician George Goschen, who the previous year had been sounded out for Prime Minister by the Queen and now brought W.G. into his after-dinner anecdotes. He spoke of 'the bore who comes to a cricket match at Lord's and makes remarks as to what is going on in the Commons. You know the reception he would have, and if he were to say the Ministry is out, there would be a cry of "Who is out?"'

'"The Ministry."'

'"Oh, I thought it was Grace."'

The second Centenary match was an altogether more frivolous affair between The Gentlemen of MCC and Eighteen Veterans over Forty, including some doughty old campaigners. At thirty-eight, W.G. just scraped into the MCC side and gave himself plenty of bowling, taking 5–87 off 56.3 overs. When MCC batted, the highlight of the innings was, for once, W.G.'s dismissal for 24 by a gentle delivery from the first ball of Mr E. Rutter's second over. 'The downfall of the great batsman at the hands of Mr Rutter caused some amusement,' said *The Times*. Three days later came the culmination of the Queen's jubilee celebrations, a service of thanksgiving at Westminster Abbey, the capital packed with her subjects keen to get a glimpse of her on the way to the Abbey. That night beacons were lit on hills the length and breadth of the kingdom.

W.G. carried on celebrating in his own distinctive fashion. For MCC he carried his bat for 81 of his side's 118 all out against Sussex, while against Cambridge University at Lord's he made a whirlwind 116 not out in 135 minutes, including one magnificent hit into the pavilion. For Gloucestershire, in addition to his brace of centuries against Kent, he made two scores of 113, both of which underlined his superiority to other mortals.

The first was against Middlesex in early June on a typically lively Lord's wicket and was made out of a total of only 197. After a few early difficulties, W.G. settled down to play an innings described as 'simply perfect' and almost carried his bat before falling lbw to A.J. Webbe. The next highest score was 25. In almost identical fashion, he held out against Nottinghamshire on an equally spiteful Clifton pitch while an almost unplayable Billy Barnes ran through the rest of the batting to dismiss Gloucestershire for 186. When the last man came in Grace was on only 82 and, wrote his biographer Methven Brownlee, 'there was a bet of a bottle of Giesler to a Jubilee shilling that he did not get his century'. As a rule, it was a mistake to bet against W.G.

He demonstrated his huge and continuing zest for the game during the Scarborough Festival when, playing for Gentlemen of England v I Zingari, he smashed a vigorous 73 and followed it by taking over the wicket-keeper's gloves and making a smart stumping off a Nepean leg-break. (This encounter has a unique place in cricket history as the only first-class match in which Queen Victoria's grandson, Prince Christian Victor, played. Then aged twenty, a former captain of Wellington College and a useful 'keeper and bat, he made 35 for I Zingari. He went on to join the army and died in South Africa during the Boer War.)

The next year, 1888, the Australians were back, led by Percy McDonnell, and like their predecessors kept running into Grace at the top of his form. The tourists' batting was weak but their bowling exceeded expectations, entirely through the efforts of two men, the right-arm medium-pacer Charlie Turner – 'The Terror' – and J.J. Ferris, a nippy left-arm seamer, both playing in England for the first time. They took an astonishing 534 wickets between them (Turner 314, Ferris 220), frequently bowling unchanged through an innings. Grace had a high regard for both of them – so much so that he hired Ferris to play for Gloucestershire in 1892 – although he dealt with them briskly enough on the field of play.

Three years later, in the book *Cricket*, which bore his name but was largely written for him by Methven Brownlee, Grace recalled: 'How those two slaved and toiled from the beginning to the end of the tour, and with what remarkable effect, is still fresh in the memories of most of us.' But Grace considered Spofforth far superior to Turner because he could choose the amount a ball would cut or swing – a few inches or a foot and a half. Turner moved the ball off the seam in prodigious fashion but never managed to produce the tiny deviations which Grace considered the most dangerous to the batsman. In effect, he swung it too much and too predictably.

They encountered Grace at his most formidable in the match against the Gentlemen of England at Lord's at the end of May, when after the tourists had made 179 he and the Surrey captain John Shuter enjoyed a thrilling partnership of 158, though it is doubtful whether the Australians did. They scored at the rate of 75 an hour and Shuter's share was 71. After Grace had completed his century (remember, this was still the first day), he 'meted out terrible punishment' and went on to make 165, one of the many candidates for his finest innings ever.

In Gloucestershire's two games against the tourists at Clifton and Cheltenham he scored 51 and 92 respectively, the latter the only score over 50 in the match. In the three Test matches he never quite came off with the bat. The first was another spectacular Lord's disaster on a wet wicket which the Australians coped with rather better than the home batsmen. The visitors batted first and W.G. was soon in action at point, snaffling a firm cut by Bannerman off Lohmann and gleefully hurling it over his head backwards all the way to third man, proof that Victorian cricketers could be as effusive in their celebrations as their late twentieth-century counterparts. Australia made 116, which proved to be the highest total of the match. W.G. struggled, along with all the English batsmen – 'Dr Grace . . . by no means seemed at home with the bowling' said *The Times* – and was finally out for 10 on the second morning. The match was wrapped up on that second day, with deplorable batting all round on a difficult pitch. England were all out for 53, their lowest total to date in a Test, Australia replied with 60, setting England 124 to win. They managed just 62. W.G. top-scored with 24, from which *The Times* drew some slight consolation:

In glancing at the feeble batting of the home team, it should be noted that Dr W.G. Grace, although falling short of the great things always expected from him, obtained more runs than any other two batsmen of the Eleven.

With England one down in the three-match series, things looked bleak. But Stoddart, who had been appointed captain for the first match, was unavailable for the vital second Test at The Oval. With defeat in the rubber looming, England at last turned to their greatest player to lead them, a few days after his fortieth birthday. He was to go on to lead his country in four out of the next five series, always against Australia as there was still no other country nearly strong enough to challenge either of them. Why did it take so long? England and Australia had played twenty-eight Tests against each other before the greatest player on either side was invited to become captain. One of the reasons was that nineteen of those games had been played in Australia during tours for which W.G. had been unavailable. But it still meant that, in those games for which he might have been considered, he was overlooked.

England's captains in those matches were Lord Harris, 'Monkey' Hornby, A.G. Steel and Andrew Stoddart – the most outstanding amateurs of their day, with one obvious exception. More to the point, they were the most upstanding, and there is a slight suspicion that cricket's top brass did not initially regard W.G. as quite up to the job socially. But there were were plenty of others who thought he wasn't quite up to it tactically. He tended to let things drift, allowing bowlers to wheel away unchanged for hours even when they were being flogged all over the ground – and there is no doubt that he over-bowled himself to a ludicrous degree. Still, he always led from the front.

His debut as captain was inauspicious – he lost the toss, but after that things improved. Australia were shot out for only 80. W.G. failed with the bat, caught at slip for 1 off the last ball of Turner's second over, but thanks to a sparkling unbeaten 62 by George Lohmann, batting at ten, England made 317 and were in control. The Australians feared their batting was not up to the standard of previous years and they were proved right: they were dismissed for 100 and the match was over within two days.

The series squared, England travelled to Manchester with renewed confidence. W.G. won the toss but when England lost two quick wickets for only six runs, crisis loomed but

Dr Grace and Mr Read by brilliant hitting soon put a different complexion on the game. To have seen the former batting one might have imagined that the wicket was perfectly true, with such ease did he play the bowling.

W.G. was brilliantly caught at long-on one-handed by Bonnor for 38, not a huge score by any standards but, as it transpired, the highest of the match and the innings that seized an initiative England were never to lose. They made 172, dismissed Australia twice in a day for 81 and 70 and won by an innings and 21 to take the series 2–1. Their new captain didn't even have time to overbowl himself, though he did take three catches in Australia's second innings, including a brilliant effort, running in from mid-off and scooping the ball close to the ground to get rid of Edwards. As the last Australian wicket fell, the crowd poured over the ropes and on to the ground, massing in front of the pavilion and refusing to leave until Peel, who took eleven wickets in the match, and W.G. appeared at a window to acknowledge their cheers. W.G. could not have started his long stint as captain of England any better.

His last match of the season against the Australians was for an England XI at Hastings, where he made an attractive 53 out of 66, though the star of the show was Turner, who took 17–50 in the match, fourteen clean bowled and two lbw. There was an amusing moment in another tour match, against C.I. Thornton's XI at Norbury, south London, when W.G., after being given out lbw to Turner to his great displeasure, was sitting among the crowd. Thornton himself drove a ball straight and high over the boundary, upon which Grace rose from his seat to catch the ball, to great amusement all round.

In 1888, Grace reached the age of forty, although he appeared older, looking by now as if he had stepped straight out of the pages of the Old Testament. His individual masterpiece that summer was his 215 for Gloucestershire against Sussex at Brighton in May, the eighth double century of his career and his first for three years. He opened the batting on the first day, by the end of which he was unbeaten on 188, out of 361–6. Sussex tried nine bowlers against him without success. Next day he completed his double century before falling to Humphreys. 'He had been in nearly seven hours,' reported *The Times*, 'and there was no falling-off from the masterly batting for which he is so famous, while he exhibited quite his old self in placing the ball.' He made only 5 in the second innings and Sussex contrived to save a game in which 1,117 runs were scored in three days.

But W.G.'s most remarkable achievement was that for the second successive season he made centuries in each innings of a match, this time against Yorkshire at Clifton. In the first innings he made 148 out of 221 while he was at the wicket, in the second 153 out of 253 to salvage an improbable draw (the most any of his team-mates managed in either innings was 47). It was the third and last time W.G. performed this feat – and remember that, at that point, he was the only batsman in the history of the game to have done it at all, never mind three times, which is one of the most telling testaments to his batting supremacy. Even the Yorkshiremen joined in the cheering when he departed the second time, each innings being chanceless. He ended the season with more first-class runs than anyone else – 1,886 at 32.51 – and the respectable haul of 93 wickets at 18.18 each, although the top wicket-taker was George Lohmann with 209 at 10.19.

In December 1888 W.G. attended the first meeting of the County Cricket Council in the pavilion at Lord's as Gloucestershire's representative. The council had been set up at a meeting at Lord's in July 1887 (when Grace could not be present because he was playing for the Gentlemen v Players) to regulate the affairs of the growing number of counties, leaving the rule-making to MCC, although many counties felt this was an area in which they too should have a voice.

The last item on the agenda was the vexed problem of exactly when a first-class match should end on the third day. One suggestion was that it should be at the discretion of the umpires if a close finish was in prospect. Grace spoke up to agree with his old friend Lord Harris, the chairman, who thought it better to start earlier in the morning. Grace proposed that matches should start at midday on the first day, and 11 a.m. on the two subsequent days although, *Wisden* reported, 'he was afraid Gloucestershire were very slack in that matter at home'.

As the 1880s came to an end Grace continued to be the most prolific scorer in the game, ending the decade in much better shape (except physically) than he had started it. In 1889 he made 1,396 runs at 32.46 with three first-class centuries, 154 for South v North and the other two in Gloucestershire's matches against Middlesex, at Lord's and Cheltenham plus a rapid 94 (out of 126) in the first innings against Surrey at The Oval. This match was noteworthy as the first to feature a declaration on the third day, a measure introduced that season to help facilitate results (along with the five-ball over, increased from four).

Back in October 1884, the Gloucestershire committee had embarked on a search for a ground of their own, appointing a sub-committee for the purpose which included W.G. They soon found a suitable area of land on Ashley Down, Bristol, but it was not until 1888 that the purchase of twenty-five acres, of which twelve to thirteen acres would be for the sole use of the cricket club, was approved by the club's annual general meeting. W.G. was appointed a director of the company that was to run the ground, and he played a big role in getting the ground in shape for the first season of cricket there in 1889. He visited it almost every day, probably driving the groundsman, John Spry, to distraction with his interventions (he had originally promised the job to Tom Gregg, coach at Clifton College, but was overruled by the committee). The first match at Ashley Down was on 22 and 23 April 1889, between a Gloucestershire XI and a Colts XXII. The inaugural first-class match was Gloucestershire v Warwickshire on 23–5 May, which the home team won by 63 runs. The county is playing there still.

In common with most new venues, the wicket took some time to settle. When the county played Sussex, W.G. was the only batsman with the technique and determination to cope with it. His 84 (more than twice as many as anyone else on either side in either innings) may have been his best innings of the summer. But 1889 marked the beginning of his decline as a consistently effective bowler. He took only forty-four first-class wickets, less than half his haul of the previous summer and his lowest total for twenty-one years. He could still winkle good batsmen out but his increasing weight and girth made him a less athletic and therefore menacing figure. In the decade ahead, his last full one at the highest level, he would never take more than sixty-one wickets in a season while the top performers raked in figures in the high two hundreds. But he was by no means finished with the bat.

Gloucestershire were in the doldrums in this period, partly because their bowling was well below the required strength, despite the efforts of William Woof, a left-arm medium-pacer who bore the brunt of the attack with W.G. in the 1880s, taking 644 wickets for the county between 1878 and 1902. They were greatly helped towards the end of the decade by another left-arm seamer, Fred Roberts, who made his debut in 1887 and toiled away until 1905, taking 963 wickets.

In 1889, the MCC commissioned a portrait of W.G. by Archibald Stuart Wortley at a cost of £300, a huge sum in those days. The money was raised by private subscriptions from members, limited to £1 each, and the portrait was exhibited at the Royal Academy. It now hangs in the MCC Museum at Lord's.

There was another, graver matter hanging over W.G.'s head. When he arrived at Ashley Down one morning after rain, he decided that the ground was too wet to play on and forbade practice until further notice. When the weather had improved and the ground had dried out somewhat, a group of young players arrived and, ignoring the notice 'No Practice Today' posted on the front gate, went in and started a practice session. Unfortunately for them, W.G. returned to the ground and was furious to see that his instructions had been ignored. He became involved in an argument with the group, one of whom must have said something cheeky or insulting. W.G. lost his temper, pulled a stump out of the ground and attacked the young man with it. From a letter which W.G. wrote on 26 May 1889 to J.W. Arrowsmith, a printer/publisher and president of the Gloucestershire committee, it appeared that the young man's father, a member of the county club was demanding compensation:

Many thanks for saying you would see White's father about the assault if I wished it. As I did not see him last evening when I saw the son, perhaps it would be as well, if not troubling you too much. The lad I know bears no ill will, but I fancy, he was kept in bed to make it look worse, you will find this out if you call. I told the boys [sic] father and mother that I was sorry I had struck the boy, but that 9 out of 10 persons would have done the same, under the provocation. I could do no more than apologise etc, which I did, and of course would pay the lad for loss of time etc. But I shall certainly not stand Black Mail being levied on me, which I fancy the father has been put up to, by some of his friends.

The father, I think you could reason with, and would after some persuasion forego proceedings which would save a lot of trouble and annoyance if it could be managed. You must not let him know, that I know you are going to see him as it may make matters worse but if you call as president of the club he belongs to, you see the son as well as the father and let me know the result. Please drop me a line at Lord's Cricket Ground, St John's Wood Road, and I shall then know how to act . . .

It would appear that Arrowsmith's mediation was successful, and the boy accepted an apology from W.G. It would certainly have been highly embarrassing for him if the affair had become public. A charge of assault could have been very awkward for a well-known city doctor, though it would have been a brave magistrate or jury who convicted W.G. of anything other than constantly wanting his own way on the cricket field.

13 · CAPTIOUS CAPTAIN RETURNS TO AUSTRALIA

1890–1892

A RELATIVELY quiet couple of seasons at the beginning of the 1890s were the prelude to W.G.'s second tour of Australia in 1891/92, eighteen years after his first. In 1890 he scored only one first-class century but still accumulated 1,476 runs, the third-highest total behind Shrewsbury and Gunn. His appetite for the game was undiminished: he completed 52 innings, and only Ulyett, with 53, went to the crease more often. Even that was not enough for Grace. C.C. Clarke recorded: 'W.G. would go anywhere to play a match if he had a spare day. Several times a telegram, on Friday evening brought him for my side on a Saturday.' The sole century came for Gloucestershire against Kent at Maidstone when he carried his bat for 109 out of 231. He just missed out on another against Yorkshire at Dewsbury, with a sparkling 98, and posted scores of 94 and 90 in his county's games against Lancashire at Old Trafford and Clifton.

The Australians were back in England, again with the relentlessly effective bowling duo of Turner and Ferris, who by extraordinary symmetry each took 215 wickets on the tour, and were now backed up by the young Hugh Trumble, on the first of his five visits to England, but their batting let them down and they lost two of the three Tests. The third, at Manchester, was abandoned because of rain without a ball being bowled.

Grace had mixed fortunes in the two matches that did finish:

in the first innings of the Lord's Test he was caught and bowled for a duck by Turner but in the second made a superb unbeaten 75 to steer England to a seven-wicket victory. In the second Test, at The Oval, he just escaped a king pair. Caught by Trumble at slip off the first ball of the first innings, in the second innings he was dropped at point by Trott off Trumble's first ball and was soon out for 16. England managed to win by two wickets. Grace's bowling recovered from the low point of 1889, and he took 61 wickets. But he was handicapped by a knee injury, which flared up again the following season and was a factor in his lowest first-class aggregate for twenty-three years, 771 against 588 back in 1868.

There was, however, no real comparison between the two eras. In 1868 he had made his runs in only nine first-class innings at an average of 65.33. By 1891 the game had developed to such an extent that Grace completed 40 first-class innings, with a top score of 72 not out, and an average of only 19.76. All in all, it was not the best preamble to a demanding tour of Australia for a man of 43. But, as so often in the past, Grace had some surprises up his ample sleeve for the critics and the sceptics.

The England tour of Australia in 1891/92 was organised and financed by the third Earl of Sheffield (1831-1909), one of the great benefactors of cricket (and many other good causes). He had created his own ground on his 5,000-acre estate at Sheffield Park, Sussex, where, starting in 1884, the Australians often opened their tours, rather as contemporary tourists do at the Duke of Norfolk's Arundel ground.

In 1887/88 two English sides had toured Australia at the same time, losing the promoters huge amounts of money (the Melbourne Cricket Club alone lost £3,000). No wonder Lord Hawke commented: 'There was never such a prominent case of folly.' There was understandable reluctance in Australian cricketing circles about bringing the Englishmen over again, but there was concern that public interest in the game in Australia was waning: it had started to grow in the 1870s and increased as the standard of cricket improved. But the wave of great cricketers who had come to full maturity in the early 1880s had passed their peak. Most had retired or were in decline and they had not been replaced by others of similar stature.

The possibility of a new English tour was first raised in discussions between Sheffield and Harry Boyle, the great fast bowler who was player/manager of the 1890 Australian touring side, towards the end of the tour. After Boyle went back to Australia, they stayed in touch on the subject. Boyle consulted with cricketing bodies and wrote to Sheffield to assure him an English side would be welcome, but the proviso was, the party had to include W.G. Grace. Nearly two decades had passed since he had first toured Australia when in his prime in 1873/74, but in all that time no cricketer had emerged in England or Australia with anything like the same ability or charisma. He was still far and away the biggest attraction in cricket.

Lord Sheffield was as keen on promoting cricket in Australia as he was in Sussex, and put up £150 for an inter-state competition, the Sheffield Shield, which commemorates his munificence to this day. He was even more generous in his attitude to the tour. He agreed to make up any losses, which in the event came to about £2,000. The tour was estimated to have cost £16,000, against receipts of £14,000, despite the tourists' getting the lion's share of the gate money. For instance, nearly forty thousand people were estimated to have watched the third game of the tour, against New South Wales at Sydney, paying some £1,800. Of this, £1,400 went to the Englishmen.

The 1891/92 tour deficit was more than accounted for by Grace's fee and expenses, which came to £3,000, double the fee he had demanded and got for his first tour. It was no wonder that seasoned old professionals should again raise the question of who was the amateur and who the professional, but there was little public grumbling, which gave W.G. carte blanche to demand what he liked. So Lord Sheffield's team, and especially W.G., had an important task to fulfil in reviving interest.

Even so, Grace was in two minds for a while about going on the tour, principally because of his fear that his injured knee would not stand up to it. But when his biographer W. Methven Brownlee quizzed him about this, his reply, quoted by Brownlee in the magazine the *Cricket Field*, was: 'The voyage and rest will put it right. I am anxious to go again, for I believe it will do the game good. A bad wicket is a rare exception there, and I feel as fit as ever.' An added bonus was that Sheffield had agreed to let Grace take his wife and two youngest children, Bessie, aged thirteen, and Charles, aged nine. It goes without saying that no one else was so favoured.

The manager of the tour was Alfred Shaw, who had retired from Nottinghamshire and was now employed by Lord Sheffield to organise matches at Sheffield Park. The tour party, of only thirteen, was almost as strong as could be mustered, with the exception of Arthur Shrewsbury and William Gunn, who did not consider the terms offered were sufficiently generous. The main batsmen were Grace, A.E. Stoddart, Abel, Read, ably supported by all-rounders Briggs, Peel and Attewell, while MacGregor, Bean and Radcliffe would be on their first visit down under. According to one Australian observer, the bowling was 'as near perfection as possible', spearheaded by Attewell, Lohmann, Briggs and Peel, who had toured Australia successfully in 1887/88, backed by Sharpe of Surrey, another newcomer to Australian conditions. They would be supported by Grace, Bean, Abel, Read, Stoddart and Radcliffe. The wicket-keepers were MacGregor and Philipson.

In the days before the tourists departed W.G. was embroiled in a bitter dispute with the Gloucestershire president, J.W. Arrowsmith, a Bristol printer and publisher, over a book they had been planning together. The plan was for it to be under W.G.'s name and would be part history of cricket, part autobiography, part W.G.'s thoughts on how to play the game, part his views on his contemporaries. Most of the actual work would be done by W. Methven Brownlee, who had written a slim biography of W.G. published in 1887. There were to be two versions: a de-luxe limited-edition for five hundred subscribers, and a much cheaper mass-market edition. He may have been content for Brownlee to write his book for him but W.G. was keenly interested in its production and how much money he would earn from it, and he was not at all happy with Arrowsmith's ideas for producing it. On 31 August he wrote to him:

You seem to have commenced the book, without my knowing exactly what you intend to do. I must see the binding and covers before giving my consent, as it must be done nicely or not at all. As to you printing it, as it is, I strongly object and I must have time to go through it carefully. Messrs Fry and Son say they have taken the back page, now I have heard nothing about any advertisement and I must know how many you intend to have in the book and what share I am to have.

Arrowsmith's immediate reply clearly did not satisfy him, for the same day he reacted furiously:

I do not at all understand the tone of your letter and think . . . that I had better not at present proceed any further in the matter.

But proceed they did, because a week later W.G. was even angrier:

. . . .I never for one instant dreamt of your doing anything I did not approve of. If you are still going to print the book as you like and not as I like then I have done with you. If you have given up the idea of printing the book just now, and won't do it at all unless I approve of it then I shall be pleased to dine with you on the 25th . . .

Arrowsmith continued to fail to mollify W.G. On 20 September, Grace exploded:

. . . You have agreed to supply the book at 6d per copy, and cannot possibly do it properly for this sum. It is not my fault but yours, and how you can suggest that I should forego my royalty I cannot understand. As I told you before, it is absurd to publish it as you propose and will bring ridicule on you and me, and I will certainly not give you my consent . . .

The day before the tour party was due to depart, W.G. appeared to have given in, albeit reluctantly:

I enclose order for two books you can please yourself about sending them, I should think that it is all right, send bill to each with book. I have put your letters in the file, and hope our private friendship will be the same as before, although in business matters we do not agree.

The tour party left by train from Liverpool Street station on 2 October 1891, bound for the Albert Docks where they were to board the P & O steamship *Arcadia*. So many well-wishers turned up at the station to see them off that railway officials had a hard job in keeping them back from the carriages. Among them were many cricketers and county representatives. Lord Sheffield, who was accompanying the party, had gone on by an earlier train while Philipson was travelling overland to Brindisi, where he was to join the ship. Many more friends and family joined the party for the hour-long train trip. There was just half an hour for final leavetakings before the *Arcadia* sailed at 12.30 p.m. Lord Sheffield had engaged a band to play on the quayside – its rendition of 'Home, Sweet Home' brought a lump to many throats – and as the ship cast off there were three cheers for his lordship and another resounding one for the England team.

The voyage was uneventful. The cricketers endeared themselves to their fellow-passengers by putting on a Christy Minstrel show, with W.G. acting as the compere, 'Mr Johnson', complete with blacked-up face and powdered beard. He must have cut an imposing figure on the stage. The part enabled him to display his droll sense of humour. In one sketch Johnny Briggs played a character who told 'Mr Johnson' a story about his little dog who had been run over in the Strand. W.G.'s response was meant to be: 'How did it occur?'

'It isn't any more of a cur than you are!' retorted Briggs.

But in rehearsals, despite careful coaching, W.G. invariably asked: 'How did it happen?' ruining the punchline and reducing his colleagues to despair.

On the night of the show, everyone was on tenterhooks, wondering how Briggs, a lively little character, would handle the situation. But when the moment came, W.G. uttered the correct line perfectly; he had been stringing them along all the while. He was in similar excellent form throughout the journey, so much so that he was unanimously voted 'the merriest heart on board'.

When they got to Australia, the tourists found a country in the grip of recession after the boom years of the 1880s during which the major cities had witnessed explosive growth. The cricketers would help to raise the spirits of a depressed nation. *Arcadia* docked in Adelaide in the second week of November, and the earl and his team were given an enthusiastic welcome, a large crowd of dignitaries coming on board to welcome them.

The next day the Mayor of Adelaide held a reception in the Town Hall at which one of the guests, having made the journey from Melbourne for the occasion, was Harry Boyle, who had played such an important role in organising the tour. The Englishmen also visited the Adelaide Oval, where South Australia were playing Victoria, and were cheered to the rafters by a large crowd. They arrived just in time to see George Giffen, known as 'the W.G. Grace of Australia', live up to the sobriquet by completing a double century. He then hit such a pulverising straight drive that it struck his brother Walter, the other batsman, on the hand as he backed up, crushing his fingers against the bat handle and forcing him to retire hurt. George Giffen went on to make 271, his highest first-class score, and take 9–96 and 4–70 as South Australia won by an innings.

The following week it was England's turn to play South Australia at the Oval in the opening match of the tour. Australian commentators had noted that it was perhaps the strongest English team ever to visit Australia and they certainly lived up to their advance billing. The weather helped: it rained heavily the night before the first day and the pitch was damp and slow, conditions which suited the English bowlers. Grace won the toss and put the home side in. The tour opened inauspiciously for the Champion: he dropped the opener Delaney at point before he had scored, but the England bowlers kept things tight all day and dismissed South Australia for 163. George Giffen laboured for two and a quarter hours over 27, and Grace claimed vehemently that he was caught at the wicket before he had scored. It was Grace who eventually held on to another chance off Peel to dismiss his great rival.

When England batted, it was a completely different story: Briggs (91), Stoddart (78) and Read (60) attacked the bowling with style and panache. Indeed, W.G., batting at three, was one of the few failures, being brilliantly caught by Reedman off Giffen for only 2; Giffen had figures of 41–5–152–7 as England scored 323, and then dismissed South Australia for only 98 to win by an innings and 62 runs, with Attewell taking 11–81. The tourists could not have got off to a better start.

On they went to Melbourne, where they arrived on 25 November, to another magnificent welcome. They were driven from the station in carriages, dressed in Lord Sheffield's colours, to the Victorian Cricket Association's headquarters where, in Sheffield's absence (he had stayed on in Adelaide for a day or two), Grace gave a little speech in response to the chairman's words of welcome. Then they were driven to the Town Hall for a reception by the Lord Mayor of Melbourne. Once again Grace had to perform the task he disliked most, making a speech, and had to do so for the third time that day at luncheon in the Melbourne Cricket Ground pavilion. There he said that if he had known he would have to give so many speeches, he would probably have stayed at home. But, he added, the team he had brought over was the best that had ever left England.

It was probably a relief to get down to some practice on the ground in the afternoon. In the eighteen years since Grace had last seen it, the MCG had been rebuilt and transformed into a stadium that could take forty thousand spectators, and he pronounced himself both impressed and saddened: 'Where are the grapevines which climbed over the wall and the wooden pavilion, and provided the players with luscious grapes?' he was reported as asking. 'Where is that famous well into which a bucket was lowered and players drank copious drafts of icy cold water after practice?'

The Australians, on the other hand, found him little changed. One journalist wrote:

As he walked from the MCC pavilion to the practice-nets, he looked what he is, the king of cricketers, and the personification of robust health and manly strength and vigour. With his flannels on, his giant-like proportions were seen to the fullest advantage, and an old cricketer who saw him here 18 years ago, remarked 'Why he is just the same as ever, except that his chest has slipped down a little.' He smote the bowling to all parts of the field, and played on under the powerful rays of a real Australian summer sun as if he throroughly enjoyed himself. Indeed, with his flowing beard, dark features and loose gait, he seemed more like an Australian than an Englishman, and would easily pass for a sun-tanned squatter fresh from the grassy downs of Queensland.

This last was a shrewd observation. Throughout the tour W.G. was subjected to a great deal of criticism by the local press. 'With the possible exception of Jardine and Larwood no English cricketer ever had such caustic treatment from the press in Australia,' wrote Australian cricket historian Keith Dunstan. No one could have mistaken Douglas Jardine for an Australian but he, Larwood and W.G. had something else in common: they played cricket like the Australians – hard and with only one object: to win. Did the Australians find that harder to take than being beaten by more self-effacing Englishmen? A century after W.G., Tony Greig and Ian Botham came in for similar treatment, and possibly for the same reason. Like W.G. they could have been mistaken for Australians, and the Australians could not forgive them for it.

The tourists' second match, against Victoria, followed the pattern of the first. The sun shone down on an exquisite scene, the ladies with their parasols and summer dresses thronging the grandstand. Victoria were shot out for 73 (Sharpe 6–40, Attewell 4–26). At lunch W.G. had to make yet another speech in reply to a toast to the visitors. Just after lunch Lord Sheffield arrived at the ground, to be greeted by the band playing 'A Fine Old English Gentleman' and a loud ovation from the crowd. (It is difficult to imagine a peer of the realm getting such a courteous welcome from an Australian crowd nowadays.)

So effective were his bowlers that Grace had no need to turn an arm over himself but he was in good form in the field. 'W.G., at point, showed wonderful agility, considering his massive frame and age,' wrote one observer. He was equally impressive with the bat, to the delight of the six thousand spectators. He opened with Abel, his huge figure dwarfing the diminutive Surrey man as they marched to the wicket to a huge ovation. Grace was quickly into his stride with a leg-side four off

Trumble and quickly accumulated runs all round the wicket, particularly with his trademark late cuts. He had one stroke of good fortune early on when Morris at third man dropped him, claiming the sun was in his eyes. It was an expensive miss, for Grace proceeded serenely on, reaching his century just before the close.

'Dr Grace's cutting was masterful, and his timing and placing up to his best form,' wrote the *Australasian*'s reporter. 'He is, of course, not as quick on his feet as he used to be, and this to some extent affects his strokes, but from first to last his display was very fine, and greatly pleased the public.' Such was W.G.'s authority that he overrode the 4 p.m. refreshment break. He was of the opinion that there were too many such interruptions in Australian cricket so when the bell went he stayed at the crease, and nobody dared countermand him, to the spectators' delight.

The following morning W.G. continued untroubled, but at a slower rate against better bowling. At lunch he was 140 not out and the score 258–7. During lunch there were yet more toasts and speeches, including three cheers for Lord Sheffield, who responded 'with the cultured ease and grace of diction charac- teristic of the true aristocrat', according to one awed observer. His speech allowed Grace off with the briefest of interventions, doubtless to his relief. As he walked out to resume his innings before a crowd estimated to have grown to fifteen thousand, the band played 'See The Conquering Hero Comes'. He struck Worrall over the long-on fence and survived a close run-out call before running out of partners. He had carried his bat for 159 out of 284; the next highest scorer was Lohmann with 39.

His return to the pavilion was a moving occasion. The *Australasian* reported:

The ovation he met with . . . was something to be remembered. Cheer after cheer went up from the thousands of throats, and as he gradually approached the gate, the immense throng that gathered there sent up a shout that woke the echoes far and wide, and scared even the cheeky minahs from their accustomed spots upon the green turf. The champion's face glowed with pleasure as he took off his hat and bent his head in response to the repeated plaudits. It was a stirring scene, and one that will be agreeably remembered for many a day .... Taken altogether his display was admirable, and showed that he is still a perfect master of the art of batting, notwithstanding his age and weight.

The Englishmen made short work of Victoria in their second innings, dismissing them for 104 to win by an innings and 107 runs. The bat W.G. used in his epic innings, made by Arthur Shrewsbury's firm in Nottingham, survives in Roger Mann's magnificent private archive in Torquay. The willow has darkened with age (and, who knows, perhaps the effects of the harsh Australian sun) but it still feels beautifully balanced and capable of meting out plenty more punishment

It was not only the Melbourne Cricket Ground that had developed out of all recognition since Grace was last in Australia. The whole country had taken huge strides forward. The 1873 tourists had been subjected to long and gruelling journeys in primitive means of transport but by 1891 there was an extensive and relatively comfortable rail network which took much of the strain out of travelling. This and a big improvement in the standard of many (but by no means all) pitches undoubtedly helped the English cricketers settle quickly into their best form.

The tour had been harmonious until the party reached Sydney for their next match against New South Wales. The Englishmen had brought an umpire with them, Cotter from Melbourne, but Moses, the NSW captain, declined to let him stand because of the long-standing rivalry between NSW and Victoria, and the start of the match was held up for an hour while Moses and Grace argued about it. Moses had his way in the end: Alfred Shaw agreed to stand instead of Cotter, but the affair left a sour taste.

The match was more hard fought than the previous two, although the tourists emerged victorious by four wickets. On the first day, before a crowd of between seven and eight thousand, NSW were dismissed for 74, Briggs and Lohmann taking nine wickets between them, but England went only 20 runs better. Opening the innings, Grace was badly dropped by Callaway off Turner on 12, but in the next over skyed a ball from Callaway straight up in the air. Turner and the wicket-keeper, Wales, both went for the catch and collided heavily but Turner, though sustaining a nasty facial injury, somehow managed to cling on to the ball, holding it aloft with both hands as he crashed to the ground. Grace declined to leave the crease until the umpire gave him out, for 15.

On the Saturday and Sunday, a total of thirty-three thousand spectators watched NSW set England 153 to win. Grace took an hour to score 19 before being caught and bowled by Turner, and at 88–6 England were in danger of defeat. But canny batting by Lohmann and Peel saw them to victory.

The party now had a swing upcountry for a series of matches against district teams. On these trips Grace liked to get in a spot of hunting or fishing. The Scottish wicket-keeper Gregor MacGregor joined him for an early-morning expedition to hunt hares by the side of the river at Bowral. W.G. suggested to MacGregor that he walk in the reeds near the river to put up any hares that might be hiding there. MacGregor demurred, for fear of the snakes he said were also lurking there. W.G. told him he was talking nonsense, and assured him there were no snakes around. A few minutes later MacGregor spotted a black snake and shot it. Grace pondered and declared: 'H'm! I don't think much of *this* kind of hare-shooting.' Shortly afterwards, MacGregor bagged another snake. 'Two black snakes in a hundred yards!' said W.G. 'It's a bit thick. I'm going home!'

On another occasion W.G. and MacGregor went out to shoot kangaroos. W.G. fired at an old 'roo and missed, at which moment a laughing jackass, which was a protected species, gave vent to the sound which gives it its name. W.G. turned to MacGregor and said: 'I tell you what, Mac – if that blessed critic doesn't mind his own business I shall shoot him, ten pound fine or not.'

The country games were two-day affairs against teams composed of twenty or twenty-two men. Grace insisted that England should put out twelve in the circumstances. The first game was against a Cumberland XX at Parramatta, when the local bowler Wilson had the distinction of dismissing Grace for a duck. The great man took 4–37 in Cumberland's second innings and the match petered out in a draw. The standard of the local players was generally very poor. Against a Camden XXII, the English XII totalled 184 on a bumpy wicket, Grace making second-top score with 36, and dismissed the XXII for 54 and 87 to win by an innings and 53 runs.

The party returned to the Sydney area to play a Berrima XXII who had the Englishmen rocking until Grace marched in as an unlikely number ten and stopped the rot with the highest score of 46, supported by the last man, Attewell (31), England finally reaching 155. The locals were dismissed for 77, England replied with 64–7 declared (Grace did not bother to bat) to set Berrima 142 to win, which was predictably well beyond their rustic capabilities and they made 76 all out. The team returned to Melbourne for a tedious drawn game against a local XVI in which Grace made only 9.

The tourists' last match before the first Test was against twenty men of Ballarat, played over three days, starting on Boxing Day. With the big game only a few days away, there was no more batting at ten for W.G. He took the opportunity to limber up by opening the batting and making a solid 62. He was outshone by Lohmann, batting at eight, who made 106 in a total of 424. The Ballarat batsmen were no match for the English bowlers, and were dismissed for 139 and 151 to lose by an innings and 134 runs. Grace took six wickets in their first innings and had 7–69 in the match.

Perhaps the Englishmen were lulled into a false sense of security by their unbeaten run since the start of the tour and the ease with which they rolled over the country teams. The first Test was a rude awakening. It started on New Year's Day 1892 and was a remarkable event in every respect. Some sixty-eight thousand people were estimated to have watched it over five days, a world record for a cricket match, ample proof that Grace's team had succeeded beyond anyone's wildest dreams in restoring public interest in the game. More than forty-six thousand paid to get in (most of the rest were not gatecrashers, but guests), generating gate receipts of more than £3,000, £2,600 of which went to Lord Sheffield's team, a magnificent windfall. Many more watched free of charge from the trees in Yarra Park. The scene on the opening day was spectacular, a perfect Australian day, and the Melbourne ground looked magnificent. 'Felix' – the Irish-born former Test player Tom Horan – rhapsodised in his column in the *Australasian*:

I have seen vast gatherings at Kennington Oval, at Old Trafford, at Bramall-lane, and at Trent-bridge; and I can honestly say that in my experience I have never seen any cricket gathering to surpass in picturesqueness and brilliance that which met my gaze on the beautiful M.C.C. enclosure on New Year's Day.

Australia were captained by the wicket-keeper Jack Blackham, who, like the young W.G., sported an imposing black beard. For the toss, he used a battered old coin which he regarded as lucky and which he had carried around for years. Sure enough, he won this time, causing a suspicious W.G. to toss it several more times to see if it could be 'fixed'. Once satisfied that all was above aboard, he led out his men to field. Australia made 240, Surrey's 'One-Eyed' John Sharpe taking 6–84, to which England responded with 264. Grace got the innings off to a good start. 'Felix' wrote:

W.G. batted in his best trim for 50. His masterful command over almost every class of ball was fully evidenced and his marked decision and excellent timing in making his strokes won the warmest praise. To cover he played with judgment and scientifically, particularly in making late cuts, in which he is a perfect adept, every ball being sent along the grass in true artistic style.

Then McLeod clean bowled Abel and Grace in successive balls.

W.G. became embroiled in more controversy over the dismissal of George Bean, who also made 50, his highest Test score. Bean was caught by William Bruce in the deep, the fielder scooping up the ball inches from the ground. Later in the pavilion, Grace approached Bruce and accused him, in effect, of cheating, because the ball in his opinion had not been cleanly taken. Naturally Bruce stood his ground. 'Felix' commented wryly: 'The umpire was of Bruce's opinion too, or he would not have given the batsman out.'

The game was turned in Australia's favour by Alick Bannerman, who batted obdurately for three hours, fifty minutes in the second innings to keep the English bowlers at bay. Eventually he was caught by Grace at point. 'Never did W.G. hug more closely or fondly any catch than that which the little stonewaller gave him,' wrote 'Felix'. Grace was full of admiration for Bannerman's display, declaring that he would have to be included in a World XI if one were picked there and then.

England were set 213 to win, and while Grace and his opening partner Stoddart were at the wicket the target seemed eminently achievable. Grace was given a 'life' by Giffen at short mid-on when he had scored seven, but otherwise looked in total command and when Blackham failed to stump Stoddart off Trott the odds swung even farther towards an England win.

The pair had put on 60 when Grace drove at Turner, failed to keep the ball down and was beautifully caught by Bannerman for 25. It was the turning point of the match. As had happened so often when W.G. was dismissed, the batting collapsed. Six more wickets fell in quick succession before stumps to leave England reeling on the ropes at 104–7. On the following day the end was not long delayed and Australia won by 54 runs. It was England's first reverse of the tour and a huge shot in the arm for Australian cricket. Equally, it was a devastating setback for the English party, who had come to take victory for granted. Worried by his bowlers' lack of penetration, Lord Sheffield suggested cabling for Arthur Mold, the Lancashire fast bowler, to bolster his armoury. On his day Mold was as quick and deadly as anyone in the game, although his action was suspect, and indeed he was forced to abandon the game in 1900 after being no-balled for throwing. Grace resisted Sheffield's proposal; he believed his side was strong enough to square the series at Sydney.

Meanwhile, the Englishmen had several gentle games – virtually exhibition matches – against Melbourne sides to help them recover from this unexpected blow to their self-esteem. One was a two-day match against a South Melbourne XVI, on that club's delightful lakeside ground, which the Englishmen declared the prettiest and best-kept they had seen in Australia. Indeed Alfred Shaw was so taken by the sight of yachts on the lake that he was said almost to have burst into poetry. A good crowd, reckoned to be about three and a half thousand, turned up on the first day, and were entertained by the police band as well as the cricketers.

At lunch, the president of the club, Mr A.D. Madden, toasted the tourists and their captain. Grace responded and took the opportunity to mention that it had been decided to restrict the match to one innings per side. One reporter noted: 'His hazel eye seemed to have a merrier look than usual, when he made this statement, as if he appeared to know that the South were in for a leather-hunting.' So it transpired. Against a weak attack the English batsmen took the opportunity, in the modern idiom, to fill their boots, amassing 438. Grace batted at seven and weighed in with a fine, though not chanceless, 69, top score and one of five half-centuries. South Australia managed to salvage a draw with an unimpressive 102–8. Grace took 1–17 but had a splendid day with the ball in the next fixture, a one-day match against a Williamstown XXII. Rain constantly affected the proceedings, but W.G. still helped himself to 11–58 as the locals were dismissed for 154. The rain restricted Lord Sheffield's XII to 43–1 and the match was drawn.

Grace nearly bagged a pair against a Melbourne Junior XX. In the first innings he was bowled for one and in the second contrived to run himself out for a duck. These minor matches were no preparation for the second Test, in Sydney, at the beginning of February. Indeed, they may have contributed to a false sense of superiority over the Australians. A commentator in the *Australasian* put it bluntly:

After winning their opening matches against South Australia and Victoria, the Englishmen had rather a poor opinion of Australian cricket, and one or two who rode the high horse expressed regret that there was no eleven in the colonies which could put them to their best. Since that time they have had reason to change their opinions.

W.G. was involved in controversy before the second Test got under way. The brilliant Australian left-handed batsman Harry Moses had picked up a bad leg injury in the first Test but was picked for the second although he was clearly not fit. W.G. was determined to square the series and warned Moses that, as a doctor, he considered his injury was too serious to allow him to play. Consequently, if he went ahead, he should not expect England to allow him a substitute in the field if he broke down. Moses tested the leg and said he was fit enough to play although many people thought twelfth man Syd Gregory should have been picked instead. They turned out to be right.

Australia won the toss and on a good wicket and in perfect weather made only 145. Lohmann was the hero for England with the excellent figures of 8–58. During his innings of 29 Moses aggravated the injury and his doctor warned him that he risked permanent injury if he fielded. But after W.G.'s pre-match warning, Blackham felt he could not ask for a substitute and poor Moses had to limp around the field, barely able to walk. The crowd protested loudly about his being forced to field, blaming Grace for it. It did not affect him in the slightest; perhaps it even encouraged him. At the close, England were 38–1 with W.G. going well.

Having made his point, next morning Grace offered Blackham a substitute after all. As a medical man, it could have given him no pleasure to see Moses struggling to walk. Blackham asked if Gregory could be substitute. As Gregory was a brilliant fielder, Grace refused the request. Eventually, they agreed on the veteran Tom Garrett. W.G. was not rewarded for his generosity when he resumed his innings. As it was Saturday, twenty thousand people had packed into the ground and they were soon celebrating the wicket they most wanted. Grace was not at his most fluent, and appeared to be cramped by the Australian tactic of posting Bruce at silly point, very close to the bat. The score had just reached 50 when he was bowled neck and crop by a beauty from his old adversary Turner for 26.

Unlike in the first Test, the English batting did not fold after his departure. His opening partner Abel carried his bat for a superb 132 and the team mustered a respectable 306 for a first-innings lead of 162. This was widely thought to be a match-winning advantage, especially when Trott was dismissed for 1 before the close. With Moses injured, Australia were effectively two wickets down – but when play resumed on Monday the crowd witnessed one of the great fightbacks in cricket history. They also gave Grace the bird again. A Sydney newspaper, the *Daily Telegraph*, had published what purported to be a letter written by him after his trip to Australia eighteen years previously, in which he was highly critical of the country and its people.

I must admit that our gentlemen players had a very scrubby fag end, but after all, we pulled through respectably, and I have the money, which is the only thing I wanted, for to tell you the truth, I care so little for colonial opinion that you may publish this letter if you like, it will show the cads what I think of them. A good deal was said about my stopping away from the lunch at various places. My reason was that I didn't want to fraternise with the tinkers, tailors and snobs who are the great guns of your cricket world. To take their money was a fair thing in return for work done, but to hobnob with a lot of scum was a far different thing. Fancy the chance of a greasy butcher on his travels walking up to me one day at Lord's with 'How d'ye do, Mr G.; I lunched with you in Australia'. My dear fellow, as far as I can see, colonial society is low, shockingly low. You have plenty of money, no doubt, but your gentlemen are yet unborn. I suppose including yourself, I met about three during the whole of my trip.

It was a hoax, written by one Richard Egan Lee, who had since died. It is difficult to see how anybody could have mistaken its coarse pastiche of an upper-class Englishman's voice for Grace's down-to-earth manner. The idea that he would have used a phrase like 'it will show the cads what I think of them' was laughable, but it appears to have convinced plenty in the Sydney crowd that it was genuine, and as a result they hurled abuse at W.G. He was so angry that he demanded that a retraction be printed, and this appeared the day after the Test finished.

He must have felt equally ill-disposed towards the Australian batsmen Lyons and Bannerman. In their contrasting style – Lyons aggressive, Bannerman the arch-stonewaller – they put on 174, a stand which turned the match. It was Grace who gave Bannerman

227

the most difficulty with what one reporter described as his 'hanging slow balls', but Lyons showed him less respect, depositing one inviting delivery in the drainage ditch for 'a fiver'. Grace eventually caught him at point off Lohmann, but by then he had scored 134. By the end of the day Australia were 101 ahead with plenty of wickets in hand.

Overnight the Australians suffered a fresh setback, to add to Moses's injury. A telegram from Melbourne announced that the bowler Charie McLeod's brother had died suddenly, aged only thirty-five. McLeod asked his team-mates what he should do. With typical Australian pragmatism, they pointed out that the next express train to Melbourne did not leave until the afternoon so he might as well bat (he made 18, highly creditable in the circumstances). There was a sequel, inevitably involving Grace. Australia made 391, setting England 229 to win. Blackham asked if a Melbourne University player named Hutton might substitute in the field for McLeod.

'Is he a better field than McLeod?' asked Grace, unimpressed by the tragic nature of McLeod's departure.

'Yes,' replied Blackham, with irreproachable honesty.

'Then get someone else,' declared Grace.

England never recovered from a dreadful start. The first two wickets, those of Abel and Bean, went down with only 6 on the board. Joined at the wicket by Stoddart, W.G. might have played cautiously to rebuild the innings. Instead, he went recklessly on to the attack. He leapt out and drove the ball straight back down the wicket like a bullet, but the bowler, Giffen, failed to hold on to the stinging chance. Grace cut the next ball beautifully for four, then slashed at Turner and was caught behind by Blackham. The whole Australian team leapt into the air to appeal, the umpire's finger went up and Grace was on his way. England were 11–3 and pandemonium followed. 'The air was thick with hats, and rent with shouting. Such a scene has, perhaps, never been witnessed on the ground before as followed the downfall of the English captain,' reported the *Australasian*. Rain spared England further humiliation that day but on the next Australia duly completed victory by 73 runs, despite Stoddart's fighting 69, and assured themselves of the three-match rubber. The result of the third and last Test, at Adelaide, was rendered a formality. It was an outcome few, not least in Australia, had anticipated at the start of the series.

Grace himself appears to have been so upset at this unexpected turn of events that he behaved badly for the rest of the team's stay in Australia, his disgruntlement taking the form of persistent disputes with umpires. After a series of upcountry matches, England returned to Sydney for the return against New South Wales, beating them comfortably by seven wickets.

The match was notable for the reappearance after several seasons in retirement of the great Percy McDonnell, former captain of Australia. He had turned down many previous entreaties to come back by the NSW selectors but meeting his old adversary W.G. again for a chat before the game persuaded him to change his mind. England amassed 414 in their first innings, Grace racing to a quickfire 45 out of 52, before playing on to Callaway. Read and Lohmann scored centuries. NSW replied with 244 (Grace 3–66) and were obliged to follow on. In their second innings they made 210 (Grace 2–29), setting England only 41 to win. Alas, opening the NSW innings each time, McDonnell made only 5 and 2.

Apart from his comeback, the main talking point was W.G.'s behaviour towards one of the umpires, Briscoe, after he turned down an appeal for a catch at the wicket in NSW's first innings. According to the umpire, a furious Grace roared: 'If we have such umpires as you we may as well go back to England.' W.G. declared that he had merely said: 'I wish you would pay attention to the game. We all heard the catch.' Even at this distance, that sounds just as insulting as the first version, and Briscoe could hardly be blamed for refusing to stand in NSW's second innings. There was a long delay while a replacement was sought. Finally, Charlie Bannerman, the former Test batsman, agreed to take over and the match could be resumed. But the incident did nothing to raise Grace's stature with the Australian public.

A two-day match against a Wollongong (NSW) XXII, ruined by rain (Grace was out for 6) was followed by a trip to Tasmania, which so captivated Lord Sheffield that there was talk that he intended to make the island his winter home. The party returned to Melbourne for the penultimate match of the tour, the return against Victoria. It was a lacklustre affair, the Victorians (137 and 100) proving unable to cope with the English batsmen, with the exception of the Test player William Bruce, who scored a half century in each innings. Grace (44) top-scored in England's first-innings total of 184 and did not bother to bat in the second when they knocked off the runs for the loss of only one wicket.

On the party went to Adelaide for the final match of their gruelling 27-match itinerary. Only two matches had been lost, but unfortunately they were both Tests, and that was how the tour would be remembered, certainly by Grace himself. The loss of the second Test, and with it the rubber, seems to have soured Grace for the rest of the time he was in Australia. 'Grace is admittedly a bad loser,' wrote Tom Horan, 'and when he lost two of the test matches in succession he lost his temper too, and kept on losing it right to the finish . . . Since that match Grace seems to have developed a condition of captiousness, fussiness and nastiness strongly to be deprecated.' These were strong words indeed from Australia's most distinguished and respected commentator, who bent over backwards to be fair to all sides.

The series may have gone but there was a lot of pride at stake at Adelaide for England: a 3–0 whitewash would be the most humiliating farewell imaginable after the high hopes, not to say arrogance, of the first weeks of the tour. The third Test saw Grace at his best as a batsman and his worst as a captain. The Australians had named Flynn, one of their most respected umpires, to stand in the game. To everyone's surprise Grace objected and would not budge. The Australians were outraged. 'His objection to Flynn was nothing short of a gratuitous insult to a first-class umpire,' wrote Horan, who also pointed out that when touring England the Australians were not allowed to object to any home umpires 'no matter how incompetent'. Ravish and Whitridge were the eventual choices; then Ravish had to stand down just before the match through illness, to be replaced by Downs.

This was not Grace's only grouse before a ball had been bowled. He boycotted an official function. He wanted the ends of the

Adelaide Oval to be roped off, to reduce the length of the boundaries, but was overruled. He didn't like the fact that the pitch was covered until the first day of the match, but was ignored. At the toss, when Blackham produced his lucky coin, Grace would not let him toss but insisted on doing so himself while the Australian skipper called. He called 'tails' and lost, to Grace's great pleasure. It was a good toss to win for the pitch, laid on clay, was in magnificent condition, hard and true, and so shiny that at first the bowlers found it hard to stay upright.

Grace and Abel opened the batting and put on 47 without trouble, Grace hitting Trott for three boundaries in his first over when he came on as first change. Though he lost Abel, stumped for 24, Grace and Stoddart went in to lunch at 65–1. Afterwards Grace continued in highly aggressive fashion, jumping down the wicket at almost every delivery and lofting the ball in to the outfield, but out of reach of the fielders. Soon after he had reached his half-century, however, he was out trying to smite a yorker from McLeod. He had hit eight fours in his 58 and walked off to a great ovation. This time England did not fold after the departure of their greatest batsman but, by the time rain curtailed play on the afternoon of the second day, had gone on to rack up a remorseless 490–9, Stoddart compiling a dashing 134, Peel made 83 and Read 57. MacGregor and Attewell rubbed salt in the wound by putting on 65 for the last wicket in steadily increasing rain.

Indeed, the rain became so heavy that the Australians appealed to the umpires several times for play to be suspended. It was only when the English players joined in that Whitridge and Downs agreed. By then the players were soaked to the skin, and it was evident that the Australians would be batting on a much stickier wicket than their fortunate opponents.

More controversy ensued on the third day, a Saturday. The rain poured down all night on the uncovered pitch, leaving it a sodden mess on which it would be almost impossible to score runs. The English were looking to get among the Australian batsmen once their own innings had been wound up, and were not at all pleased to hear that the umpires, having inspected the wicket, decreed that the start of play should be delayed for an hour.

W.G. was outraged. He marched into the Australian dressing-room and demanded that Blackham accompany him out to the wicket so that they, and not the umpires, should decide whether play should begin. Blackham declined, and Grace departed in high dudgeon, threatening to pull his team out of the match if he did not get his way. 'Who told the umpires to inspect the wicket? I didn't,' was his parting shot. 'Disagreeable insinuations were made by Grace and a couple of the [English] professionals,' wrote the *Australasian*'s reporter. These were apparently to the effect that the umpires had bowed to Australian pressure in taking their decision.

The Australians denied this, saying the Blackham in fact went out of his way to avoid talking to the umpires. Grace later claimed he had meant that pressure had been exerted from people who had been betting on the match and not by the Australian players, but the damage was done. In the Australian view, Grace had hoist himself with his own petard by making such a fuss about the umpires before the match started. Having successfully objected to Flynn, he could hardly complain about the decisions of the pair who eventually stood. All he succeeded in doing was in insisting that they inspect the wicket every quarter of an hour.

When tempers cooled and play resumed, MacGregor and Attewell put on a further 9 to take their stand to 74 before MacGregor was given run out going for the single which would have taken the score to 500. As it was, England's 499 was their highest Test score against Australia until then.

As they feared, the Australians could not cope with the conditions and were shot out for 100 and 169, to lose by an innings and 230 runs, their heaviest defeat. On Saturday, the crowd showed what it thought of Grace's conduct by subjecting him to mock applause whenever he touched the ball. 'It was made abundantly clear that Grace is by no means as popular with Australian crowds as he was at the commencement of the tour,' commented the *Australasian*.

England wrapped up the match on the fourth day, Monday, leaving them a day's rest before they sailed for home on the Wednesday.

Although he ended the tour under a cloud, there was no doubt that from a playing point of view it had been a success for W.G. He topped the tour party averages in eleven-a-side matches, with eleven innings (once not out), an aggregate of 448 and an average of 44.80. (Abel was second with 38.80, while Stoddart scored two more runs – 450 – but averaged 37.50.) He was also top of the averages with the following figures: innings: 31; runs: 921; highest score 159 not out; not out: 3: average 32.89. It was a tremendous achievement, which surprised and impressed informed Australian observers. When he first toured Australia in his prime twenty years earlier he had averaged 35.11 in all matches, admittedly on far worse wickets. Still, it was evident that he had maintained an extraordinarily high batting standard for a man of forty-three.

The same could not be said for his bowling. He bowled little in eleven-a-side matches, taking only five wickets at 26.80. He fared better in the other matches, against primitive batting, with a haul of forty-eight wickets at only 9.52. As for his fielding, the *Australasian*'s tour summary commented: 'W.G. Grace, despite his weight and stomach, acquitted himself creditably at point, and accepted more than one hot chance.'

On the original aim of the tour, to revive interest in cricket, Tom Horan was in no doubt: 'It is now the concurrent testimony of all that the visit has caused a cricket revival which has surpassed even the most sanguine anticipations of those who viewed the tour favourably when it was first proposed.'

The English party left Adelaide bound for home on the steamship *Valetta*. It was Grace's last look at Australia. He never went back to the land where they mixed awe and dislike for him in about equal measure.

14 · RESURRECTION
1892–1897

IT might have been expected that the forty-three-year-old W.G. would return from the gruelling Australian tour exhausted. Nothing could have been further from the case. Perhaps the long sea voyage home helped to restore him – that and his naturally robust constitution. At any rate he returned to the English scene reinvigorated, rather as he had done in 1874.

He and his fellow tourists were back in action together a week after landing, against the Rest of England in a benefit match at Trent Bridge for their manager Alfred Shaw. Rain severely curtailed proceedings, as it always seemed to whenever his colleagues tried to raise money for Shaw, but Grace still managed to make a fine 63 in even time out of 80. It was the start to a consistent, if not outstanding season, in which he again failed to make a century in England. This time he missed out on that milestone by only one run, for Gloucestershire against Sussex at Gloucester. He was stuck on 99 for several overs until he lost patience, tried to hit his fellow Australian tourist, George Bean, back over his head and was caught and bowled. It was only as he walked back to the pavilion that he noticed from the scoreboard that he had been so close to three figures, and demanded crossly of his brother E.M.: 'Ted, why ever you didn't you tell me? I could have scored off any of those balls.'

'Aye, aye,' replied E.M., 'and if I had told you, you would have been the first to complain.'

Although hampered for much of the season by a bad knee, which severely reduced his mobility at the wicket and in the field, he played many other good innings for Gloucestershire. For the first time, the nine teams in the county championship played each other home and away and Gloucestershire had high hopes of doing well, particularly as the Australian fast bowler J.J. Ferris, who had always played well in England, had qualified for the county by residence. In the event, he was a great disappointment. By modern standards, he performed excellently, with eighty first-class wickets at 24.80 each, but that left him only twenty-first in the averages. Grace considered that Ferris' poor summer had a discouraging rather than encouraging effect on his team-mates, who had hoped for so much from their new recruit.

Surrey carried all before them to emerge as champions. Gloucestershire could manage only seventh place, third from bottom. Grace also finished seventh in the first-class batting list, totalling 1,055 runs at an average of 31, making 47, 72 not out (at Lord's) and 89 (at Lord's) against Middlesex, and 41 and 54 in two appearances for the Gentlemen v Players at Hastings.

Both the public and the committee were getting fed up with Gloucestershire's continuing poor performances, and there was no doubt in the minds of many where the blame lay – with the captain and his selection policy. There was no doubt that W.G. was a very astute judge of a cricketer, but when it came to picking the Gloucestershire team he had a preference for public-school and university men over local club players. In the mid-1890s this was to pay off, particularly with his selection on slender evidence of Charles Townsend and Gilbert Jessop, who were to prove two pillars of the county side. But many of the players W.G. picked were not worthy of their place.

In 1892 the county's future was looking bleak, and opposition grew towards the authoritarian captain. The outcome was that in December 1892 some members of the committee proposed a selection committee. No decision was taken, but W.G. brooded on this unprecedented challenge to his authority over Christmas and by the time of the next meeting in January 1893 he had communicated his resignation from both committee and captaincy.

The committee immediately retreated. 'They beg to remind him of the assurance then given him, that the Committee did not wish to take any action distasteful or antagonistic to him as they still have the same confidence in his captaincy now as previously to the meeting on 9 December . . .' W.G. did not withdraw his resignation. He merely played – and captained – on.

The following season, 1893, Grace registered a further improvement, finishing fifth in the first-class averages on 35.75. His total of 1,609 was bettered by only two other batsmen (Gunn and Stoddart, who both passed 2,000). He made only one century, 128 for MCC v Kent at Lord's, but was in cracking form in the first Gentlemen v Players game, at The Oval, with 57 and 68 against top-quality bowling. 'After twenty-nine years of continuous work in first-class cricket, he is still the noblest Roman of them all,' marvelled the 'Pavilion Gossip' writer of *Cricket: A Weekly Record of the Game*.

W.G. reserved some of his best performances for his appearances against the Australian tourists, again led by Blackham, who were a powerful batting side let down by their bowling. Grace and Stoddart had four century opening partnerships for MCC and England, and two others of 75-plus. Grace set the tone for the summer with 63 for Lord Sheffield's XI in the opening match of the tour. He did not, however, have it all his own way against the Australians. They took 503 off Gloucestershire at Bristol, condemning W.G. and his team to two long days in the field. The grey-haired George Giffen confirmed his reputation as the W.G. of the southern hemisphere with 180, his highest score in England. W.G.'s bowling figures were 57–22–137–2. When the county side finally batted, they put up a dismal display and were shot out for only 41. Batting at number ten, W.G. contributed an unbeaten four. Only rain saved Gloucestershire from defeat on the most monumental scale.

In the tourists' next match, against a Grace-led MCC team, J.J. Lyons produced one of the most memorable innings of that or any other summer, a storming 149 in 95 minutes to help save the game, which lingered as long in the folk memory as Ian Botham's identical score in 1981 against Australia was to do. Grace made 13

236

in MCC's first innings total of 424, and 33 in the second innings when he and Stoddart put on 72 for the first wicket against bowlers who found it difficult to grip the ball after an interruption for rain. In the end, a match that England looked to have in the bag finished in an exciting draw. In the return match, Grace made 75.

For South of England he scored 66, during which he passed 40,000 runs in first-class cricket, completed in 967 innings, at an average of more than 41. No other cricketer had compiled even half that total at that time. He added to the total in Arthur Shrewsbury's England XI at Trent Bridge – Shrewsbury's benefit match – when he and Stoddart put on 114 for the first wicket, Grace's contribution being 49. He was in his best form, hitting six boundaries until, going for his half-century he skyed a delivery from Turner and was caught by Giffen circling behind the bowler. Shrewsbury himself made an unbeaten 52 and his XI, which was virtually the full England team, thrashed the Australians by an innings and 153 runs.

Grace had to pull out of the first Test Match proper, at Lord's, because of an injured finger – it was the first Test he had ever missed in England, and was otherwise notable for the debut of F.S. (later Sir Stanley) Jackson, the brilliant young Cambridge captain, whose fag at Harrow had been one Winston Spencer Churchill, and who marked his first performance with 91.

Grace was fit again for the second Test at The Oval in which he took back the captaincy from Stoddart. The Surrey club generously made the game Maurice Read's benefit, although he was not playing; it was the first time the 'gate' for an official Test had been made over to a player in this fashion. W.G. won the toss and shared a resolute opening partnership of 151 with Stoddart against tight and hostile bowling in punishing heat. Most of their runs at first came from edges through the slips and 'four balls out of five had to be played with the utmost caution, not to say diffidence', according to one report. 'Giffen seemed especially difficult, and while Stoddart generally dropped down on him very late, Grace played him as a rule forward.' At lunch they were undefeated on 134, but were late coming out afterwards, while both the Australians and the umpires lay down on the grass 'to wait for the time when it might please the batsmen to put in an appearance. There were ominous rumours that Grace's finger had again broken down, and that Stoddart had sunstroke.' Happily neither rumour was true. At 151, Stoddart was out for 83, and Grace followed without further addition to the score, caught at slip off Trumble for 68. 'Though he never seemed comfortable, and was often beaten, he showed much of his old skill.'

Then Jackson capped his first Test performance with a brilliant century in England's total of 483 and Australia were shot out for 91. Following on, they made a much more respectable 349 but England still won by an innings and 43 runs. The weather was extremely hot throughout the match and the *Cricket Field* noted:

As the majority of the players on both sides wore wide white hats, which threw their faces into deep shadow, it became a work of difficulty to recognise them while they were in the field. W.G. was the only exception, for, owing to his beard, his patch of black was very much bigger than that of anybody else.

It was the decisive result of the series, for the final match, at Old Trafford, ended in another draw. In Australia's first innings, Grace caught Trott at third man: 'Grace ran in with all the vigour and dash of his youthful days and captured the ball close to the ground,' reported the *Sportsman*. When England batted, he compiled a slow 40 after running Stoddart out for a duck; he was eventually bowled off his pads by Bruce. In the final innings, England were set a target of 198 in 135 minutes; Grace and Stoddart rattled up 78 at almost a run a minute before Stoddart went for 42. Grace was caught by Trott off McLeod for 45 with the score on 100, and the match petered out with England 80 short and six wickets still in hand.

But while England's fortunes had revived, Gloucestershire's were going in the opposite direction. They finished bottom of the county table, although Grace headed the averages, and produced several fine performances, notably 96 against Middlesex, 75 against Sussex, and a 61 against Surrey, when the rest of the side managed only 44. On the plus side for Gloucestershire was the debut in August 1893 of W.G.'s godson, Charles Townsend, then still a

Clifton College schoolboy. Son of Frank Townsend, who had played with the Graces during Gloucestershire's formative years, Townsend was to become the deadliest leg-spinner in the English game and subsequently one of its finest left-hand batsmen.

Another county debutant the same month was Grace's eldest son, W.G. junior, who had a good record with the bat for Clifton College. While Townsend's selection at the age of only sixteen was a risk which came off triumphantly, W.G.'s choice of his son was a classic example of the weakness for which he had attracted so much criticism, for young W.G. was no more than a good public-school player. Typically, Grace blamed Gloucestershire's disastrous summer partly on his own bad luck in losing the toss ten times out of sixteen.

There was still the matter of his future to decide. In September he withdrew his resignation but the committee again raised, somewhat gingerly, the question of a selection committee. Would he be prepared to consider the idea? His reply was unambiguous: 'I will have nothing to do with it.' That was the end of the matter, for a few years at least. The chores of captaincy were not confined to battles with the committee. There were always more mundane matters to attend to, as a letter to a Charles Blundell, now in the Lord's archives, demonstrates (with W.G.'s usual lordly indifference to grammatical niceties):

You asked me for the County ground for the match today. I had a pitch prepared and luncheon ordered 1/- per head. Yesterday my son heard that the match was at Bath. Whose fault is this. It is very awkward to tell the caterer there is no luncheon after ordering it.

Things were no better for Gloucestershire and Grace in 1894. The county again finished bottom of the table and Grace's form was lamentable. In 16 innings for his county he managed an average of only 18.9. His highest score was a rapid 88 against Sussex at Brighton in May, and he made 61 against Nottinghamshire at Trent Bridge but his highest score in the home matches was only 49.

In all first-class cricket he scored 1,293 at an average of 29.38 but many of these were 'soft' runs. He hit two of his three centuries of the summer for MCC against Cambridge University, who had a notably weak bowling attack, including his highest-ever score at Lord's, 196. There was now a family connection with Cambridge: W.G. junior had gone up to Pembroke College the previous autumn and had high hopes of a Blue as a freshman after a good record at Clifton, but although he scored 88 in the freshmen's trial match, he was not picked for the university side in his first year.

It cannot have been easy being the son of the most famous player in the game, a problem that has been faced by many sons of distinguished players since then. As so often happens, W.G. junior was a perfectly competent player who had none of his father's extraordinary talent (how could he?), or even that of his uncles Ted or Fred. 'He was a very useful all-round cricketer,' said Gilbert Jessop, who made his Gloucestershire debut in 1894, and was a generous soul, 'being an especially fine mid-off.'

Although there is plenty of evidence that W.G. was a kindly man towards children, he seems sometimes to have been less than charitable towards his eldest son. One Bristol club cricketer remembered getting into a cab with them when W.G. junior accidentally stepped on his father's foot. 'W.G. stormed and raved at his son for a good five minutes. The son meekly expressed his regret and, eventually, managed to appease the great man's wrath.'

W.G. senior fell into the familiar parental trap of taking too great an interest in his son's sporting progress. A notable Bristol athlete, J.W.S. Toms, recalled:

'W.G.' was very keen for his son, young 'W.G.', to win the Public Schools' quarter-mile championship and asked me to help in his preparation. The training was on the County Ground and very drastic it was, too. 'W.G.', believing in stamina, would make me run 350 to 400 yards all out. Then he would yell until the finish, 'Come on, lazy bones!'
To 'W.G.'s' disappointment, his son was second in the fastest time recorded up to that date.

W.G. overdid the pressure when it came to cricket too. When his son was not picked for the University's match against the MCC at Fenner's, he picked him for MCC instead. Father and son opened the batting for MCC only for W.G. junior to suffer the humiliation of a duck. W.G. senior showed the difference in class by making 139. To rub salt in the young man's wound, exactly the same thing happened in the return match at Lord's: he was dismissed without scoring while his father went on to make 196. W.G. junior did make 54 in the second innings, but it was off an exhausted Light Blue attack.

However, to his father's pride and delight, he managed to get his Blue the following year, and performed creditably in the University match, opening the innings and making 40 and 28, W.G. parading in the Long Room in a new hat and coat. Unfortunately, in his final year, W.G. junior reverted to type – he made a 'pair' against Oxford. As he trudged back to the Lord's pavilion after his second duck, his mother and sister Bessie, who had made the journey from Bristol to watch him, sat in silence, tears streaming down their faces.

A quiet, bespectacled man who had none of his father's ebullience and indeed seemed unlike anyone else in the extrovert Grace clan, W.G. junior played little first-class cricket after that. He was saddled with the unfortunate nickname 'Sally' and broke with the family tradition of going into medicine. A brilliant student, who was Fifth Senior Optima in the Mathematical Tripos of 1896, he became a schoolmaster, first at Oundle, then at the Royal Naval College, Osborne, on the Isle of Wight. He died in 1905, aged only thirty, after an emergency operation for appendicitis.

W.G. senior's best batting against quality bowling in 1894 came, yet again, for the Gentlemen in their three games against the Players: 71 at The Oval, a particularly meritorious 56 on a rain-affected pitch at Lord's, and a spectacular 131 at Hastings, although he had the good luck to play the ball on to his stumps and get away with it before he had scored. It was one of the rare bright spots in an otherwise unremarkable season, another being a nine-wicket haul against the first South African team to tour England, although they were not good enough to merit first-class status.

It looked to the world as if Grace was in gradual decline, and he could not even please the Gloucestershire folk who had followed him so adoringly for so long. When Sussex came to Bristol on the August bank holiday, heavy overnight rain followed by another downpour during lunch caused play to be abandoned at 3 p.m. without a ball being bowled. Thinking he would placate the large crowd which had waited patiently for play to begin, W.G. organised an impromptu football match on the practice ground but badly misjudged the spectators' mood. When he and his team ran out in what Jessop described as 'hastily improvised accoutrement', the crowd took it badly and, gathering in front of the pavilion, demanded their money back. The demonstrators would probably have dispersed had the haughty young C.B. Fry, of Sussex, not appeared and 'cocked a snook' at them. They jostled the players as they tried to leave, and one group even took their anger out on a section of the pitch.

In 1894 MCC supervised the biggest shake-up the county championship had ever seen, setting in place for the 1895 season the framework of the system that has survived, with a few additions and amendments, to the present day. Derbyshire, Warwickshire, Essex, Hampshire and Leicestershire were granted first-class status and admitted to the championship, making a total of 14. The new counties brought an influx of promising new players to the game, to add to a fresh generation of outstanding cricketers like Archie MacLaren and Ranjitsinhji who were already making their mark in the older counties and the universities. But Grace was not ready to cede the stage to them just yet.

The omens for the 1895 season were not good. In his opening first-class innings, for MCC against Sussex at Lord's, Grace was dismissed for 13, but after that he barely made another mistake all summer. That first match was laden with potential symbolism, for it marked the county debut of Ranji, whose silky batting skills had come to their notice in the service of Cambridge University. Sure enough, Ranji glided to a wonderful 150, upon which the MCC captain, Arthur Hornby, tossed the ball to the forty-six-year-old Grace. He dismissed Ranji with his first delivery to him and in MCC's first innings proceeded to demonstrate to the young master that he was far from finished by hitting a fast century. To complete the symbolism, Ranji dropped Grace in the slips when he had made only 14.

The Champion's century set the the scene for an extraordinary May and an equally astonishing season which showed that he had lost none of his old power. In its achievement, it was second only to his *annus mirabilis* of 1876 and, taking the ageing process into account, it ranked equal with that record-breaking season. As a start, Grace scored 1,000 runs in May, the first batsman to reach a goal which was to become one of the most eagerly sought but hardest to reach landmarks in the first-class game. Grace's achievement was all the more outstanding for he scored all his runs in the twenty-one days between 9 and 30 May.

After the Sussex match, he made scores of only 18 and 25 for MCC against Yorkshire at Lord's. Then came Gloucestershire's match against Somerset at Bristol and Grace's biggest score for twenty years, a herculean 288, which was also his hundredth hundred in first-class cricket and the first time that landmark had ever been reached. No contemporary batsman was even close to such an achievement – Abel, for instance, made a total of 74 centuries in his entire career, Shrewsbury 59. The only member of the 'hundred hundreds' club whose career seriously overlapped with Grace's was Tom Hayward, who reached the magic figure in 1913.

Grace's record came on Friday 17 May, the second day of the Somerset match. The visitors had made 303 in their first innings, W.G. bowling forty-five overs for a return of 5–87. Demonstrating yet again his extraordinary robustness, he made 38 not out before stumps on the first day. On the Friday morning snow fell over Bristol and a bitter cold persisted throughout the day, but it did nothing to hamper W.G., who swiftly demonstrated that his eye was well and truly in, and moved inexorably towards the record. As he neared it, nerves appeared to get the better of him, a sight no one present could recall. Charles Townsend, who was batting with him at the time, remarked: 'This was the one and only time I ever saw him flustered.' The Bristol county ground still did not have a proper scoreboard and two spectators remembered W.G. bellowing to the scorers, 'How many does Charlie want for his century?' (the answer was 'Two' which he failed to get) and then, 'How many have I made?'

Finally, Sammy Woods attempted to put batsman and crowd out of their misery with a slow leg-side full toss, clearly deliberately designed to give Grace the record – but even that generous gesture nearly went wrong because the ball's trajectory was lower than Woods intended, 'and the least mistake on W.G.'s part might have deferred the consummation of one of the feats which every one [sic] present will never forget,' reported the *Cricket Field*. Fortunately, his nerve held steady enough to despatch the ball to the boundary for the record, amid deafening cheers. Woods, one of the most extrovert and sportsmanlike characters in the game, was the first man to shake W.G.'s hand.

The Bristol ground had never seen anything like it. 'Old and middle-aged men became boys for the time,' added the *Cricket Field*, 'while relations and close friends sought for isolated spots to keep down the throb in their throats that might result in hysterical laughter or tears.'

If the Somerset bowlers had hoped W.G. might reciprocate Woods's gesture, they were mistaken. That had never been his way. He now proceeded to slaughter the bowling in majestic fashion. At lunch he was 159, and as news spread of his doings, spectators flocked to the ground. When he reached his double century, in only 220 minutes, E.M. carried out to the middle a tray bearing two bottles, or a magnum, of champagne (eyewitness accounts differ). The Somerset players toasted W.G. and he helped himself to plenty of it too. Thus recharged, on he went towards his triple century, which was only thwarted when Tyler at mid-off leapt to hold on to a stinging off-drive one-handed.

'At the wickets five hours and a half, he had played perfect cricket, and at no time did he give anything like a chance,' reported the *Daily Telegraph*. It was the third highest score of his first-class career, 'a performance', according to another correspondent, 'that perhaps no one will live to see equalled, let alone excelled . . . "W.G." played the noble game with an amount of vigour and dash that brought to mind his doings in the "seventies".' One remarkable fact was that, according to the

Somerset wicket-keeper, A.P. Wickham, W.G. allowed only four balls to pass through to him during his entire innings, which would be utterly inconceivable in the twentieth-century game.

Gloucestershire wrapped up the match just after 4 p.m. on the Saturday, much to W.G.'s delight, for it meant he could jump on a train to London in order to attend a dinner in honour of his England team-mate and fellow opener A.E. Stoddart. (W.G. scandalised an old lady in his compartment by changing into his white tie and tails on the way).

The dinner was given by the Hampstead club, for whom 'Stoddie' had once made 485, then the highest score ever recorded in a cricket match. Grace was very fond of Stoddart, and claimed credit for having 'invented' him as a bowler (he was a useful performer who took 278 first-class wickets in his fifteen-year career). He derived huge pleasure from describing how Stoddart, when being collared by a batsman, once exclaimed, 'All right, hit away, but it's all your fault, W.G., and I wish I had never bowled a ball in my life.'

The Rev. R.S. Holmes, author of 'Cricket Notes' in the magazine *Cricket: A Weekly Record*, recorded W.G.'s arrival, fresh from his latest exploit: 'What a reception we gave him as he rolled in a few minutes late, as fresh as a new pin, and as brown as a berry.' When W.G. rose to make the main speech at the end of the evening, he spoke of Stoddart's achievements and their times together, particularly against Australia, but made no mention at all of his own recent deeds. 'W.G.'s speech was like his cricket,' commented Holmes, 'entirely devoid of meritorious ornamentation. It was the man, and was effective just because it was guilelessly natural. He did not orate, he simply talked.'

Just as in 1876, getting one huge score only seemed to whet Grace's appetite for more – much more. After a spirited 52 against Cambridge University for Gentlemen of England, he travelled to Gravesend for Gloucestershire's match against Kent. He and his men had to endure long sessions in the field while Kent accumulated 470, Grace suffering the indignity of being twice hit over the pavilion by a newcomer, Percy Northcote. But he made the Kent bowlers pay for such an outrage. The

Sportsman's correspondent was almost lost for words if not split infinitives:

Were we to exhaust all the adjectives at our command, it would be difficult for us to sufficiently express our admiration of the grand athlete who yesterday treated the 5,000 people on the Bat and Ball enclosure at Gravesend to a display which it is unlikely that any of them will ever erase from their memories.

W.G. batted all day, piling up his second double century within a week, going in first and finishing the day undefeated on 210. The next highest score was Kitcat's 52. W.G. was twice dropped behind the wicket, on 41 and 81, but was otherwise in his most resplendent form, cutting and driving with all his old panache. As the *Sportsman* continued:

In short, it was just such an innings as 'W.G.' might have played when in the zenith of his fame and before half the present generation of cricketers were born. To the close of a long and tiring day for him 'W.G.' played the game with the keenness of a schoolboy, and never hesitated to start for a run when there was the least chance of getting one.

He took four hours to make his century, and then accelerated, posting the next 50 in only thirty-five minutes, and racing to his double century in only half an hour more. It was his eleventh double century in first-class cricket, and he was not finished by a long way. Next day he made another 47 before being last out for 257, caught in the long field off the only lofted shot he hit in the whole innings. The epic had lasted seven and three-quarter hours.

Gloucestershire still had a first-innings deficit of 27 when a late luncheon was taken. With only the afternoon and evening sessions left, on a pitch on which 913 runs had been scored so far, everything pointed to a tame draw, but fired up by W.G.'s example, Gloucestershire shot Kent out for only 76 in their second innings. That still left an improbable target of 104 to win in seventy-five minutes. Surely not even W.G. could manage that after his exertions so far?

By now he was on a roll. In an hour, he rattled up a superb 73 not out and the game was won by nine wickets with time to spare, the first time a side facing more than 400 in the first innings had rallied to win the match. Grace, at forty-seven, had been on the field for every minute of an absorbing game. More than that, he had uttterly dominated it. It is worth quoting at length from the *Sportsman*'s report of Monday 27 May, for its vivid description of a remarkable day's play.

Kent's defeat would not have been accomplished had not the champion, for champion he is, despite the vapourings of silly scribes, accomplished an achievement which was worthy of anything he has ever done before in the course of his long and honourable career. More praise than this we cannot bestow on one who throughout thirty years of cricket never played better than when his side went in to get 104 runs to win in an hour and a quarter. It was a race against the clock in which the scythe-bearer was always a bad second. Grace's cricket was perfectly amazing. To set the field for him was actually impossible. First he started placing the ball on the on-side in his old sweet way, and then when the captain of the opposing team put his men in that direction he just as promptly cut or drove the ball to the opposite side. There was really no end to his resources, and when at the end of an hour he had scored seventy-three off his own bat, and enabled Gloucestershire to win the game, the spectators went perfectly frantic. Although their side was beaten the partisans of Kent cheered the marvellous batsman in a manner that did one good to listen to it. Shouts of 'Bravo, Grace!' came from 4,000 throats at once, and the Gloucestershire captain had a reception when he returned to the pavilion which will not readily fade from his memory. While he was dresssing the crowd waited for him, and following him to his cab gave him three hearty cheers as he made his way along the street to his hotel. His was a triumphal procession, indeed, through the town, and that he thoroughly deserved it all his opponents were the first to admit . . .

Grace is not as other men, however, and therein lies the secret. With him time seems to stand still, and he almost seems to have learned the secret of perpetual youth. He was as lively as a kitten during his last period at the wickets, and the way in which he ran between the wickets when bustled would have put many a younger man to the blush.

With one match to play before May was out, W.G.'s total for the month was 847. The setting for his attempt on the record could not have been more appropriate: his favourite stamping ground, Lord's, where he took his county on 30 May to play Middlesex. Although the match started on a Thursday, some eight thousand spectators turned out to see if their champion could reach his unique target. Fortunately for them, and him, W.G. won the toss and was thus able to proceed at once towards his goal.

It was soon clear from his cautious approach that he was determined to get there. He took no risks against the bowling of Hearne and Nepean and by lunch he was 58 not out, still 95 short of his target. After the interval, he endured a trying spell from Nepean, and was twice within a whisker of being caught off mishits. Gradually he got on top of the bowling again, then slowed down as he approached his century. After he hit Hearne for four and two in the same over, his old friend Stoddart was brought back on at the pavilion end. 'Stoddie's' trundlers were all that W.G. needed: two blows to the square-leg boundary saw him to his century, out of 198.

That seemed to relax him, as he now began to play more freely, ably backed by A.J. Dearlove, a Bristolian making his county debut, who could scarcely have imagined that it would be in such auspicious circumstances. He fell, however, to a brilliant one-handed catch by Webbe at mid-off, Jessop came and went swiftly on his Lord's debut, and it fell to Captain A.R. Luard, who had played only four games for the county the previous season, to support his captain at this vital period of the innings.

W.G. was visibly tiring, but Luard seized the initiative and with some flashing stroke play rattled up a swift half-century. The dashing captain took the pressure off Grace at just the right time, as he inched towards his target. With 4 more still needed, Nepean produced a leg-side long-hop which Grace seized on with relief and despatched to the fence, bringing up his 150 and his 1,000 runs to the great relief of the crowd, who had lived every run of the day with him. 'Fully three-quarters of the great company stood up and cheered, frantically waving their hats and showing other signs of delight at the champion's great achievement,' went one report. 'Shouts of "Bravo, Grace," were heard on all sides, and the applause lasted for minutes.' Luard was out for 64, but W.G. played resolutely on. Jessop, who had never seen W.G. play a big innings before, watched in rapture from the pavilion. He wrote later:

Though the attack was never loose . . . he hit it when and where he liked. The wickets that day were pitched on the top side of the ground, but despite the added distance the 'Old Man' planted two from Jack Hearne in the same over through the window of the Committee-room . . . It was afterwards my pleasure to see many other big innings of the 'Old Man's' but none of them succeeded in giving me quite the joy that this one did.

It looked as if W.G. might carry his bat to round off a momentous day, but with only ten minutes left before stumps, after nearly five and a quarter hours at the crease, he finally succumbed, bowled by Dr George Thornton for 169, and departed to another great ovation. The crowd was not finished yet. At close of play, thousands gathered in front of the pavilion to acclaim their hero, who came out on to the balcony to acknowledge their cheers.

To mark these two milestones, the *Daily Telegraph* launched a national testimonial for Grace, urging its readers to donate a shilling apiece to the great man. It raised £5,381 9s 1d., demonstrating the deep affection which the ordinary public felt for Grace.

On 8 June, W.G. wrote to 'the proprietors of the *Daily Telegraph*' from his home in Victoria Square, Clifton:

Words fail me to express as I should my hearty thanks for the leader with which you have honoured me in your paper of today referring to the part I in common with so many others have been permitted to take in popularising our great national game. I have still further to thank you for the list you have started in your paper and headed with so princely a donation towards a national testimonial and I think I should be less than human if I did not wish it unbounded success however unworthy I may be that it should be so . . .

But not everybody approved. Some felt it inappropriate for a newspaper to solicit shillings on behalf of a national treasure and would have preferred the MCC to have been its instigators. One such was Grace's England colleague, A.G. Steel, who wrote afterwards:

I am bound to say I was not altogether pleased with the *Daily Telegraph* testimonial. A national testimonial in honour of the greatest cricketer the world has ever seen, on his completion of a performance which may be a 'record' for all time, was indeed fitting. Surely the greatest cricket club in the world – the MCC – was the proper initiator of the testimonial to the greatest cricketer. Day after day, as one read of the flood of shillings pouring in, accompanied by such varied correspondence, one could not but feel a little alarm for the dignity of our great game.

Belatedly, the MCC realised the same thing and joined forces with the *Telegraph*, contributing £2,377.2s.6d. from its members. Gloucestershire, too, got in on the act, and an appeal to their members raised a further £1,436.3s.8d., making a total of £9,073.8s.3d., worth at least £250,000 in today's money. Ever shrewd in financial matters, Grace asked that two-thirds of this windfall should be invested for him; the rest he took as a lump sum.

A particularly sour note was struck by Max Beerbohm, who clearly did not approve of the wave of national hysteria and the rush to hurl money at a man who, arguably, didn't need it. He produced a cartoon showing Grace trousering a cheque while the funeral procession of one of his patients passes by. But Grace's fellow doctors did not share Beerbohm's view. That sober periodical, the *British Medical Journal*, was infected by the national mood and urged doctors to give to the *Telegraph*'s shilling fund:

In this truly national testimonial it is peculiarly fitting that the members of the medical profession, to which Dr Grace belongs, should take part. As doctors, we feel an interest in the great cricketer as a splendid example of what exercise and training, under the guidance of a knowledge of the laws of health, can do for the development and presentation of physical vigour; and as Englishmen we are not less proud of him as a representative of all that is best and most wholesome in manly sports.

Plenty of doctors obviously agreed, for the *BMJ* raised 906 shillings (£45.6s.), which was sent on to the *Telegraph*.

Dinners in Grace's honour were held in Bristol, presided over
by the Duke of Beaufort, and London, where the menu at the
Sports Club bore a poem:

> Now the hundredth hundred's up,
> W.G.,
> You have filled the bowler's cup,
> W.G.,
> You have filled his cup of sorrow,
> Solace he of hope can't borrow,
> For you'll do the like to-morrow,
> W.G.

And indeed he did. He made five more centuries in 1895, to give
him nine for the season, his best since 1871, when he compiled
his record of ten. Three of them were at Lord's. For MCC v
Kent, he made a careful 125 on a difficult wicket. He followed
that with 101 not out against I Zingari, in that club's jubilee
match against Gentlemen of England, which won the game for
the Gentlemen, who had been set 172 to win. Thanks to W.G.,
they did so by ten wickets. And to cap his marvellous Indian
summer, he made his customary century for the Gentlemen v
Players, though oddly enough it was his first at headquarters
in that fixture since that other golden summer of 1876. His
only other century for Gloucestershire in 1895 was 119 against
Nottinghamshire at Trent Bridge and he rounded off his season
with 104 for South v North at Hastings.

His aggregate was a magnificent 2,346, at an average of 51,
comparing very favourably with his figures of 1876 earlier (2,622
and 62.42). He picked up only sixteen wickets, but only the
brilliant newcomer Archie MacLaren, of Lancashire, headed him
in the batting averages, thanks largely to his world record innings
of 424 against Somerset at Taunton which finally eclipsed W.G.'s
344, also made in 1876. For the Champion, it was almost as if the
twenty intervening years had never happened. Small wonder that
the *Cricket Field* should summarise the year thus:

For a time nothing was heard of but the powers of Mr Grace. In the
church and the music hall reference was made, though in different
ways, to the example he set to the youth of the world, and it is not

251

too much to say that, for the time being, the affairs of the world at large had to take a second place.

There was a footnote to W.G.'s epic year. In a letter of 23 September, he wrote:

I played nearly all the year with the same bat for which I have already been offered £20 but money won't purchase it although I did tell a gentleman at The Oval that he could have it for £1,000.

Imagine the price it would fetch nowadays.

It would have been asking a great deal of W.G. to equal his achievements of 1895, but in 1896 he continued in much the same vein, recording his first triple century (301 for Gloucestershire v Sussex at Bristol) since 1876, and fifth double century (243 not out, against the luckless Sussex bowlers again, for his county at Brighton). The double century came first, in the by now traditional fixture between the two counties starting on Whit Monday. W.G.'s 243 was made out of a total of 463. The return match, starting at Ashley Down on the August bank holiday, attracted a huge crowd, eager to see W.G. and Ranji, the two finest batsmen of the era, pitted against each other. W.G. had picked W.G. junior to open the batting with him, but all he succeeded in doing was to emphasise the yawning gap in class between them. His bespectacled son was soon out for one, while he himself made precisely 300 more. By the end of the first day he had made 195 in brilliant fashion, and was pursued off the pitch by the jubilant crowd. Next day he was ninth out for the third highest score of his career, another monument to his astonishing skill, patience and sheer physical strength. Sussex were beaten by an innings and 123 runs.

Gloucestershire saw the best of him that summer. He also made centuries against Somerset (186 at Taunton) and Lancashire (102 not out at Bristol), and good scores against Yorkshire (at Bristol) and Kent (at Gravesend and Cheltenham). But it wasn't all plain sailing. Grace was an unwitting and unwilling participant in the most controversial incident of the year, indeed of the decade – the professional strike before the third Test Match against the visiting Australians at The Oval, which left a bitter taste for years. Perhaps it was a hangover from W.G.'s cash windfall of the previous summer. That had served to remind professional cricketers that the only man making big money from the game was ostensibly an amateur. The fee for playing for England was £10 but the professionals suspected that Grace was receiving a lot more than that, despite his amateur status.

On the eve of the match, five of the England team – Gunn, Lohmann, Hayward, Abel and Richardson – demanded double the previous fee or they would refuse to play. It was widely reported that Grace's fees and expenses were the main cause of their resentment. Four of the protesters were on the Surrey staff and the Surrey committee, in charge of the match, stood firm. Faced with this attitude, three of the strikers backed down on the morning of the match and were allowed to play. But Lohmann and Gunn stuck to their guns, and the match went ahead without them. So disturbed was the Surrey club at the incident that it issued a statement:

The Committee of the Surrey County Cricket Club have observed paragraphs in the Press respecting amounts alleged to be paid, or promised to Dr W.G. Grace for playing in the match England v Australia. The Committee desire to give the statements contained in the paragraphs the most unqualified contradiction. During many years, on the occasions of Dr W.G. Grace playing at The Oval, at the request of the Surrey County Committee, in the matches Gentlemen v Players and England v Australia, Dr Grace has received the sum of £10 a match to cover his expenses in coming to and remaining in London during the three days. Beyond this amount Dr Grace has not received, directly or indirectly, one farthing for playing in a match at The Oval.

W.G. himself was deeply angered by his team-mates' action, referring later to 'many irritating statements of an absolutely false character . . . made with regard to prominent amateur cricketers', and described the strikers' attitude as 'dictatorial', an odd word to use in the circumstances. As usual, there was right on both sides: W.G. undoubtedly earned more money from the game than any professional, but he was still the game's greatest attraction, capable of putting thousands on the gate for a mere county game in which he was playing. The professionals were poorly paid and badly looked after by the sport. None of them received national testimonials from newspapers although the takings from their benefit matches had improved. One or two of the richer counties had started paying their professionals a small weekly stipend over the winter months but most of them got nothing at all from the game out of season. But Grace could reasonably argue that he did more than any other cricketer to support his professional colleagues' benefits. He would go anywhere to help them, and pull in large numbers of spectators who would add vital extra income for the beneficiaries.

The editor of *Wisden*, Sydney Pardon, sat on the fence when he pondered the issue after the season had ended. 'The earnings of the players have certainly not risen in proportion to the immensely increased popularity of cricket during the last twenty years,' he wrote, 'but to represent the average professional as an ill-treated or down-trodden individual is, I think, a gross exaggeration.' As for 'the thorny question of amateurs' expenses', no doubt there were 'some abuses', but a distinguished county captain had assured him that he knew of 'not more than half-a-dozen men, playing as amateurs, who make anything out of the game'. He concluded: 'Mr W.G. Grace's position has for years, as everyone knows, been an anomalous one but "nice customs curtsey to great kings" and the work he has done in popularising cricket outweighs a hundredfold every other consideration.'

The strike was an unfortunate climax to a gripping Test series in which W.G. was once again England's captain. Like England, Australia had a highly promising new generation of players, and in the first Test at Lord's one of them produced what was perhaps the most famous single delivery W.G. faced in his long career. Ernest 'Jonah' Jones was a twenty-seven-year-old miner from South Australia on his first tour of England, a stocky right-arm fast bowler who could extract fearsome bounce, and proceeded to do so against W.G. with a snorter which reared up, brushed the great man's beard (and the top of his bat handle), soared over the wicket-keeper's head and raced to the sightscreen for 4. Jones followed through and arrived level with Grace, who was variously reported as saying, 'Whatever are ye at?' and 'What do you think you're at, Jonah?' Jones was said to have replied sheepishly: 'Sorry, Doctor, she slipped.'

Grace was visibly shaken by the ball and took some time to recover his composure while the excited crowd buzzed. However, there was nothing W.G. liked better than demonstrating to a touted young player that he was still capable of a thing or two. He settled down and saw Jones off, with a dogged 66. 'The first ball I sent whizzing through his whiskers,' said Jones afterwards. 'After that, he kept hitting me off his blinkin' ear-'ole for four.' England won the match by seven wickets.

The Australians squared the series by winning the second Test, at Old Trafford, despite a brilliant 154 by the star of the summer, Ranjitsinhji, who with 2,780 runs went on to beat by 61 W.G.'s record aggregate for a season, in 1871.

One incident at Old Trafford showed Grace at his shrewdest as captain. His new wicket-keeper, 'Dick' Lilley, occasionally turned his arm over and had taken 6–46 for Warwickshire against Derbyshire the previous week. Looking for someone to break a useful stand between Hill and Trott, Grace summoned Lilley who took off the gloves and pads and tried his arm. Although he was inaccurate and expensive, Grace kept him on and was rewarded when Trott edged a catch to Jack Brown, the temporary keeper. His object achieved, Grace instantly removed Lilley from the attack with the words, 'I shan't want you to bowl again. You must have been bowling with your wrong arm.' Lilley's first Test wicket was to be his last.

It was Grace's captaincy that was the deciding factor in England's winning the decider at The Oval, though the visitors gained a measure of revenge against Gloucestershire, dismissing the county at Cheltenham for only 17 (their lowest score ever), of which Grace made 9.

The side which the Gentlemen put out against the Players in 1896 is widely regarded as the strongest ever, and they duly did the 'double' over the Players at The Oval and Lord's. W.G made half-centuries in both matches, both innings playing a crucial part in his side's victory. At Lord's he got the Gentlemen, chasing 224 on a difficult wicket, off to a brisk start with 54 after being missed at short leg off the first ball he faced. The young bloods, Jackson and Ranji, finished off the job.

There was a famous confontation between W.G. and MacLaren at Old Trafford that summer. MacLaren went back to play the ball, but before setting off for a run trod on his wicket when he had scored 2. There was no appeal from the Gloucestershire fielders, but when MacLaren made no move to leave the crease W.G. exclaimed, 'What? Ain't you going, Archie?' MacLaren replied that he wasn't, as he believed he had broken his wicket after completing his shot. W.G. then appealed to the umpire, William Shrewsbury, brother of Arthur, who sided with MacLaren. W.G. was incredulous and then extremely angry, and could not put the incident out of his mind for the rest of the match, muttering furiously to himself out in the field, as was his custom when things went against him.

Ranji may have dominated the season, but Grace still topped the 2,000 mark, totalling 2,135 at 42.70 to finish fifth in the averages. He also took fifty-two wickets, his best haul for five years.

W.G. still had two more seasons at the top of the first-class game, which took him, incredibly, through to his fiftieth birthday in 1898. After that there was a slow but inevitable decline.

His performances in 1897 were steady after an odd start to the season, which had *Wisden* baffled. As if determined to show his critics he still had all the energy of a man half his age, Grace's first few innings were marked by an impetuosity which was all the stranger from a player whose patience was a byword. 'So long did he continue to play in a manner quite foreign to his normal methods as to create a feeling of dismay,' remarked cricket's bible. However, normal service was resumed with 66 for the Gentlemen against a strong Players' attack at Lord's which reduced the brilliant new generation of amateurs to impotence, but not the Old Man.

Nottinghamshire felt the full weight of his bat in both their matches against Gloucestershire. He made 126 at Trent Bridge and an even better 131 in the return at Bristol, and hit a third county championship century of the summer (116 also at Bristol) against Sussex. His only other century (113 at Bristol again) was perhaps fortunate to be categorised as first-class, for it was made for Gloucestershire against the third Philadelphian touring team from the United States who, it rapidly became apparent, were out of their depth against the MCC, county and university sides against whom they were pitted. Their batting was weak (Grace took 7–91 against them) but their bowling was a litttle stronger – they had the distinction of dismissing the hitherto rampant Ranji for a golden duck.

Grace compiled a satisfactory 1,532 runs at 39.28 – only six batsmen scored more – to finish tenth in the national averages. He also took fifty-six wickets, four more than in 1896, at 22.17.

15 · A BIRTHDAY TREAT
TO REMEMBER

IN the autumn of 1897 the *Sportsman* had an idea. On 18 July 1898, W.G. would celebrate his fiftieth birthday. What better way of celebrating it than by postponing the start of the Gentlemen v Players at Lord's, the fixture with which Grace was uniquely associated, from the second week of July to the great day itself? The proposal quickly won support. When the county cricket secretaries gathered in December for their annual meeting they agreed unanimously that the match should begin on Monday 18 July. Furthermore, there would be no other first-class fixtures arranged for that period so that the strongest possible teams could be selected from the amateur and professional ranks. The scale and nature of the tribute were unprecedented, and showed, if proof were needed, the reverence and respect in which Grace was held by his peers.

There was a lot of cricket to be played in 1898 before the great game. W.G. was in reasonable but by no means spectacular form in the early part of the season, warming up with 146 not out in a practice match against twenty-two County Colts, and 65 for MCC against Sussex at Lord's. With less than a fortnight to go to his Jubilee game, he took his Gloucestershire team to Leyton for what turned out to be an epic encounter with Essex. It was the first time Gloucestershire had played there, and only W.G.'s second visit. His face was unfamiliar to at least one local, the policeman on duty at the pavilion entrance, who at first refused him admittance because he did not have a member's ticket (clearly a role model for generations of Lord's gatemen ever since). It was also a head-to-head confrontation between W.G., at forty-nine the doyen of English batsmen, and the fearsome Charles Kortright, at twenty-seven the finest fast bowler of the younger generation. As amateurs, they were due to play together for the Gentlemen at Lord's. At Leyton, however, there was no love lost between the pair. The elder man claimed all the early honours. 'It was "W.G.'s" day with a vengeance,' reported the *Sportsman*, 'as besides taking seven wickets for 44 runs, the cricketer of this or any other age flogged the Essex bowling to the extent of one hundred and twenty six runs.' On what was generally reckoned to one of the country's plumbest batting wickets, W.G. bamboozled the powerful Essex batting line-up, who had made 497–5 against Derbyshire in their previous match. 'Deceiving the batsmen with the flight of the ball, "W.G." stuck up the opposition in a manner almost unaccountable, and one and another of the team returned to the pavilion in a silence that was almost depressing.'

His victims included Percy Perrin, with what almost everyone else on the field thought was a caught and bowled taken on the bounce, and Kortright, no mean batsmen, leg before. Essex were all out for 128 by 2 p.m., and had not Walter Mead indulged in some late hitting (including three mighty leg-side blows off Grace), W.G.'s figures would have been even more remarkable. It was widely felt that the young Essex batsmen, who had never faced him before, were simply bamboozled by him. The journalist W.A. Bettesworth commented on this phenomenon later in the month:

When men had once become accustomed to his bowling he was often pretty severely treated, but he was always likely to break up a partnership. To a man who has never been opposed to him he is almost invariably fatal, however good he may be, and old cricketers were not at all surprised when the Essex men could make neither head nor tail of him.

Kortright did not take this blow to his county's pride lying down. When Gloucestershire batted, bowling at his fastest and fiercest, he pitched the ball persistently short, and several times rapped Grace painfully on the hands. After one delivery, W.G. pointedly walked half-way down the pitch and vigorously patted it with his bat, which caused some amusement, though not presumably to Kortright. Mixing gritty defence with judicious attack, W.G. played an innings which evoked his greatest years, reaching his century out of 153, and his total of 126 out of 203. He was finally out to a tired shot, not surprising when one thinks of what he had acomplished in less than a day's cricket, skying an attempted pull straight up in the air to be caught by wicket-keeper Russell.

He was cheered all the way back to the pavilion and several men ran on to the field to congratulate him. Kortright took five wickets but not the one that mattered. Many years later, he told John Arlott: 'The Old Man made me look as simple as dirt. He wasn't attempting to hit the ball with his bat outside the off-stump, but was punching it – punching it – with his thick felt gloves through the slips, and I was bowling fairly fast then . . . Everyone was much surprised at it.'

In Gloucestershire's second innings, when they needed only 148 to win, Kortright was even more lethal. Jessop later recalled:

Here we had the fastest bowler in the world bowling with a determination which I never saw exceeded. Even W.G. during the hour and a half in which he batted . . . was constantly at fault in his timing, once so much as to receive one of Kortright's fastest deliveries in the stomach. The bruise . . . was quite the most extraordinary extravasation of blood that I have ever witnessed. The seam of the ball was quite clear, and you could almost see the maker's name impinged on the flesh. The horrid thud of the impact could be distinctly heard in the pavilion.

As well as demonstrating his durability and courage, Grace was the beneficiary of further dubious umpiring decisions. When he had made only six, he appeared to be caught and bowled. It seemed so clearly out that, at first, no one bothered to appeal. When W.G., who thought it was a bump ball, stood his ground, Mead appealed and the umpire, George Burton, gave him out. W.G. roared, 'What, George?' and Burton changed his mind. In W.G.'s defence, Burton's view was obscured by the bowler and Cyril Sewell, the other batsman, thought W.G. was correct.

As angry as the rest of the Essex team, Kortright now bowled as fast as he had ever done. With Gloucestershire on 96–3, he reached within himself for one more lethal salvo. First, he trapped W.G. plumb lbw, but the umpire, presumably totally cowed by now, declined to give it. Grace edged the next one to give a catch behind, but again the umpire was the only other man on the field not to see or hear it. Infuriated, Kortright pounded in and produced an unplayable ball which knocked two of Grace's stumps out of the ground, one of them cartwheeling through the air and landing yards away. W.G. was one short of his half-century. As he slowly turned to leave the crease, the triumphant Kortright approached and remarked: 'Surely you're not going, Doctor – there's still one stump standing.'

W.G. walked off in high dudgeon, telling one and all he had never been so insulted. There was plenty more drama to come. Gloucestershire inched towards the target, but steadily lost wickets. With two runs needed, the ninth wicket went down, leaving only the old professional, Fred Roberts, a fine bowler but total rabbit with the bat, and Kortright rampant. Determined to win, W.G. instructed Roberts he was not to move his bat or run away.

'But what about my wife and family, Doctor?' Roberts is said to have asked.

'Oh, they'll be all right,' remarked W.G. 'Kortright may hit you but he can't kill you and if we win, there'll be an extra £1 for you. But if you get out, you'll never play for Gloucestershire again.'

This dire warning did the trick. Gloucestershire scraped home by one wicket, Jessop hitting Kortright for four to seal the narrowest of victories. This may have been the last straw for Kortright, who was so incensed by Grace's behaviour that it was only the intervention of the Essex and former England amateur 'Bunny' Lucas that persuaded him grudgingly to accept his invitation to appear for the Gentlemen in Grace's Jubilee Match. He was ever afterwards glad that he did.

There were still eight days to go before the great day, but W.G. had no thought of conserving his energy. He played cricket on six of them, first against Warwickshire (at Birmingham), against whom he made 24 and took 2–27 and 4–46, then against Somerset (at Bristol), maintaining his good form with a twelve-wicket haul (7–85 and 5–53) to add to 20 with the bat.

There was huge public expectation in the days before the Jubilee Match, stoked by long articles and profiles about Grace in the sporting newspapers. On the morning of Monday 18 July a large crowd started gathering at Lord's well before the gates were due to open at 10.30 a.m.(the match was to start at noon). Gloucestershire supporters were not to be left out. Hundreds came up from the West Country, on special excursion trains laid on for the occasion. As the crowd poured into the ground, it soon became apparent that there would not be room for all in the stands and seats, and it was decided to allow the overspill on to the grass all around the ground. The official paying attendance figure was 17,423, so at least 20,000 were estimated to be crammed into the ground for this historic day.

W.G., with his wife and daughter, Bessie, arrived just before eleven o'clock and found extreme difficulty in getting through the crush, as everyone wanted to shake his hand. Inside the ground, there were hundreds of congratulatory telegrams for him.

It was a beautiful day, the wicket hard and true, and no surprise that Shrewsbury elected to bat. Unless Kortright ran through the professionals within the day, the crowd would have to be satisfied with seeing Grace in the field but not at the crease on his birthday.

Just after the ground clock had struck twelve, W.G. emerged from the pavilion. His descent of the stairs took some time, as so many members wanted to shake him by the hand, but when he finally stepped out on to the grass, wearing his familiar red and yellow striped cap, he received a tremendous ovation; his team followed at a decent distance to allow him to savour this great moment. It was an incredible thirty-three years since he first walked out for the Gentlemen at Lord's – but it was a very different figure who now made his way to the middle: the lithe young athlete with the dark beard had given way to a ponderous, stooping, twenty-stone colossus with an impressive girth, whose beard had long turned grey. He still fielded at point but now had difficulty in reaching down for the ball, although his huge hands were still as safe as ever when anything catchable came straight at him. On this day, too, he was hampered by a bruised heel, which soon obliged him to return briefly to the pavilion for treatment.

He and Kortright were still not on speaking terms, but the Essex man did as he was told and bowled a terrifyingly quick spell, without any luck, to get the match off to a flying start. Grace was at first cheered whenever the ball went to him in the field, and delighted the crowd when he brought himself back on for his second spell with the ball and induced 'Long John' Tunnicliffe to edge a catch to Gregor MacGregor behind the stumps.

But the day was something of an anticlimax, after the torrent of publicity beforehand. Scoring was slow, prompting one observer to remark that 'many of the batsmen seemed to be overweighted by the sense of their responsibility'. Grace's limelight was rather stolen by one of his oldest adversaries, Billy Gunn, who compiled a patient 139, a record for a professional in this fixture at Lord's, but W.G. led the applause when he reached his century.

A brief piece of newsreel footage survives to commemorate the great day. Wearing a dark-striped blazer over his white flannels, his MCC cap perched on his massive head, W.G. strolls towards camera behind one of the stands, dwarfing Arthur Shrewsbury, captain of the Players, beside him. As they pass the cameraman, W.G. grins and genially raises his cap before passing out of shot. Behind them come the rest of the players in a sort of crocodile, many of them smoking pipes or cigarettes (perhaps they have just emerged from lunch). Behind them straggle a crowd of men, dressed very formally, wearing top hats, bowlers or boaters, and a few boys in Eton jackets. There is just one woman in a white hat and long white dress.

It was a historic day in more than one sense. Shortly after lunch, W.G. left the field again, not from a recurrence of his injury, but to attend a meeting of representatives from all the counties, under the chairmanship of the President of the MCC, the Hon Alfred Lyttelton, MP (and former England wicket-keeper, whom W.G. had replaced behind the stumps in the Oval Test of 1884). The meeting voted to set up a new body to control Test matches in England, later to be called the Board of Control.

At 6.30 p.m., with the Players on 328–9, W.G. led his men off the field, to the total surprise of everyone else, as play was supposed to finish at 7 p.m. No one objected. That evening, the MCC held a banquet in his honour in the pavilion.

On Tuesday morning the Players were soon dismissed for 335, the pick of the bowlers being W.G.'s protégé Charles Townsend, with 4–58. Grace himself took 1–34 off 12 five-ball overs. Then came the moment another huge crowd had come to see: the fifty-year-old Champion emerging from the pavilion to open the innings, in tandem with his old accomplice Stoddart. But there was no gentle full toss or long-hop to get him off the mark, even from that model professional and sportsman, Jack Hearne, the Middlesex and England medium-pacer then at the height of his career. Instead, W.G. scratched around, was twice beaten and barely survived the first over. With barely a run scored, he was dropped twice, by Lilley behind the stumps and by Hearne off his own bowling, to the crowd's great relief. Clearly troubled by his bad heel, he looked every year of his age.

A few more aggressive blows got him going at last but it was always hard graft, and he was further inconvenienced by a delivery from Haigh which reared up and struck him painfully on the left hand. Still, he and Stoddart completed the 50 partnership before the Middlesex man was out for 21. With the score on 79, Lilley made amends for his earlier drop by holding on to an edge off Lockwood and W.G. was gone for 43. It was enough to satisfy the crowd, who gave him a great hand as he limped benignly off.

Helped by a fighting 50 from Archie MacLaren, the Gentlemen got to 303, only 32 behind, and then reduced the Players to 42–2 by the close, thanks largely to another wicked session from Kortright, bowling flat out in the gathering gloom: he knocked Bobby Abel's leg stump out of the ground and Bill Storer's bat out of his hands three times in ten minutes. Everything pointed to an exciting final day's play.

For the second consecutive evening, W.G. was honoured with a dinner, this time at the Sports Club in St James's Square, attended by 150 cricket dignitaries, with the Attorney-General, and President of Surrey, Sir Richard Webster, QC, MP, in the chair. W.G. was flanked by his contemporaries, Sammy Woods and Archie MacLaren to his right, Stoddart, MacGregor, Jack

Mason and Kortright, swallowing his pride, to his left. Webster ran through the guest of honour's career, telling a few of the old chestnuts along the way. There was no man in England, he observed, whose doings were more closely watched than Grace's. Why, only the previous evening in the Commons, Mr A.J. Balfour, speaking from the Treasury Bench, had proudly mentioned that he was the same age as 'the champion'. He ended with the hope that 'in days to come . . . W.G., from his fireside, would be able to contemplate with satisfaction his cricket days, in which he has not thought of himself, but set an example, and would die as he had lived, admired of the British nation as a straightforward type of an Englishman.'

If W.G. found this a touch morbid, he kept the thought to himself and responded in his familiar style, at once shy and humble, gruff and amusing. 'I wish I had Stoddart's happy knack of saying the right words in the right place' he said, but he managed it, none the less, without the distraction of notes. He went on: 'If I cannot say the right words, I feel them' and never said a truer word.

One delightful anecdote typified his style:

Sir Richard Webster said I was always very good to young players. Well, I remember, many years ago, when I was playing for MCC against Surrey at Lord's, they brought up an unfortunate colt who had taken a few wickets in a match the week before. He bowled one over. The first ball I played back quietly to him. The next went into the garden, down by the old armoury. The third followed suit, and the fourth and fifth went into the pavilion. They never bowled that poor fellow again. If you call that giving advice to a young cricketer, well . . .

The rest of the sentence was drowned by laughter from his fellow diners.

It was overcast and chilly when the Gentlemen walked out on to the field to start the third and final day, minus Grace, whose left hand and heel were both troubling him. There were fewer spectators than on the first two days, but the crowd was still respectable enough and grew through the day to around twelve thousand (compared with more than seventeen thousand on the Monday).

Kortwright, Sammy Woods and Jack Mason could not break through as they had the previous evening, Shrewsbury decided against a sporting declaration, and the Players were eventually all out for 263. That left the Gentlemen a target of 296 in 150 minutes, so a draw looked odds-on.

To general disappointment, Grace did not open the innings, nor did he appear even though wickets started to tumble, and the rumour spread around the ground that he would be unable to bat because of his bruised hand. When the seventh wicket went down with only 77 runs on the board, the Gentlemen were staring ignominious defeat in the face, for there were still fifty-five minutes to go until the officially advertised finishing time of 6.30 p.m. However painful his ageing limbs were, this was not the moment for Grace to duck a challenge, and his familiar figure appeared on the pavilion steps, to a great ovation. Before another run had been scored, the batsman at the other end, Johnny Dixon, was on his way, swiftly followed by MacGregor, leaving the lame and sore Grace at the wicket and only – of all people – Kortright to bat. Fortunately, he and W.G. had by then patched up their differences; indeed Grace had referred jocularly to 'my friend Kortright' in his speech the previous evening.

'Korty, don't be nervous, play your usual game,' advised Grace as their paths crossed.

'All right, Doc, I'll do my best,' replied the volatile fast bowler, and he proceeded to do so, striking the ball cleanly around Lord's while Grace, restricted by his hand injury, played more defensively. As the minutes ticked away, the crowd became more and more excited. 'There was no getting away from the fact that the sympathies of the vast throng were on the side of the batsmen,' as one report had it. Certain defeat might yet be avoided – and looked to have been when Kortwright survived what was generally assumed to be the last over, of Storer's very occasional leg-spin. A pitch invasion from the jubilant spectators looked a certainty as, with the score on 130–9, Kortright headed triumphantly for the pavilion, only to be waved back. Like almost everyone else on the ground, he was unaware that Grace and Shrewsbury had earlier in the day agreed to play an extra half-hour, until 7 p.m., if either side was in a position to win at 6.30 p.m. Grace had somehow managed not to inform Kortright of the new plan while they were together at the wicket.

However, Kortright settled down again, and played as calmly as before. Shrewsbury kept trying new bowlers, but to no avail, and the tension mounted again. With only four minutes left, Shrewsbury tried one last gamble, bringing his opening bowler Lockwood on from the Pavilion End.

Kortright had made 46, and perhaps the thought that he might reach his half-century as well as save the match was his undoing. He drove at Lockwood's third ball, but instead of despatching it to the boundary succeeded only in skying it high on the off side for Haigh to pocket the catch, running back. All out for 158, the Players had lost by 137. The last-wicket pair had put on 78 and W.G. was left on 31 not out. He walked slowly back to the pavilion, arm-in-arm with Kortright, their feud finally at an end, as the crowd surged around them, slapping them on the back. They would not disperse from in front of the pavilion until W.G. and Kortright appeared on the players' balcony to acknowledge their cheers. Certainly, the Press was ecstatic. 'By general consent the match was one of the best ever seen at Lord's,' said the *Daily Telegraph*. As a Victorian melodrama, it could hardly have been bettered.

After such an exciting game, two late nights and his injuries, Grace could have been forgiven for wanting a long rest. Nothing gives a better idea of his extraordinary stamina and continuing enthusiasm for the game than the fact that the very next morning he turned out at Trent Bridge to open the batting for Goucestershire – and finished the day on 143 not out, although he could barely walk (he was eventually dismissed next day for 168 out of a total of 307). His appearance attracted a larger crowd than usual to the ground on which he had first played nearly a quarter of a century previously. It was he, of course, who had scored the first first-class century there, and his latest display, and his after-dinner speech during the Lord's match, provoked yet another poem in his honour, entitled 'The Lay of the Oldest Cricketer':

The day was long, the air was warm
The Doctor was in splendid form;
'Twas like his cheek, the Notts men say,
To keep them in the field all day;
The bat, with which he made his score
To them seemed wider than a door.
Most ancient of all players he,
The fifty-year-old 'W.G.'
Ah, well a day! the times are gone
When he but weighed a dozen stone;
But still from morning's light till dark
He carols like the blithesome lark.
At Sports Club, courted and caressed,
High placed in hall, a welcome guest,
He boldly stepped into the breach,
With unpremeditated speech.
Old times are changed, old manners gone,
But Dr William still keeps on;
The youngsters of these modern days
Look on with rapture when he plays.
A wondrous batsman, calm and cool,
Admired by dukes and boys at school,
While earls and peasants in the ring
Applaud him as they would a king.

Gloucestershire experienced a welcome revival in 1898, to finish third in the county table behind Yorkshire and Middlesex.
W.G. made one more century for them, 109 against Somerset at
Taunton. What neither he nor anybody realised at the time was
that his fifty-first hundred for Gloucestershire would also be his
last for the county of his birth.

Sussex would have been the recipients of that award, had not
Grace suddenly declared Gloucestershire's innings closed when he
was 93 and looking certain for a century. The reason was that, until
then, 93 was the only score under 100 he had not made in first-class
cricket. He was well aware that his great career had almost gone full
circle, and wanted to tie up the loose ends. This unique deed shows
that he was, in his way, as obsessed with statistics as most cricket
lovers, whether active or passive. The difference with the rest of
them is that he was in a position to do something about his own.

W.G. may have been honoured and feted by the cricket world in his Jubilee year but no official recognition came his way, despite the Prince of Wales's admiration. The obvious acknowledgement would have been a knighthood, which would surely have been forthcoming in modern times. The explanation is probably that sportsmen were not regarded as serious people, and certainly not by Queen Victoria. If any sovereign were to honour W.G. it would have been the sporting figure of Edward VII, who came to the throne in 1901, but the call from the palace never came. Lord Hawke regarded it as a surprising omission on the government's part, particularly when such an influential Cabinet Minister as A.J. Balfour was frequently in attendance at Lord's and indeed became Prime Minister in 1902. W.G. had to rest content with the undying affection of the common people.

16 · CLOSE OF PLAY

1898–1915

A T first everything seemed set fair. The Jubilee had capped half a century of uninterrupted success, the country had paid homage – and good money – to its Champion. Then life turned sour for W.G. On 11 October 1898, The *Sportsman* announced the establishment of the London County Cricket Club by the Crystal Palace Company. It was intended to be a blue-chip venture: the executive committee included Sir Richard Webster, the Attorney-General, who had presided over W.G.'s Jubilee dinner in July, although Webster's new appointment sat oddly with his presidency of the Surrey club of which the new outfit was meant to be a rival; A.J. Webbe, who had retired the previous month as captain of Middlesex after fourteen years in the job and who had often opened the batting with W.G. for various teams; and Sir Arthur Sullivan, the celebrated composer. However, the biggest name involved was the Secretary and Manager: W.G. Grace himself, who, it was announced, would move to the London suburb of Sydenham and 'devote his whole time' to getting the new venture off the ground.

Its backers thought they saw what would now be called 'a gap in the market': there was a large catchment area of potential cricket-watchers who were a long way from The Oval or Lord's. London County would play on the Crystal Palace ground in Sydenham, south-east London, which had been laid in 1857 as part of the development of the site following the relocation of Joseph

Paxton's great Crystal Palace there in 1854 (it had originally been erected in Hyde Park as part of the Great Exhibition of 1851).

The news was not well received from the Crystal Palace club, which already played on the ground, but it came as a bombshell to Gloucestershire, for Grace was still its captain. How could he do both jobs properly? Grace was in no doubt that he could; but it did signal the end of his medical career. He may not have minded too much, for local government boundary changes in Bristol had altered the area served by his medical practice, and he was involved in a dispute with the Bristol Board of Guardians over compensation. The offer from Crystal Palace meant he could resign and devote himself entirely to cricket. He would certainly not lose out financially: his salary was said to be £1,000 a year. He also persuaded the Engineering School at Crystal Palace to take in his youngest son, Charles, as a student.

By Christmas Dr and Mrs Grace and family had moved into their new home, St Andrew's, in Lawrie Park Road, Sydenham. But hardly had they settled in when tragedy struck. In February 1899, their only daughter, Bessie, who had moved to London with them, died of typhoid, which was still a constant menace to the public. She was only twenty and W.G.'s favourite child, bright, bouncy and a talented sportswoman. Much as he loved his three sons, he loved Bessie the most for she was the most like him in character. How strange that a disease which he had helped to combat in Bristol for twenty years should carry away his daughter only months after he had ceased to practise medicine. He and Agnes were devastated. On 19 March W.G. wrote to Cyril Sewell, a talented, South African-born amateur who had made his debut for Gloucestershire in 1895:

I must thank you for your kind letter of sympathy with us in our great trouble and for so kindly attending the funeral on such a dreadful day . . .

But W.G. was nothing if not practical. He went on to enquire whether Sewell would be available to play for London County in the forthcoming season and added:

The Club is going strong, over 200 members already joined. The pavilion is half up and ground looking well . . .

Preparations for London County's new season were indeed proceeding apace. The new pavilion was soon completed, at a cost of £3,000, and more money was spent on improving the pitch and outfield, under the supervision of the old Gloucestershire bowler Bill Murch, by then rather deaf. W.G. converted him into a makeshift wicket-keeper, commenting in a letter a few years later: 'Murch kept wicket for us, he would be very good but his hands would not stand much fast bowling.'

At first, it looked as if Grace would be able to carry out his responsibilities in Gloucestershire and London. He played in Gloucestershire's first four games, all away from home, but back in the West Country there was deep unhappiness about his divided loyalties, which may have been brought to a head by the London club's first game, against Wiltshire at Swindon on 5 and 6 May. Including Grace, there were four Gloucestershire players in the London team: the others were Townsend, Brown and Troup. (Five more came from the Crystal Palace club, with which London shared their home ground.) Two days later, Grace pulled off something of a coup by bringing the Australians, led by the inspirational Joe Darling, to Crystal Palace for their opening match of their tour, against the South of England. The match was drawn, the brilliant newcomer C.B. Fry top-scoring for the South with 81.

The Gloucestershire committee met on 16 May to decide what to do about their wayward captain. They resolved to ask him which county matches he was going to play in that season. Ten days later, they communicated their request by post. They might as well have sent him a letter bomb. Grace's reply, written on 28 May 1899, is worth quoting in full:

To the Committee of the Gloucestershire County Club.

Gentlemen, in answer to yours of the 26th, re resolution passed on the 16th and kept back from me for reasons best known to yourselves, I beg to state that I had intended to play in nearly all our matches, but in consequence of the resolution passed and other actions of some of the Committee, I send in my resignation as Captain, and must ask the Committee to choose the teams for future games, as I shall not get them up.

I have always tried my very best to promote the interests of the Gloucestershire County Club, and it is with deep regret that I resign my captaincy. I have the greatest affection for the county of my birth, but for the Committee as a body, the greatest contempt.

> I am,
> Yours truly, W.G. Grace

After that, there was no going back. When the Committee met to consider W.G.'s thunderous missive, it came up with the following resolution:

That while the Committee are conscious of the great services rendered by Dr Grace to the Gloucestershire Cricket Club as well as to cricket generally, and feel deep regret at his severance from them in spite of the efforts which have been made by them to avoid it, they feel they have no course open to them but to accept his resignation.

It was an abrupt and unexpected end to W.G.'s playing days for the county with which his family's name was virtually synonymous. He had captained the side since its inception in 1870. Gilbert Jessop wrote later:

The news came as a complete surprise to me, for relations between the County Committee and himself had always struck me as being particularly friendly. There seemed to be strong reason why they should be anyway, for the majority of them were close personal friends of the "Old Man".

But even the closest of friends can fall out. His successor was Walter Troup, who tried, together with J.A. Bush, a member of the committee, to talk W.G. out of quitting but he refused to withdraw his remarks or his resignation.

The saddest side to the affair was that, according to a letter of 19 April to J.J. Sewell, uncle of Cyril, he was on the point of retiring anyway.

Your nephew says he cannot play at all this year, this is a very sad blow to me, it is my last year and I was in hopes of leading Gloucestershire to a few victories during this season . . . I must ask you to consent to his playing at Blackheath, The Oval, Lords and Brighton, do please grant this request for the good of the poor old county.

A few months later, W.G. was still seething. On 12 July he wrote to Sewell:

. . . I am glad to hear I am not the only one who the committee dislike, from what I hear, they cannot speak the truth, they are a bad lot and the less you have to say to them the better for you.

But he usually calmed down after his explosions and, true to form, he came to regret his precipitate resignation. Gloucestershire was his first and only love, and he maintained a keen interest in its affairs. E.M., after all, was still the club secretary, and W.G. stayed in contact with other influential figures, like Arrowsmith. He also plundered the county for players, whenever possible, to make up his teams at London County. To the relief of all concerned, the rift between W.G. and Gloucestershire did not last long, as we shall see. Troup captained the side for the rest of the summer and was then replaced by Gilbert Jessop, who led the county until 1912. Although he got Troup to play for London County, W.G. did not rate him very highly as a cricketer, as he revealed in a letter to Arrowsmith a year or two later:

. . . to give Troup what the club did was simply money wasted. What Jessop gets is another thing as he draws the public which Troup never did and never will.

The summer of 1899 signalled the end of another chapter for W.G. – his England career. On 1 June, the first Test against Australia began at Trent Bridge. It was also the first Test to be played at the Nottingham ground and the first five-Test series to be played in England. That led to another notable novelty: the England team for all five Tests would be chosen by the same selection committee. Until then, there had been three Tests per summer: at Lord's, The Oval and Old Trafford, with the teams picked by the MCC, Surrey and Lancashire committees respectively. Naturally, W.G. was on the new body, chaired by Lord Hawke, and although approaching his fifty-first birthday was once more selected as captain.

This was hard luck on Arthur Shrewsbury, the idol of Trent

Bridge and a mere forty-four, for, as C.B. Fry related, 'the team could not carry both W.G. and him, since both of them could field at point and nowhere else'. So Shrewsbury was the unlucky one, to his chagrin, and Billy Gunn (only forty-two) was chosen. Their generation was being pressed hard by the outstanding newcomers. Ranji was already an automatic choice, and Fry and MacLaren were pressing hard for inclusion.

In his autobiography, Fry recalled how he was Grace's first name on the batting list for Trent Bridge on the strength of his 81 against the Australians for London County. Not only that: Grace co-opted him on to the selection committee despite the fact that the twenty-seven-year-old Fry had not yet made his Test debut. In doing so, Grace was to prove the unwitting architect of his own downfall.

The Australians had sent their most powerful team since the all-conquering squad of 1882 and they had much the better of the first Test. On a beautiful summer's day, there were fifteen thousand people in the ground to watch the start of the historic match. 'Nottingham has not been so full since the Church Congress,' commented *The Times*. Australia batted all day for only 238, attracting some criticism for their slow play. They were out for 252 on the second morning; Grace gave himself twenty overs, in which he conceded only 31 runs.

He opened the batting with Fry, two giants of the game, one of the past, the other of the future. As they walked out to the middle, Grace said to his partner: 'Now, Charlie, remember that I'm not a sprinter like you.' However, in contrast to the dour Australians, the two amateurs attacked from the outset on a hard, true wicket. They put on 75 in brisk fashion but as Fry wrote later, 'Had I been in with Joe Vine of Sussex the score would have been over 100. We lost innumerable singles on the off side, and I never dared to call W.G. for a second run in the long-field.' It was looking good for England but, as *The Times* related:

They had hit the bowlers off their pitch and were getting runs quickly, but just when everything was going well a kind of 'rot' set in . . . The turning point of England's fortunes began with the dismissal of Dr Grace, who treated Noble's bowling much too cheaply and turned the ball into the wicket-keeper's hand.

275

W.G. had made 28. Fry went on to make 50, Ranji 42, but England were all out for only 193. They had gone into the match deprived by injury or unavailability of all their fast bowlers and in their second innings the Australians took full advantage. The tourists declared at 230–8, Clem Hill top-scoring with 80. Crucially, W.G. missed him at point 'which he could have taken with ease if he could have bent', said Fry. Grace's immobility attracted some barracking from the crowd, and although he did eventually manage to get down to another sharp chance to dismiss Hill, by then the damage was done. Set 290 to win, England were four wickets down in less than an hour, including Grace's, bowled by a sharp break-back from Howell for one.

Nobody realised it at the time, but that one run was W.G.'s last in Test cricket. Ever the realist, he himself read the writing on the wall earlier than anyone else. He was getting on, and Australia had a fit and formidable attack in the shape of Jones (who had slipped that famous ball through Grace's beard the last time he was in England), Trumble, Noble, McLeod and Howell. An imperious undefeated 93 by Ranji saved the match and England's face but Grace was not fooled. Immediately the match was over, he confided in F.S. Jackson: 'It's no use, Jacker. I shan't play again.'

He was right. But did he perhaps have second thoughts when it came to picking the side for the second Test, at Lord's? Fry related how he arrived at the Sports Club in St James's Square for the selection committee meeting on the Sunday before the match was due to start. He was a few minutes late and as he walked into the room, W.G. said: 'Here's Charles. Now Charles, before you sit down, we want you to answer this question, yes or no. Do you think that Archie MacLaren ought to play in the next Test match?'

'Yes, I do,' replied Fry without thinking, having a high regard for the young Lancashire man.

'That settles it,' said W.G., and Fry went on:

I sat down at the table. Then, and only then, did I discover that the question W.G. had asked me meant, 'Shall I, W.G. Grace, resign from the England eleven?' This had never occurred to me. I had thought it was merely a question of Archie coming in instead of one of the other batsmen, perhaps myself. I explained this and tried to hedge, but the others had made up their minds that I was to be confronted with a sudden casting-vote. So there it was. I who owed my place in the England team to W.G.'s belief in me as a batsman gave the casting-vote that ended W.G.'s career of cricket for England.

Fry continued:

Fortunately for my peace of mind I found out afterwards that W.G. himself felt that he ought to retire, not because he could not bat or bowl to the value of his place, but because he could not move about in the field or run his runs.

But surely if W.G. had really been convinced it was time for him to quit, the obvious course would have been to inform his fellow-selectors that he did not wish to be picked again. This he did not do, although he accepted the choice of MacLaren with a good grace. It may well have been that he regretted his outburst to Jackson at Trent Bridge and would happily have gone on playing for England if the selectors had backed him.

W.G. lost not only his place to MacLaren but the captaincy too, although Jackson was felt by some to have a greater claim. The change did not bring the desired result. Australia won the Lord's Test decisively and managed to avoid defeat in the remaining matches of the rubber to take it 1–0.

W.G. had played twenty-two Tests (all against Australia, the only other Test-playing country) over nineteen years, scored 1,098 runs at an average of 32.29, with five centuries and a highest score of 170, taken nine wickets at 26.22 each and held 39 catches. What figures might he have recorded if countries like South Africa, India and the West Indies had also been playing Test cricket in his era?

The result of these dramatic events was that for the rest of 1899 W.G. was able to devote himself to the affairs of London County. A second match against the Australians at Crystal Palace was arranged for immediately after the fourth Test at Old Trafford, although the home team was billed as Dr W.G. Grace's XI. Both Alec Hearne and Len Braund scored centuries for him but the match ended in a draw. W.G. was in fine form for his new team for the rest of the summer. He made 1,092 runs for them at an average of 84 and four centuries, including 175 not out against the new first-class county of Worcestershire, and also picked up fifty wickets. But these runs or wickets did not count towards his career statistics as none of London County's twenty-seven games was granted first-class status.

As the century came to its end, Grace could look back on twelve months in which his medical, county and international careers had also been wound up.

London County applied to be admitted to the county championship to open the new century but were turned down, hardly surprising in view of their brief history and tenuous financial prospects. Attendances during their first season had been by no means overwhelming and cricket's administrators, notoriously conservative at the best of times, could be forgiven for requiring much more evidence of London County's long-term prospects. W.G.'s only consolation was that London's matches against first-class counties, MCC and the universities would be counted as first-class fixtures. He managed to arrange thirteen of them, plus a further fifty-seven games.

He also recruited his old friend and adversary, forty-six-year-old W.L. 'Billy' Murdoch, the former Australian captain, who had settled in England, captained Sussex for six seasons and even played one Test for his new country (in South Africa). If W.G. had one bosom buddy in the last decade of his cricketing life, it was W.L. Although the Australian was six years younger, they had had remarkably similar careers, and held roughly similar roles within the game in their respective countries. In the first Test match played in England, back in 1880, they had had almost identical scores, Murdoch's 153 pipping Grace by 1 run. Like Grace, Murdoch was both a massive accumulator of runs, and a genial and popular father figure. Once Murdoch had moved to England in 1893, he and Grace often socialised and played golf together.

W.G. found it difficult, however, to recruit a regular line-up of other good players, although he himself had a productive season with bat and ball: 2,273 runs and 133 wickets in all games. He made centuries against Worcestershire and MCC, and half-centuries against Derbyshire, Warwickshire and Cambridge University. He was of course free to play in other matches: his finest display in 1900 was 126 for South v North at Lord's, in a benefit match for the dressing-room superintendent.

One of his most enjoyable matches for London County that summer was against Whitgift Wanderers at Crystal Palace on 26 June when he took seven wickets, scored 111 not out and put on 100 in less than an hour with his youngest son, Charles, aged eighteen, who made 60. 'My son also scored 120 on June 24th for Old & Present Students of the Engineering School at the Crystal Palace,' his father proudly wrote to the cricket statistician and historian F.S. Ashley-Cooper on 3 July. For the last decade of his cricketing career W.G. kept Ashley-Cooper informed of his achievements on the field.

He was as keen to see all his scores and wickets recorded, however minor the game, as he had been in his heyday. Thus, on 13 December 1900, he reflected on the past season in a note to Ashley-Cooper: 'I should have scored 1,000 runs only I injured my foot at Lord's on August 19 and played only twice . . . afterwards.' On the reverse he noted: 'In 1900, W.G. Grace scored 713 runs. He had 21 completed innings and averaged 33. He took 110 wickets average 13 runs per wicket. He played one three-figure innings for London County . . .'

In truth, London County was never the serious cricketing project its backers had envisaged but more of a jolly swansong for the Champion in his twilight years. If the committee really wanted it to be a commercial and cricketing success, it may have been a mistake, ironically, to appoint the greatest name in cricket to run it. Perhaps a younger, more ambitious man would have been more successful in the long term. As it was, W.G. and the club's supporters had a lot of fun during its brief life but it never threatened to join the game's élite.

It was more like a precursor of the International Cavaliers, who enlivened Sunday cricket in the 1960s, an *ad hoc* group of players ranging from the great to the quite good, whose main purpose was to entertain the public. But it did enable many young players to break into the first-class game, which might otherwise have been closed to them. W.G.'s best young capture was the all-rounder Len Braund, who had played two seasons for Surrey and then been released. He played the 1900 season for LCC and, having qualified for another county, moved to Somerset, where he was an immediate success and became a permanent fixture in the England team, while still turning out occasionally for London County.

On 29 May 1902, came the first move in making peace between W.G. and his old county. He took a London County team to Bristol to play a Charles Townsend XI in a charity match to raise money for the NSPCC. In November he expressed his appreciation to Arrowsmith:

After the kind way you treated us at Bristol last season, I must say I should like to come again . . . If you will play us I shall be very pleased and it will be doing us a good turn, I think the match would pay well . . .

The match to which he referred was indeed arranged. The following season London County played two matches against Gloucestershire. The first was at Crystal Palace. A.G. Powell, who accompanied the Gloucestershire team to London, set the scene:

While walking across the ground before the game started the dear old man caught sight of me and came hurrying across with outstretched hand to welcome me, then catching hold of my arm lugged me away on a tour of inspection, for he was very proud of his ground, especially the bowling green. He was unfeignedly delighted to have his old team as guests, and those who played will not soon forget the lavish hospitality bestowed under his direction.

Nobody forgot the part he played in the match either. Gloucestershire batted first and piled up a large score, but W.G. still managed bowling figures of 6–80. He then proceeded to score 150 and despite a large deficit on first innings London County eventually won by seven wickets. Although the breach had now been healed, W.G. could be forgiven for relishing the result. London won the return match at Gloucester by five wickets, a remarkable double. To complete the peace, Gloucestershire made him a Life Member of the club.

It was in September 1902 that W.G. took his first ride in a

motor-car, courtesy of Harry Preston, the hotelier, who was then dividing his time between Brighton and Bournemouth. W.G. was playing at Bournemouth and had to go on to Hastings. He asked Preston if he could drive him to Brighton. Preston agreed, but added they would have to leave by midday, for the journey took four hours and he did not want to be driving in autumnal gloom. W.G. told him to be at the ground at 11 a.m. He batted first, and allowed the second ball to hit him on the body and then the stumps.

'Out!' cried the umpire, and before the amazed crowd, and the still more astounded bowler, had realised what had happened, 'W.G.' was halfway back to the dressing-room, and a few minutes later he was beside me in the car.

We reached Brighton safely, and the 'Old Man' enjoyed every yard of the drive.

Its impressive results against Gloucestershire gave a false impression of London County's progress. The new club's effective life lasted only until the end of the 1904 season, with an annual programme of about a dozen first-class fixtures and between eighty and ninety lesser games. W.G. made a total of seven centuries in its colours but it never achieved its aim of acceptance into the County Championship and was even turned down by the Minor Counties, at the end of 1904.

Because of confusion among officialdom, none of its fixtures for 1905 was granted first-class status and that effectively killed the club off. Grace and Murdoch were also ageing, and the lack of first-class status meant it could no longer attract promising younger players.

For the four first-class fixtures which London County should have played in 1905, the club had to change its name to Gentlemen of England. One of them, on Easter Monday, was against Surrey, led by Tom Hayward. For the county it was an early-season run-out against Grace's XI, which had a particular significance naturally lost on everybody involved. It was the first-class debut of a young man from Cambridge by the name of Jack Hobbs, who was to become the third first-class player to make a hundred hundreds.

The other two were W.G. Grace and Tom Hayward. Hobbs gave notice of his talent with scores of 18 and 88, the top score in the match.

For W.G. the year was overshadowed by the death in March of W.G. junior. He was only thirty, just a few months older than G.F. had been.

In 1906 the skeleton of London County had just three first-class games, all as Dr W.G. Grace's XI, two against Cambridge University and one against the West Indies, who were touring England for only the second time. His teams had varying fortunes against Cambridge. In the first match, at Fenners from 4–6 June, W.G. was in astonishing form for a man of his age as his team inflicted the university's defeat of the season by seven wickets. He opened the bowling in Cambridge's first innings, and returned the respectable figures of 2–45, the undergraduates being shot out for 107. Then he marched out to open the batting as well and put the students' bowling to the sword in his old style. *The Times* reported:

Dr Grace played magnificent cricket, batting with perfect ease all round the wicket, and although he was missed in the long field off Mr Napier's bowling, he seemed to have no difficulty in playing all the bowlers. It was quite a glimpse of his old form he gave.

The unlucky Napier finally made amends, catching him for 64, but in his second innings W.G. carried on as before, remaining undefeated on 44 in his side's total of 114–13.

But he could not sustain his form in the return match at Crystal Palace twelve days later when his side was considerably weaker. Indeed, he appears to have been unable to raise more than ten men at first. His son Charles Butler Grace was presumably co-opted, for he was listed as batting at number eleven in the second innings, having been 'absent in the first innings'. W.G. made 0 and 1 and his team was beaten by an innings and 41 runs.

Between the two matches against the undergraduates came the fixture against the West Indians, led by H.B.G. Austin and including the brilliant young batsman, George Challenor, only eighteen years of age, and Lebrun Constantine, father of the legendary Learie. The opening match of their tour, it was played at Crystal Palace, and showed their lack of match practice for they were soundly defeated by 247 runs, W.G. scoring 23 and 9. More extraordinarily, he opened the bowling and took 4–71 and 4–74, his second innings victims including Constantine caught and bowled for a duck and Challenor bowled for 4.

He had one more big match to come, which must rank as one of the most remarkable performances by an individual player. It was the Gentlemen v Players at The Oval, for which Grace was selected at the request of H.R. Leveson-Gower. By now the pressures of county cricket meant that there was a growing movement to drop the second playing of the famous fixture, for it was becoming increasingly difficult to recruit enough good players. In 1906, only two of the amateurs and six of the professionals who had played in the match at Lord's the previous week were selected for The Oval. In those circumstances, it was not so strange that a place should be found for W.G.

The match began on Monday 16 July, two days before his fifty-eighth birthday, and an incredible forty-one years since he had first played in the fixture at the Surrey ground. To compensate for the second-rate nature of many of the players, the Surrey committee cut the admission price to 6d. It did the trick to some extent, as more than six thousand spectators paid to see the opening day, when the Players made 365 all out and were criticised for dull play, although present-day spectators would be delighted to be subjected to such a scoring-rate. In the Gentlemen's first innings, W.G. batted at number seven and was out for four.

The Players appeared to be terrified of losing, and having made 335 in their second innings (Grace 7–1–23–1) set the Gentlemen the ridiculous target of 443 in four and a half hours on the third day, W.G.'s fifty-eighth birthday. This time, he opened the batting, with C.J.B. Wood, using a bat he had picked out of George Beldam's bag. Beldam, who played for Middlesex and was a pioneer of sports photography, told him he could use it but if he made a century he had to sign it and return it. W.G. did his best to oblige, giving the crowd something to remember him by, an innings of 74 in three hours which afforded them the occasional glimpse of his past greatness. Let *The Times* tell the story:

His was a great physical effort . . . While making the first fifty, he played extremely well, watching the ball with much of his old skill and placing it on the leg-side with great certainty. It was but natural that he should tire, and, although his innings had been chanceless he might twice have been caught in the slips before he was caught there. The crowd for a very long time received the strokes he made with enthusiasm, and it was only when the taking of a very long tea interval convinced them that there was no serious effort to bring the match to a serious conclusion that their enthusiasm waned. However, they applauded Dr Grace warmly when he at last got out after what must be regarded as a wonderful batting feat for any man in any class of cricket to accomplish on his fifty-eighth birthday.

As he re-entered the dressing-room he threw down Beldam's bat and said, 'There, I shan't play again.' He wasn't quite accurate about that, but it was certainly his last big match and he had gone out like the lion he was. (Despite not making a century, he returned the bat to Beldam anyway, duly signed.)

In 1907 and 1908, London County's (alias Gentlemen of England) fixture list had dwindled to one early-season match against Surrey at The Oval. In 1907 W.G. made 16 and 3. In October 1907, he dutifully sent his season's statistics to Ashley-Cooper: 'Batting: Innings 25 Not Out 3, Runs 1051, Average 47; Bowling: Wickets Taken 104, Average per wicket 13.

W.G.'s first-class career ended in 1908, not in the balmy atmosphere of a late summer evening but with an early-season match interrupted by snow and sleet, but it was a gallant exit none the less. The game between his Gentlemen of England XI and Surrey at The Oval starting on a chilly 20 April was the opening first-class fixture of the 1908 season. Surrey took advantage of the Gentlemen's frozen fingers to score 390, though Hobbs made a duck. Opening the innings, W.G. made a cautious, patient 15 in an hour and a half before being bowled. But when the Gentlemen followed on 171 runs behind, the old W.G. went into action in his best style. It must have been a memorable cameo. *The Times's* correspondent wrote:

Dr Grace was only at the wickets for half an hour for his runs and his driving and pulling was an object lesson to many a young player. He put plenty of power into his strokes, and his play was really wonderful considering his age. He was seldom at fault in his timing and his placing generally was very accurate.

All good things come to an end. He was bowled by Busher for 25, the outgunned Gentlemen subsided to defeat by an innings, and W.G.'s first-class career was over, although the press was more preoccupied with the death on the same day of Sir Henry Campbell-Bannerman, who had resigned as Prime Minister just 16 days earlier.

W.G. celebrated his sixtieth birthday in July 1908 with a two-day charity match at Chesham between his XI and Mr W.F. Lowndes's XI. Because of rain, it ended in a draw; W.G. was run out for a single. On 17 August, he made his final appearance for London County, against MCC in the only setting that was appropriate – Lord's.

He opened the batting in London County's first innings, but the finale was not destined to be a glorious one: he made only a single before being bowled. A young Parsee named Kanga whom W.G. had uncovered from somewhere provided the fireworks with a sparkling innings of 46. Set 146 to win, London County made the runs with four wickets in hand to give W.G. a winning send-off, but, perhaps exhausted from his exertions in the field, he did not bat again.

At the end of 1908, the Crystal Palace Company wound up the cricket club, and the following year the company itself went into receivership.

In his sixties, W.G lived the life of a retired gentleman. He and his wife moved to Mottingham, also in south-east London, and he indulged himself in his new passions – golf, bowls and curling in the winter – and followed the Worcester Park Beagles, as enthusiastically as he had tramped the fields of Gloucestershire in his boyhood. He wrote to Charles Blundell: 'I was out with the Beagles at Chelsfield on Saturday, had good sport for the hounds running about two and a half hours and killed in the end.' To an old friend, Dick Bell, he wrote in 1911: 'I beagle Mondays and Fridays, so do not come on those days.'

Gilbert Jessop has left a delightful cameo of Grace and Murdoch playing golf at Rye, where he was accustomed to play on the Sunday of the Hastings Festival. W.G. brought to golf all the gusto he had given to cricket for the previous forty years. The match in question was at the very beginning of W.G.'s love affair with golf; Jessop reckoned that he and Murdoch had played no more than half-a-dozen games previously. W.G. lashed his tee shot into the 'Hell' bunker, a notorious hazard on the Rye course, and seemed likely to win the hole comfortably because Murdoch had already taken seven to get on to the green. W.G. started to climb the steep face of the bunker but 'the weight of his incoming tread . . . caused his ball to roll down towards him. To arrest its progress, W.G. took an almighty swipe at it – and I rather fancy that when he fetched up at the bottom with a bump the ball had just beaten him in the ensuing race . . . The match was halved, Billy winning the hole in twelve to thirteen.'

Murdoch, who was also a solicitor, travelled back and forth between Britain and Australia. In January 1910, W.G. added a postscript, ungrammatical as ever, to a letter to Ashley-Cooper: 'I had a postcard a few days ago from W.L. Murdoch he is in Australia again but I believe is coming back again.' On Saturday, 18 February 1911, Murdoch was watching the fourth Test of the Australia–South Africa series at the Melbourne Cricket Ground, where he was a revered figure. In the break after Australia's second innings had ended during the morning session, the genial old Australian captain predicted that South Africa would lose five wickets before lunch. His forecast was uncannily correct.

While lunching with the committee, Murdoch remarked: 'I'll never make another prophecy again. I've brought bad luck on those boys.' He never spoke a truer word. Shortly afterwards, he complained of feeling ill, and pitched forward on to a table. He died later that afternoon in hospital without regaining consciousness, aged only fifty-four.

Three months later, W.G. suffered an even greater loss when E.M., who had been in poor health for some time, died.

W.G.'s enthusiasm for cricket remained undiminished. On 12 October 1910, he summarised the past season for Ashley-Cooper:

'I played in 17 matches during the season and had 15 completed innings, scoring 418 runs, average 27.13. My highest score was 71. I only bowled in a few matches but took over 20 wickets. Hoping this will enable you to make up a small paragraph . . .'

His eye for a cricketer was as shrewd as ever. In August 1911 he wrote to Francis Lacey, secretary of the MCC, who clearly wanted to know his opinion of the Nottinghamshire all-rounder Ted Alletson. Earlier that season Alletson had made an astonishing 189 in 90 minutes against Sussex, the last 142 taking an incredible 40 minutes. Presumably Lacey wanted to know whether Alletson would be suitable for the MCC ground staff, and was doubtful about his action. W.G.'s letter shows his generous nature, and his distaste for slow play:

. . . he has a peculiar action, but I did not think he threw at all when I saw him bowl. He told Jessop that West the umpire said his action was suspicious and told or asked R.O. Jones to take him off. He seems a very quiet and well behaved young fellow, and can just hit and no mistake. I saw him and Jessop together, and the differing styles were very interesting to watch. One crouching down and the other standing straight up and making the most of his height. I think you should engage him, and if you don't like his action, don't bowl him in a match. His very fine hitting can induce others to play a fast game, instead of pottering about like most Pros do now. Another young Pro, Haywood of Northants you might engage, he is a good all round young fellow and very good practice bowler.

In the event, Alletson was taken on to the Lord's payroll in 1914.

W.G. had no wish to be involved in controversy in his twilight years, as he made plain in April 1911 when Ashley-Cooper wanted his opinion on the players who would make up the best side of an unstated era. He singled out Willsher, Jupp and Alfred Shaw but added: 'I certainly do not want to be dragged into any controversy about the best team, so must ask you not to make any remark on what I say . . .'

In November 1914, when Ashley-Cooper, who was writing a biography of E.M., wanted more information about a row involving the Coroner, W.G. replied: 'I should not mention it, it can do no good.' Inserted in the letter was a sheet of paper detailing W.G.'s record in 1911: 'Batting: Innings 16, runs 352, highest score 79, average 22. Matches bowled in: 8. Wickets taken: 30.'

W.G. still turned out regularly for the Eltham club. A photograph taken in 1913 at Gravesend shows him on-driving imperiously, well out of his crease, head steady, eyes following the ball's progress, still a model for any youngster. On 23 June 1914, he was one of the 250 guests at a dinner to mark the centenary of the establishment of the Lord's ground at St John's Wood. Lord Hawke, President of the MCC, presided. He paid tribute to one of England's greatest players, A.G. Steel, who had died only eight days earlier, wondered whether the slow run-rate then prevalent was not due to better field placing and batsmen's unwillingness to take risks (shades of 1996), grumbled about the tea interval, declared his belief that unfair bowling had been banished for ever and then reached the climax of his speech.

Never had English cricket had so many great names to conjure with as in the epoch of 'the Grand Old Man', the mere mention of whose name brought a rousing cheer from the tables, Ranji, Stoddart (who was, alas, to shoot himself the following year), Jackson, Sammy Woods, Jessop (W.G.'s protégé) and Hirst. The diners probably did not realize that Hawke had just delivered the memorial address for the Golden Age of cricket – and that they were also cheering and raising their glasses to the Champion in his presence for the last time.

W.G. played his last game of cricket, for Eltham, a month later, on 25 July. Astonishingly, he made 69 not out, against Grove Park on a bad pitch. He was sixty-six years old, and looks every year of his age in the team photograph taken for the occasion. He and his team-mates had good reason to look sombre. On the Continent, the clouds of war were gathering. A few days later W.G. went to Jack Hobbs's benefit match at Lord's, where it had been switched because Hobbs's home ground, The Oval, had been requisitioned by the War Office. On the night of 3–4 August 1914, German forces invaded Belgium. On 4 August, Great Britain declared war on Germany. The First World War was to cast a deep shadow over W.G.'s last year of life and may have hastened his death.

As the German army threw back the French divisions and the British Expeditionary Force sent to defend Belgium, Grace's deep sadness at the turn of events was evident in a letter he sent to the *Sportsman*, which was published on 27 August.

Sir, – There are many cricketers who are already doing their duty, but there are many more who do not seem to realize that in all probability they will have to serve either at home or abroad before the war is brought to a conclusion. The fighting on the Continent is very severe, and will probably be prolonged. I think the time has arrived when the county cricket season should be closed, for it is not fitting at a time like this that able-bodied men should be playing day after day, and pleasure-seekers look on. There are so many who are young and able, and are still hanging back. I should like to see all first-class cricketers of suitable age set a good example, and come to the aid of their country without delay in its hour of need.

Yours, etc

W.G. Grace

It was the first time that W.G. had publicly shown any interest in events outside cricket. This was perhaps understandable. The year of his birth, 1848, had been a year of turmoil and revolution on the Continent, but for Britons of his generation, their country remained serenely untouched by events beyond its shores for the next half-century and more. Great Britain may have been involved in war and the problems of subduing a mighty empire but it all happened a long way from home. Now for the first time in Grace's lifetime, this domestic immunity from the infection of war was threatened.

The wish he expressed in the letter was quickly granted. The county championship was terminated early, leaving Surrey as champions, and first-class cricket was not resumed until the spring of 1919.

Most of the last images of W.G. are affected by the war. On Whit Monday 1915 a charity match was held at Catford Bridge to raise money for Belgian refugees. W.G. had been invited to play but on arrival at the ground felt unwell and decided to withdraw. But he offered to take a collecting box around the ground, and presented

289

a bat to the man of the match. A photograph shows him sitting on a chair in front of the pavilion, leaning forward to deposit a coin in a collection box carried on the back of a dog, accompanied by a soldier in unform. Looking on is a moustachioed cricketer in flannels, blazer and cap, who may be Archie MacLaren. Another photograph taken around the same time shows W.G. in his garden (where he loved to potter about), flanked by MacLaren and Ranji, both in uniform.

While working in the garden on 9 October 1915, W.G. suffered a stroke, somehow struggled indoors and took to his bed. Mrs Grace was clearly worried but in a letter on 12 October to F.S. Ashley-Cooper, the cricket historian and statistician, who had written a biography of E.M. and was working on the definitive version of W.G.'s career figures, was optimistic that he would recover.

The doctor is ill and may not do anything in the way of going through your proofs for a week at least from now – he was taken ill on Saturday but read the first lot of proofs through and told me of a lot of mistakes but they are not marked and I am sure that I could not remember all, he would be very sorry for it to be published with such a number of errors . . .

The following night, 13 October, saw the biggest Zeppelin raid of the war on the capital and outlying towns. Five of the giant German airships wreaked massive damage on central London, Woolwich Arsenal and Croydon, killing 71 people and injuring 128. The Zeppelin L13, captained by Kapitanleutnant Mathy, dropped several bombs, mainly incendiaries, on the Woolwich barracks and arsenal, not far from Mottingham, causing extensive damage. The explosions did nothing to improve W.G.'s condition.

H.R. Leveson-Gower twice visited W.G., at Mrs Grace's request, soon afterwards. 'I don't like these 'ere Zeppelins,' complained W.G. Trying to comfort him, Leveson-Gower jokingly wondered why a man who had stood up to the world's fastest bowlers on rough wickets without a tremor should fear the odd German airship.

'Yes, quite true,' replied W.G. 'But then I could see the fast balls. I can't see those confounded Zeppelins.'

On Tuesday 19 October *The Times* reported that 'Dr W.G. Grace is suffering from slight cerebral hemorrhage, affecting the speech centre only. His condition yesterday was stated to be satisfactory.' The following day he was said to be 'making good progress and his condition is now quite satisfactory'. A similar note appeared on 21 October, but then his condition worsened and he died peacefully at home in the morning of Saturday 23 October.

His death was attributed to heart failure, and was said to have been reported by the German press, and attributed to the effectiveness of their mighty Zeppelins. The issue of *The Times* which reported his passing carried several columns of death notices of officers cut down in Flanders. Much space was devoted to the international outrage aroused by the execution of Nurse Edith Cavell a few days earlier. The King appealed for more volunteers 'in order that another may not inherit the free Empire which their ancestors and mine have built'. He added: 'The end is not in sight.'

Among the pages given over to news of the war, the paper found space to pay lavish tribute to 'a cricket career that has not been equalled by any cricketer in the past and is not likely to be in the future'.

The funeral took place at Elmer's End Cemetery three days later. There was a good turn-out of cricketers past and present, considering the demands of the war, headed by those two giants of the game, Lords Hawke and Harris, and the uniformed Ranji, plumper now than the lithe figure of two decades previously. W.G. was laid to rest beside his children, W.G. junior and Bessie.

W.G.'s will was published in December 1915. He left estate worth £7,278 (£6,590 net). Probate was granted to Mrs Grace and their son, Captain Charles Butler Grace, then serving with the Fortress Engineers. He left everything to his widow, and his canniness was evident to the end: he had made the will on 24 November 1914, in his own handwriting on a sixpenny form, dispensing with the need for a solicitor.

Agnes Grace survived him by fourteen years, dying at her home in Hawkhurst, Kent, in 1930. His two surviving sons did well in life but did not live much longer than their mother.

Henry Edgar Grace had a distinguished career in the Royal Navy, commanding a series of cruisers and the aircraft-carrier *Vindictive* during the First World War and being commended for service in action at Gallipoli, rising to Vice-Admiral. He served in Berlin and Hong Kong, became an ADC to the King, was Rear-Admiral of Submarines and was promoted Admiral in 1934 after his retirement. He died suddenly at Devonport in 1937, aged sixty-one.

The youngest, Charles Butler, was an electrical engineer, tall and bearded like his father, about whom he loved to tell stories, and an enthusiastic club cricketer all his life, a good batsman and lob bowler like his uncle E.M. As managing engineer of the Weald Electricity Company in Kent, he started a works team which grew into a strong local side. He died in a manner one feels his father would have approved. Playing at Sidley, Bexhill, on 6 June 1938, he collapsed at the wicket seconds after hitting the boundary which brought up the 300, his team's highest-ever score. At first it was assumed he had merely fainted in the excitement of the occasion but the players rapidly realised it was a lot more serious than that. He was only fifty-six.

There are surprisingly few memorials to England's greatest cricketer. The main one is, fittingly, at Lord's: the Grace Gates, the main entrance, opened in 1923. They were designed by Sir Herbert Baker, who also designed the Grand Stand at Lord's, demolished at the end of 1996. There was some discussion in 1996 of whose statue might occupy the fourth plinth at the corner of Trafalgar Square, which remains empty. To mark the one hundred and fiftieth anniversary of his birth in 1998, it would be entirely appropriate if a statue of W.G. Grace was erected there. It would make up, belatedly, for the knighthood he deserved but never received. It would also mark the changed perception of the importance of sport's role in society. And who embodied the finest English qualities better than W.G.?

W.G.'s grave was at one time neglected but was restored, thanks to an initiative by the Forty Club. Surprisingly, in view of their importance to the history of the area, the Grace family graves in the churchyard at Downend were in very poor condition when I visited them in the summer of 1996. No casual passer-by would have any idea that here lie the remains of such an important family, including two of the greatest cricketers of the Victorian era, E.M. and G.F. Grace.

There are five Grace family graves situated in the plot, none of them well tended. The biggest one, topped by a cross, is of that of Henry Grace, W.G.'s oldest brother. On it are carved the words, 'Physician and Surgeon of Kingswood Hill, who died Nov 13 1895 aged 62. A truly unselfish man deservedly beloved and regretted by all who knew him.' Buried with him is his widow Leanna, who died on 16 October 1898, aged sixty-nine. It was extremely dilapidated: one of the iron railings had fallen down and lay on top of the grave, which was almost obscured by thorns, dock leaves and ivy.

Next to it is a less impressive, triangular-topped grave, that of Fred and his mother Martha. It also commemorated Dr Henry Mills Grace, who is buried in the church. The tombstone of E.M. and his first wife, Annie White Grace, who died in 1884, aged only thirty-seven, also bears the names of seven of their children who predeceased him. Five died in infancy – Maud, Ada, Sybil, John and George Frederick, who bore the Christian names of his late uncle but lived only sixteen days. The record of all those children dying so young is a reminder of the sadness that Victorian families had to bear; being the children of a doctor was no defence against the deadly illnesses of the age.

Two of W.G.'s sisters also lie there: Alice Rose, who had married the schoolmaster (and W.G.'s tutor) Mr Bernard, and died in 1895, aged forty-nine; and Fanny, who died in 1900 aged sixty-two. In a different part of the churchyard is buried 'Uncle Pocock' – Alfred Pocock, who had coached W.G. in the orchard of The Chestnuts and lived until the ripe old age of eighty-four, but of their connection with England's greatest cricketer there is no sign.

At least E.M. and G.F. lie within the sound of willow on cricket ball. On the other side of the churchyard wall is a cricket ground, that of Downend Cricket Club. Formerly a farmer's field, it was rented from Lady Cave in 1893 and converted for cricket. There was a strong Grace connection – the club's first president was the Rev. John Dann, vicar of Downend and W.G.'s brother-in-law.

W.G. brought the Gloucestershire side along for a match in 1896 which attracted a big crowd. Alas, the village's favourite son was bowled for only 3 by the Downend captain, Ted Biggs, a carpenter. The club flourished and provided the county with some fine cricketers. In 1921 the club bought the ground for £600 and the following year a new pavilion was opened by Mrs Blanche Dann, W.G.'s sister, and the ground was renamed The W.G. Grace Memorial Ground.

More recently, in 1977, Downend won the Western League, a very strong and hard-fought competition set up in 1970, with the aid of a young Australian who had written to the club asking if he could play for it for a season to broaden his experience. His name was Allan Border, and although he played a big role in Downend's greatest season, nobody at the club thought he would one day go on to play Test cricket, let alone become one of his country's most successful captains and score more Test runs than anyone else in the history of cricket.

Dr Grace would have approved, for Border was just his type of cricketer – devoid of frills, hard, brave and competitive. He also possessed a dry wit that the doctor would have appreciated. In one match for Downend, he held on to a catch in the gully but the batsman stood his ground. 'Why don't you go?' called Border. 'It's people like you who give people like me a bad name.'

The Australian connection is maintained. When I visited the ground on a summer evening in 1996, a match between Downend and an Australian touring team had just concluded, and the tall, blond young visitors were standing outside the pavilion nursing glasses of lager and chatting to the local men. Across the road at the far end of the ground still stands the house where the Champion cricketer was born a century and a half earlier.

It was easy to imagine his spirit hovering over the scene, and to visualise him standing around after a thousand such games, discussing the day's play with his usual gruff enthusiasm. What is certain is that his own memory will be treasured by everyone connected with cricket for as long as the game is played.

As his obituary in *Wisden* recorded: 'When he was in his prime no sun was too hot and no day too long for him.'

APPENDIX

W.G. GRACE - FIRST-CLASS CAREER STATISTICS

Season	Innings	NO	Runs	Average	100s	Wickets	Runs Conceded	Average
1865	8	1	189	27.00	0	20	268	13.40
1866	13	2	581	52.81	2	31	483	15.58
1867	6	1	154	30.80	0	39	293	7.51
1868	11	2	588	65.33	3	44	639	14.52
1869	24	1	1,320	57.39	6	73	1,189	16.28
1870	38	5	1,808	54.78	5	50	785	15.70
1871	39	4	2,739	78.25	10	79	1,345	17.02
1872	29	3	1,485	57.11	6	56	678	12.10
1873	32	7	1,805	72.20	6	75	1,093	14.57
1874	32	0	1,664	52.00	8	139	1,757	12.64
1875	48	2	1,498	32.56	3	191	2,473	12.94
1876	46	4	2,622	62.42	7	130	2,457	19.04
1877	40	3	1,474	39.83	2	179	2,293	12.81
1878	42	2	1,151	30.28	1	152	2,208	14.52
1879	28	3	880	35.20	2	105	1,414	13.46
1880	27	3	951	39.62	2	84	1,480	17.61
1881	22	1	792	37.71	2	45	879	19.53
1882	37	0	975	26.35	0	101	1,754	17.36
1883	41	2	1,352	34.66	1	94	2,077	22.09
1884	45	5	1,361	34.02	3	82	1,762	21.48
1885	42	3	1,688	43.28	4	117	2,199	18.79
1886	55	3	1,846	35.50	4	122	2,439	19.99
1887	46	8	2,062	54.26	6	97	2,082	21.46
1888	59	1	1,886	32.51	4	93	1,691	18.18
1889	45	2	1,396	32.46	3	44	1,020	23.18
1890	55	3	1,476	28.38	1	61	1,182	19.37
1891	40	1	771	19.76	0	58	973	16.77

Season	Innings	NO	Runs	Average	100s	Wickets	Runs Conceded	Average
1891/2	11	1	448	44.80	1	5	134	26.80
1892	37	3	1,055	31.02	0	31	958	30.90
1893	50	5	1,609	35.75	1	22	854	38.81
1894	45	1	1,293	29.38	3	29	732	25.24
1895	48	2	2,346	51.00	9	16	527	32.93
1896	54	4	2,135	42.70	4	52	1,249	24.01
1897	41	2	1,532	39.28	4	56	1,242	22.17
1898	41	5	1,513	42.02	3	36	915	25.41
1899	23	1	515	23.40	0	20	482	24.10
1900	31	1	1,277	42.56	3	32	969	30.28
1901	32	1	1,007	32.48	1	51	1,111	21.78
1902	35	3	1,187	37.09	2	46	1,074	23.34
1903	27	1	593	22.80	1	10	479	47.90
1904	26	1	637	25.48	1	21	687	32.71
1905	13	0	250	19.23	0	7	383	54.71
1906	10	1	241	26.77	0	13	268	20.61
1907	2	0	19	9.50	0	--	--	--
1908	2	0	40	20.00	0	0	5	--
TOTAL	1,478	104	54,211	39.45	124	2,808	50,982	18.15

Catches: 875 Stumpings: 5

FIRST-CLASS CENTURIES (124)

1866	224*	England v Surrey	The Oval
	173*	Gentlemen of the South v Players of the South	The Oval
1868	134*	Gentlemen v Players	Lord's
	130 and 102*	South of Thames v North of Thames	Canterbury
1869	117	MCC v Oxford University	Oxford
	138*	MCC v Surrey	The Oval
	121	MCC v Notts	Lord's
	180	Gentlemen of the South v Players of the South	The Oval
	122	South v North	Sheffield
	127	MCC v Kent	Canterbury
1870	117*	MCC v Notts	Lord's
	215	Gentlemen v Players	The Oval
	109	Gentlemen v Players	Lord's
	143	Gloucestershire v Surrey	The Oval

	172	Gloucestershire v MCC	Lord's
1871	181	MCC v Surrey	Lord's
	118	Gentlemen of the South v Players of the North	West Brompton
	178	South v North	Lord's
	162	Gentlemen of England v Cambridge University	Cambridge
	189*	Single v Married of England	Lord's
	146	MCC v Surrey	The Oval
	268	South v North	The Oval
	117	MCC v Kent	Canterbury
	217	Gentlemen v Players	Brighton
	116	Gloucestershire v Nottinghamshire	Nottingham
1872	101	MCC v Yorkshire	Lord's
	112	Gentlemen v Players	Lord's
	117	Gentlemen v Players	The Oval
	170*	England v Notts & Yorkshire	Lord's
	114	South v North	The Oval
	150	Gloucestershire v Yorkshire	Sheffield
1873	158	Gentlemen v Players	The Oval
	145	Gentlemen of the South v Players of the North	Prince's
	134	Gentlemen of the South v Players of the South	The Oval
	163	Gentlemen v Players	Lord's
	192*	South v North	The Oval
	160*	Gloucestershire v Surrey	Clifton
1874	179	Gloucestershire v Sussex	Brighton
	150	Gentlemen of the South v Players of the South	The Oval
	104	Gentlemen of the South v Players of the North	Prince's
	110	Gentlemen v Players	Prince's
	167	Gloucestershire v Yorkshire	Sheffield
	121	Gloucestershire & Kent v England	Canterbury
	123	MCC v Kent	Canterbury
	127	Gloucestershire v Yorkshire	Clifton
1875	152	Gentlemen v Players	Lord's
	111	Gloucestershire v Yorkshire	Sheffield
	119	Gloucestershire v Nottinghamshire	Clifton
1876	104	Gloucestershire v Sussex	Brighton
	169	Gentlemen v Players	Lord's
	114*	South v North	Nottingham
	126	United South v United North	Hull
	344	MCC v Kent	Canterbury
	177	Goucestershire v Nottinghamshire	Clifton
	318*	Gloucestershire v Yorkshire	Cheltenham

1877	261	South v North	Prince's
	110	Gloucestershire & Yorkshire v England	Lord's
1878	116	Gloucestershire v Nottinghamshire	Nottingham
1879	123	Gloucestershire v Surrey	The Oval
	102	Gloucestershire v Nottinghamshire	Nottingham
1880	106	Gloucestershire v Lancashire	Clifton
	152	England v Australia	The Oval
1881	100	Gentlemen v Players	The Oval
	182	Gloucestershire v Nottinghamshire	Nottingham
1883	112	Gloucestershire v Lancashire	Clifton
1884	101	MCC v Australia	Lord's
	107	Gentlemen of England v Australia	The Oval
	116*	Gloucestershire v Australia	Clifton
1885	132	Gloucestershire v Yorkshire	Huddersfield
	104	Gloucestershire v Surrey	Cheltenham
	221*	Gloucestershire v Middlesex	Clifton
	174	Gentlemen v Players	Scarborough
1886	148	Gentlemen of England v Australia	The Oval
	104	MCC v Oxford University	Oxford
	110	Gloucestershire v Austalia	Clifton
	170	England v Australia	The Oval
1887	113	Gloucestershire v Middlesex	Lord's
	116*	MCC v Cambridge University	Lord's
	183*	Gloucestershire v Yorkshire	Gloucester
	113*	Gloucestershire v Nottinghamshire	Clifton
	101 and 103*	Gloucestershire v Kent	Clifton
1888	215	Gloucestershire v Sussex	Brighton
	165	Gentlemen of England v Australia	Lord's
	148 and 153	Gloucestershire v Yorkshire	Clifton
1889	101	Gloucestershire v Middlesex	Lord's
	127*	Gloucestershire v Middlesex	Cheltenham
	154	South v North	Scarborough
1890	109*	Gloucestershire v Kent	Maidstone
1891/2	159	England v Victoria	Melbourne
1893	128	MCC v Kent	Lord's
1894	139	MCC v Cambridge University	Cambridge
	196	MCC v Cambridge University	Lord's
	131	Gentlemen v Players	Hastings
1895	103	MCC v Sussex	Lord's
	288	Gloucestershire v Somerset	Bristol
	257	Gloucestershire v Kent	Gravesend
	169	Gloucestershire v Middlesex	Lord's

	125	MCC v Kent	Lord's
	101*	Gentlemen of England v I Zingari	Lord's
	118	Gentlemen v Players	Lord's
	119	Gloucestershire v Nottinghamshire	Cheltenham
	104	South v North	Hastings
1896	243*	Gloucestershire v Sussex	Brighton
	301	Gloucestershire v Sussex	Bristol
	186	Gloucestershire v Somerset	Taunton
	102*	Gloucestershire v Lancashire	Bristol
1897	126	Gloucestershire v Nottinghamshire	Nottingham
	116	Gloucestershire v Sussex	Bristol
	113	Gloucestershire v Philadelphians	Bristol
	131	Gloucestershire v Nottinghamshire	Cheltenham
1898	168	Gloucestershire v Nottinghamshire	Nottingham
	126	Gloucestershire v Essex	Leyton
	109	Gloucestershire v Somerset	Taunton
1900	126	South v North	Lord's
	110*	London County v Worcestershire	Crystal Palace
	110	London County v MCC	Crystal Palace
1901	132	London County v MCC	Crystal Palace
1902	131*	London County v MCC	Crystal Palace
	129	London County v Warwickshire	Crystal Palace
1903	150	London County v Gloucestershire	Crystal Palace
1905	166	London County v MCC	Crystal Palace

* Not Out

SUMMARY OF CENTURIES

England: 5	Gentlemen of South: 7	Gloucestershire & Yorkshire: 1
Gloucestershire: 50	South: 10	London County: 7
MCC: 19	United South: 1	Single Men of England: 1
Gentlemen: 15	South of Thames: 2	
Gentlemen of England: 5	Gloucestershire & Kent: 1	

Note: W.G. is still generally credited with 126 first-class centuries, the figure compiled by his diligent contemporary F.S. Ashley-Cooper and approved by *Wisden* but extensive research by later investigators and the Association of Cricket Statisticians discounted two: 152 for the XI that had just toured Canada and the USA against an MCC XV at Lord's in 1873, and 113 for Gloucestershire against Somerset at Clifton in 1879, because Somerset were not regarded as a first-class team at that stage.

APPENDIX

TEST CAREER (All against Australia)

Played: 22

Batting	Bowling
Innings: 36	Wickets: 9
Not Out: 1,098	Runs: 236
Highest Score: 170	Average: 26.22
Centuries: 2	Fielding
Average: 32.29	Catches: 39

MINOR CRICKET (1857-1914)

Runs: 45,283   Wickets: 4,578   Catches: 656

SELECT BIBLIOGRAPHY

Altham, H.S., *A History of Cricket* (George Allen & Unwin, 1926)

Arlott, J., *Jack Hobbs: Profile of 'The Master'* (John Murray and Davis-Poynter, 1981)

Bowen, R., *Cricket: A History of its Growth and Development throughout the World* (Eyre & Spottiswoode, 1970)

Brookes, C., *English Cricket* (Weidenfeld and Nicolson, 1978)

Brownlee, W.M., *W.G. Grace: A Biography with A Treatise on Cricket contributed by W.G. Grace* (London, 1887)

Cross, F.G., *A Panorama of the British Medical School* (University of Bristol, 1993)

Daft, R., *Kings of Cricket* (J.W. Arrowsmith, 1893)

Darwin, B., *W.G. Grace* (Duckworth, 1934)

Davie, M., and Davie, S., (eds), *The Faber Book of Cricket* (Faber & Faber, 1987)

Dunstan, K., *The Paddock That Grew: The Story of Melbourne Cricket Club* (Cassell & Co, 1962)

Ellis, C., *C.B.: The Life of Charles Burgess Fry* (J.M. Dent, 1984)

Fitzgerald, R.A., *Wickets in the West, or The Twelve in America* (London, 1873)

Frith, D., *England versus Australia: A Pictorial History of the Test Matches since 1877 (Lutterworth Press, 1977)*

Fry, C.B., *Life's Worth Living* (London, 1939)

Grace, W.G., *Cricket* (London, 1891)

———*Cricketing Reminiscences* (London, 1899)

Green, B., *A History of Cricket* (Barrie & Jenkins, 1988)

———(ed) *The Wisden Papers 1888–1946, (Stanley Paul, 1989)*

———(ed) *The Concise Wisden: An Illustrated Anthology of 125 years* (Macdonald/ Queen Anne Press, 1990)

Green, D., *The History of Gloucestershire County Cricket Club* (Christopher Helm Ltd, Bromley, 1990)

Harris, Lord, *A Few Short Runs* (London, 1921)

Harte, C., *A History of Australian Cricket* (Andre Deutsch, 1993)

Hawke, Lord, Harris, Lord, and Gordon, Sir H., *The Memorial Biography of Dr W.G. Grace* (Constable, 1919)

Hawke, Lord, *Recollections and Reminiscences* (London, 1924)

SELECT BIBLIOGRAPHY

James, C.L.R., *Beyond a Boundary* (Stanley Paul, 1963)

Jessop, G.L.A., *A Cricketer's Log* (Hodder & Stoughton, 1922)

Kynaston, D., *W.G.'s Birthday Party* (Chatto & Windus, 1990)

Leveson-Gower, Sir H., *Off and On the Field* (Stanley Paul, 1953)

Martin-Jenkins, C., *World Cricketers: A Biographical Dictionary* (Oxford University Press, 1996)

——*The Wisden Book of County Cricket* (Queen Anne Press/Macdonald Futura, 1981)

——(ed) *A Cricketer's Companion* (Smallmead Press, 1992)

Midwinter, E., *W.G. Grace: His Life and Times* (George Allen and Unwin, 1981)

Moorhouse, G., *Lord's* (Hodder & Stoughton, 1983)

Morris, Capt J., *German Air Raids on Great Britain 1914–1918 (London, 1925)*

Munro Smith, G., *A History of the Bristol Royal Infirmary* (Bristol, 1917)

Parker, G., *Gloucestershire Road: A History of Gloucestershire County Cricket Club* (Pelham, 1983)

Perry, C.B., *The British Medical School* (Historical Association, Bristol branch)

Powell, A.G., and Canynge Caple, S., *The Graces (E.M., W.G. and G.F.)* (The Cricket Book Society, 1948, republished by Cedric Chivers Ltd, Bath, 1974)

Preston, H., *Memories* (Constable, 1928)

Ranjitsinhji, K.S., *The Jubilee Book of Cricket* (London, 1897)

Rayvern Allen, D., *Cricket with Grace: An Illustrated Anthology on 'W.G.'* (Unwin Hyman, 1990)

Sale, C., *Korty: The Legend Explained* (Ian Henry Publications, Hornchurch, 1986)

Steel, A.G., and Lyttleton, the Hon R.H., with contributions by Lang, A., Grace, W.G. and Mitchell, R.A.H., *Cricket* (London, 1904)

Thomson, A.A., *The Great Cricketer* (Robert Hale, 1957)

Walker, F., *The Bristol Region* (Nelson, 1972)

West, G.D., *The Elevens of England* (Darf Publishers, 1988)

——*Twelve Days of Grace* (Darf Publishers, 1989)

——*Six More Days of Grace* (Darf Publishers, 1992)

Woods, S.M.J., *My Reminiscences* (Chapman & Hall, 1925)

Dictionary of National Biography

Scholae Medicine Bristol: Its History, Lecturers & Alumni 1833–1933 (University of Bristol, 1933)

The Association of Cricket Statisticians, *Gloucestershire Cricketers 1870–1979* (1979)

Newspapers and Journals: *Wisden; Cricket Scores and Biographies: Cricket Lore; The Bristol Medico-Chirurgical Journal: The Times; The Daily Telegraph; The Australasian; The Sporting Gazette; The Sportsman; The Sporting Clipper; Bell's Life in London; The Cricket Field; Cricket: A Weekly Record; The Clifton Chronicle and Directory; The Bristol Evening News; The Bristol Mercury.*

INDEX